not away from the everyday world of interdependence, but to a wiser, more selfless, more compassionate engagement with our infinite relatedness to others and the infinite consequentiality of our every action. If you want a way through the maze of today's pop spirituality to find the real path to full awakening, read this book!"

ROBERT A. F. THURMAN, PHD
professor of Tibetan studies at Columbia University, president of Tibet House US and Menla Mountain Retreat, and author of *The Jewel Tree of Tibet*, *Inner Revolution*, and *Essential Tibetan Buddhism*

"Looking back over my own spiritual path, there were many times I felt I was being pushed through a brick wall in order to gain the understanding that would enable me to manifest the life and freedom I have attained. I applaud Dr. Neale for this wise, thoughtful, and generous approach to becoming what we were put here to be: balanced and whole human beings."

DAMIEN ECHOLS
author of *Life After Death*, *Yours for Eternity*, and *High Magick*

"Dr. Miles Neale's new book is a road map to enlightenment. Drawing on his many years as a psychotherapist and Buddhist meditator, he guides the reader through all of the stages one needs to go through in order to heal traumas, come to terms with our lives, and find true love, compassion, forgiveness, and authenticity in our hearts. Dr. Neale writes in an accessible and profound way, elucidating precious teachings of Buddhist literature that guide us in how we should live, act, and think in order to find and spread happiness. It is a beautiful and inspiring book that will no doubt bring guidance to all who are seeking an awakened mind and life."

EDDIE STERN
founder of Ashtanga Yoga New York and author of *Yoga Mala*

D1262387

"In the near future when we have built more equitable and sustainable societies, it will be because humanity embarked on a process of awakening with each of us not becoming Buddhist but more fully human, wise, and compassionate. Miles offers this inspiring vision, and *Gradual Awakening* provides a training manual for the spiritual revolution that will help catalyze global systems change."

ROBERT-JAN VAN OGTROP, MBA
founder and chairman of Circle Economy and founder
of the Foundation for Natural Leadership

If you're tired of simply following your breath and want to follow in the footsteps of the Buddha and his heirs, up the path that will bring you unerringly to the source of your own fully embodied, fully human awakening, then this is the guide you've been waiting for!"

JOSEPH LOIZZO, MD, PHD
assistant professor of psychiatry at Weill Cornell Medical College, founding director of the Nalanda Institute for Contemplative Science, and author of *Sustainable Happiness*

"This is a brilliant book. In a voice that is fierce yet gentle, erudite but earthy, Dr. Miles Neale combines a beautifully laid Buddhist road map for human awakening with modern neuroscience and psychotherapy. Not only incredibly useful for those interested in harnessing the transformative potential of Tibetan power tools like visualization, *Gradual Awakening* also speaks to the urgency of our time, reminding us that our personal journey of healing is not optional if we have any chance of helping a society that has lost its way."

ETHAN NICHTERN
author of *The Road Home: A Contemporary Exploration of the Buddhist Path*

"Dr. Miles Neale gives a refreshing interpretation of an ancient classic through a modern neuropsychological lens—a hipster's road map to throw into your backpack on life's grand adventure."

WADE DAVIS, PHD
professor of anthropology at the University of British Columbia, explorer-in-residence at the National Geographic Society, and author of *The Serpent and the Rainbow* and *The Lost Amazon*

"This is a wonderfully readable, fresh, and personal exploration of the traditional teachings within Lama Tsongkhapa's 'Gradual Path.' Dr. Neale's experience and insights as a Western psychotherapist blend beautifully with his deep knowledge of the Dharma. *Gradual Awakening* is a rich, thorough, and insightful guide for anyone new to the Tibetan tradition and a refreshing reiteration for older practitioners. Dr. Neale expertly shows how Buddhist understanding and practice can challenge and genuinely address our contemporary alienated spiritual malaise."

ROB PREECE

author of *The Wisdom of Imperfection* and *The Psychology of Buddhist Tantra*

"Dr. Miles Neale leads us on our own journey with neuroscience and psychotherapy, drawing us back to spirit. He illuminates traditional teachings for reflection and action, from aspiration and refuge to radical altruism. This is strong and effective medicine. *Gradual Awakening* is a true friend and guide for bringing liberating values to life."

SHARON SALZBERG

author of *Real Happiness* and *Real Love*

"Dr. Miles Neale's *Gradual Awakening* offers a much-needed answer to the proliferation of popular spiritual teachings that promise some sudden enlightenment, as if awakening were the ultimate escape from the inexorable relativity and messy impermanence of the human condition. He begins by challenging the 'easy enlightenment' that mistakes experiences of oneness, timeless presence, or self-loss for the final goal, and goes on to explain why these routine meditative states must be skillfully harnessed to free the mind for psychological insight and the embodiment of compassion. Dr. Neale's book eloquently presents the Tibetan tradition of teaching a gradual path to enlightenment, which weaves meditation together with wisdom and ethics in a consummate practice that fosters fully awakened humanity. The path we travel in its chapters dates back to the systematic curriculum of India's great contemplative universities like Nalanda, and from there back to the Buddha's original Noble Eightfold Path. Inspired by a brief text from the Tibetan Renaissance genius Tsong Khapa, this guide maps out thirty steps on the way from our common human condition of confusion and addictive emotions to the complete awakening of perfect Buddhahood. True to the legacy of Shakyamuni and the Nalanda masters before and since Tsong Khapa, this path leads

GRADUAL
AWAKENING

Also by Dr. Miles Neale

Advances in Contemplative Psychotherapy:
Accelerating Healing and Transformation,
with Joe Loizzo and Emily J. Wolf

GRADUAL

AWAKENING

THE TIBETAN BUDDHIST PATH OF BECOMING FULLY HUMAN

MILES NEALE PsyD

foreword by Geshe Tenzin Zopa

sounds true

BOULDER, COLORADO

Sounds True
Boulder, CO 80306

© 2018 Miles Neale
Foreword © 2018 Geshe Tenzin Zopa

Sounds True is a trademark of Sounds True, Inc.
All rights reserved. No part of this book may be used or reproduced in any
manner without written permission from the author and publisher.

Published 2018

Cover design by Jennifer Miles
Book Design by Beth Skelley

Illustrations © 2018 Duane Stapp
Cover photo © Cory Richards/National Geographic Creative

Printed in Canada

Excerpt(s) from The Power of Myth by Joseph Campbell, copyright © 1988 by Apostrophe
S Production, Inc., and Bill Moyers and Alfred Van der Marck Editions, Inc., for itself and
the estate of Joseph Campbell. Used by permission of Doubleday, an imprint of the Knopf
Doubleday Publishing Group, a division of Penguin Random House LLC. All rights reserved.
Any third-party use of this material, outside of this publication, is prohibited. Interested
parties must apply directly to Penguin Random House LLC for permission.

Translations of the Three Principles of the Path and prayers are used by permission of Joseph
Loizzo, translator.

"Geluk Refuge Field with Tsongkhapa," Central Tibet; ca. late 18th-early 19th century,
pigment on cloth, Rubin Museum of Art, gift of Shelley & Donald Rubin Foundation,
F1997.41.7 (HAR 571) used by permission of the Rubin Museum of Art.

"Shakyamuni Buddha," Eastern Tibet; 16th century, pigment on cloth, Rubin Museum of Art,
gift of Shelley & Donald Rubin Foundation, F1997.1.5 (HAR 39) used by permission of the
Rubin Museum of Art.

Library of Congress Cataloging in Publication Data
Names: Neale, Miles, author.
Title: Gradual awakening : the Tibetan Buddhist path of becoming fully human /
    Dr. Miles Neale.
Description: Boulder, Colorado : Sounds True, 2018. | Includes bibliographical references and index.
Identifiers: LCCN 2018003042 (print) | LCCN 2018031039 (ebook) |
    ISBN 9781683642107 (ebook) | ISBN 9781683642091 (pbk.)
Subjects: LCSH: Lam-rim. | Spiritual life—Buddhism. | Enlightenment (Buddhism) |
    Buddhism—Doctrines. | Buddhist philosophy. | Buddhism—Psychology.
Classification: LCC BQ7645.L35 (ebook) | LCC BQ7645.L35 N38 2018 (print) |
    DDC 294.3/4435—dc23
LC record available at https://lccn.loc.gov/2018003042

10 9 8 7 6 5 4 3 2 1

To my Jewel Tree lineage of mentors . . .
His Holiness the Dalai Lama
Professor Robert Thurman
Dr. Joseph Loizzo

And to my heroes, each a lamp on the path . . .
Acharya Godwin Samararatne
Kyabje Gelek Rinpoche
Kyabje Lama Zopa Rinpoche
Venerable Geshe Tenzin Zopa

Shakyamuni Buddha

CONTENTS

FOREWORD

A little knowledge is a dangerous thing. The great eleventh-century Nalanda pandit Lama Atisha understood this well, and with a mighty heart of wise compassion he set out to marshal the Buddha's eighty-four thousand teachings—found in hundreds of scriptures and thousands of verses—into a logical, sequential, and practical road map to help guide spiritual seekers on the path, from ordinariness to liberation on to full and final awakening. This unique style of teaching came to be called Lam Rim, or the Gradual Path to Enlightenment, and, attesting to its beauty and effectiveness, has been preserved in all lineages and schools of Tibetan Buddhism for the past thousand years.

One of the unique features of the Lam Rim is that it recognizes an alternative to the path of sudden, spectacular enlightenment and instead proposes a more modest, gradual awakening. From the beginning of Tibet's history of receiving dharma transmissions from India, with the great debates involving the eighth-century Indian scholar Kamalashila, it was clear that for the masses the gradual process of studying, contemplating, and embodying insights over the course of a sustained, lifelong practice would be most appropriate and beneficial. While all methods have their validity and are useful for practitioners of various dispositions, the gradual approach explained in these pages is as relevant to modern students as it was to Tibetans centuries ago.

According to Lama Je Tsongkhapa (1357–1419), the essence of the entire path to awakening can be distilled into three main realizations: *renunciation*, the mind that relinquishes distortions, afflictive emotions, and compulsions, as well as their unfavorable results; *Bodhicitta*, the mind set on awakening for the benefit of others; and *wisdom*, the mind that directly perceives the ultimate reality of emptiness and interdependence. This book presents those three essential realizations along with contemplation topics and meditation techniques designed to ease their integration.

Gradual Awakening is generously offered by the learned teacher and psychologist Dr. Miles Neale, who has devoted himself to scientific and Buddhist philosophical training for the past twenty years, and whose life is a living example of the Bodhisattva conduct that the Lam Rim teachings were intended to manifest in all of us. Along with sophisticated philosophical insights and complex visualization practices, I am happy to see that Dr. Neale has also presented some of the traditional Tibetan rituals, prayers, and liturgy. Rather than abandoning these cultural aspects to make the Lam Rim more accessible to the West, Dr. Neale has used neuroscience and other familiar Western psychological concepts, as well as personal stories, to reveal their deeper meaning, make them relevant to a wider audience, and ensure their vitality is preserved during the current wave of the dharma's cross-cultural transmission.

Dr. Neale and I have studied the Lam Rim from a common source and lineage that have been realized, preserved, and passed down directly from mind to mind for at least six hundred years, from the great early masters Lama Atisha and Je Tsongkhapa, to modern masters such as Pabongkhapa Déchen Nyingpo, Lama Yeshe, and Geshe Lama Konchog, all the way to our current gurus His Holiness the Dalai Lama and Kyabje Lama Zopa Rinpoche. Despite the reproducible nature of the Lam Rim teachings that have continued unbroken over the centuries, there remains room for flexibility, ingenuity, and skillful adaptation. I very much enjoy Dr. Neale's fresh interpretation of the profound Lam Rim teachings that he has thoughtfully and respectfully examined through the perspectives of neuroscience and psychotherapy. Because of his long years of committed study, practice, teaching, and synthesis done with a sincere, altruistic motivation, I trust this book will reach many people who might otherwise not have had the fortune to be exposed to and to derive benefit from the dharma.

Furthermore, I am delighted with the manner in which Dr. Neale turned this book, along with its companion audio compilation of guided meditations, both published by Sounds True, into a vehicle to raise awareness and support for the nuns of Khachoe Ghakyil Ling Nunnery—the largest Tibetan Buddhist nunnery in Nepal—in order that they might pursue their wish to study dharma and reach enlightenment. This is an unbelievable act of generosity, and it shows that Dr. Neale has a deep understanding of the teachings on karma, emptiness, and compassion that are at the heart of the Lam Rim. I rejoice in his meritorious activities, and I pray that this book serves you well on your gradual journey of awakening and that the dharma continues to flourish in the West.

For more than 2,500 years, wherever across the planet Buddhism has been transplanted, it has influenced and been influenced by the dominant worldviews and practices of the various cultures it has entered. This continues to be the case as Buddhism migrates West and engages with the powerful disciplines of science, medicine, and psychology. As we all know, the world is facing many challenges—economic, sociopolitical, and environmental—and greater interfaith and interdisciplinary dialogue among different groups is critical if we are to build bridges, create harmony, deepen understanding, and collaborate to find solutions. In light of this, I am particularly pleased by the work of Dr. Neale and his colleagues at the Nalanda Institute for Contemplative Science, who are offering a bridge across time and space, between East and West, ancient and modern, spiritual and scientific, so that we might all share and receive mutual benefit from the rich cultural perspectives, techniques, and technologies of one another.

May these teachings benefit numberless sentient beings as vast as space and sow the karmic seeds of enlightenment in everyone fortunate enough to encounter them.

> May all beings have happiness and the causes of happiness.
> May all beings be free from suffering and the causes
>   of suffering.

May all beings never be separated from the supreme
   happiness of enlightenment.
May all beings abide in equanimity, free from clinging
   to close ones and aversion to others.

With sincere prayers for all,

GESHE TENZIN ZOPA
Touring Geshe
Foundation for the Preservation of the Mahayana Tradition (FPMT)
Kopan Monastery, Kathmandu, Nepal
2017

INSPIRATION

STANDING ON THE SHOULDERS OF GIANTS

If I have seen further than others, it is by standing on the shoulders of giants.
SIR ISAAC NEWTON, letter to Robert Hooke, February 15, 1675

Enlightenment is possible—*for everyone*. However, I don't think we will all awaken spontaneously in the way contemporary spiritual teachers Krishnamurti or Eckhart Tolle did. Most of us will never experience a voice from on high, a flash of life-altering insight, stigmata, or a transcendent miracle. Anything is possible, but the odds are not in our favor. What these teachers experienced is like winning the lottery.

Yet, from the Buddhist perspective, most of us have already won the lottery: against all probability, we have been born as human beings with intact senses and a bit of interest in pursuing something spiritual. This is even more remarkable when we consider the obstacles and temptations of our materialistic culture, in which spirit is thrown out with the bathwater of religious dogma, God is proclaimed dead, consciousness is reduced to epiphenomena of the brain, and life's purpose is made a hedonic scramble on a treadmill to nowhere. What is far more likely than sudden enlightenment is gradual awakening. Following a systematic educational process like a college curriculum, gradual awakening builds on incremental insights into who we truly are, learning to care for ourselves and others, and discovering creative ways to engage the problems we all face. This gradual process of awakening doesn't offer an escape hatch to another realm of reality or disavow our human wounds, limits, and foibles in this realm; rather it embraces and transforms them, because *the only way out is through*.

The Gradual Path, or Lam Rim, Tibetan Buddhism's alternative to instantaneous awakening, serves as the backbone of this book. In the style of Joseph Campbell's monomyth *The Hero's Journey*, the Lam Rim method is ancient and relevant, spiritual and scientific, and complete and systematic—holding a comprehensive set of universal insights, meditative arts, and practical tools I have spent my entire adult life studying and making as accessible to modern Westerners as it was thousands of years ago to the Asian cultures of its origin. After two decades of exploration, critical self-reflection, and refinement, I'm prepared to share what I've learned. I don't claim to be awakened, to be a guru, or even to be someone special, but I do assert that the Gradual Path is a unique teaching that can progressively awaken *you*, and through you, this planet. The Lam Rim has saved my life and the lives of the clients and students I have had the privilege to work with, and it could save yours.

Much (if not all) of my spiritual growth was cultivated and punctuated by my encounters with a succession of incredible teachers. A qualified mentor is essential as we find our way from suffering to freedom, from spiritual darkness to the transcendent light of Divinity. This is one of the primary themes of this book. As I look at my mentors, I don't necessarily think they've all reached the pinnacle of enlightenment—although I could be wrong—but they do seem to be living more meaningful and fulfilling lives than most people. They've evolved through their commitment to the Gradual Path, which has been handed down in an unbroken lineage from teacher to student, from Buddhist Master Atisha in the eleventh century to Je Tsongkhapa in the fifteenth century, all the way to the current Dalai Lama, and from him to my mentors—Robert Thurman and Joseph Loizzo.

My intention, alongside theory and practice, is to share my story by focusing on a unique, although often misunderstood, aspect of Tibetan Buddhism called guru yoga, or mentor bonding. I've marked the milestones of my own hero's journey by my fortunate encounters with remarkable guides and the generous, life-affirming gifts they bestowed upon me. Westerners tend to have a cultural resistance toward gurus, a carryover from a legacy of religious manipulation and broken trust, so rather than shy away from the topic of gurus with distaste and suspicion, I'd like to engage it in a practical, therapeutic way by inquiring into and working through hang-ups and unfavorable associations. When I first encountered Buddhism, like many Westerners, I had a weird, unhealthy mix of guru idealization and guruphobia. This might resonate for you as well. That's okay. It's understandable to be concerned, given our culture's overemphasis on independence that leaves us bereft of guidance. This lack of guidance has led us to idealize the elder archetype on one hand, whereas the history of religious hypocrisy and misuse of power has left us suspicious and critical on the other. However, we are missing an enormous opportunity if we deny ourselves a wholesome, mature reliance on those who have evolved to what we aspire to become. As Sir Isaac Newton urged, we can evolve best by standing on the shoulders of giants, getting closer to truth by building on the discoveries of those luminaries who came before us. As you move through this book, acknowledge whatever complicated feelings arise, but see them as an opportunity to expose and work through your wounds, preconceptions, and defense adaptations, as well as the social memes and implicit propaganda of our materialistic and conformist society.

My hero's journey began when I met my first Buddhist teacher, the late Sri Lankan lay Vipassana master Acharya Godwin Samararatne. I traveled to India in 1996, when I was twenty years old, to live and study in a Burmese monastery at the site of Buddha's awakening at Bodhgaya. Although I was there for educational purposes under the auspices of Antioch University's Buddhist studies program, I truly was searching for relief from the tumult of my childhood traumas and disillusionment with modern acquisitive culture.

Godwin was not a guru, had no entourage, was not even a scholar, and did not teach philosophical complexities from a dais. Rather, he was a down-to-earth layman, a librarian who offered the simple and direct methods of mindfulness and loving-kindness—the two foundational tools of self-healing—which we all need at the outset of our path. More importantly, Godwin embodied the presence, attunement, and guidance I had not consistently received when I was growing up, and therefore did not internalize. In Buddhist terms, Godwin was a *kalyana-mitra*—a spiritual friend and confidant—a perfect first step between my isolation and the distant peak of a guru figure, someone who could walk beside me on the path. Godwin allowed me to connect with my humanness—wounds and all—thawing the frozen pain of my wintry past in the warmth of genuine intimacy. He was a mirror clear enough to reflect and illuminate the best of myself, a healing ally who didn't judge, manipulate, or need anything from me and, therefore, was an exemplar of unconditional love.

I have two memories of experiences with Godwin that will never fade. The first occurred when he called me to his room in the monastery after I had complained about not being able to sleep, a condition that had plagued me since childhood. We spoke through the evening, sharing stories, and when it grew late he invited me to rest in his room in the attendant's bed, recommending I lie on my right side, as it is said the Buddha did when he passed from this life. I slept deeply that night for the first time in a while, but I don't think it was about posture—it was about Godwin's presence, his grace, and the effortless, platonic connection we shared. Refreshed, we rose before sunrise and walked in silence, spontaneously hand in hand, from the monastery, through the darkness, and down a dirt road to the Bodhi tree where the Buddha reached enlightenment. Sitting together in meditation under the branches, dawn broke to the resonance of monks chanting, an endless stream of prayers thousands of years old and echoing through the ages. That was the first time I came to know what the word *love* meant. The person, the place, and the moment all felt like finding home. It was pure magic.

The second experience occurred two years later. I had returned to Asia to study with Godwin at his Nilambe Buddhist Meditation Center, outside of Kandy, Sri Lanka. During the silent retreat, participants were encouraged to meditate alone outdoors for periods of time. I found a spot on a bluff overlooking the lush tea terraces I had named the Garden of Eden. It was in solitude there, bathed in sunlight, mindfully listening to the morning birdsong, that I had my first so-called breakthrough meditation experience. My sense of self, its incessant inner monologue of self-loathing, receded and collapsed into a crystalline *selfless* presence. I was no longer an observer noticing sound, but instead became the birdsong itself. With this dissolution of separation arose indescribable relief. Boundaries melted and a freedom emerged unlike anything I had known before.

That unifying insight—what the Zen Buddhists call *kensho*—didn't last long, yet while I was in it, it could have been eternal. When consciousness receded and I reassumed the separateness of my ordinary self, a tremendous sense of exhilaration lingered because of what I thought I had discovered. Was this awakening?

I stayed on that bluff for hours as I reflected on what had occurred. I came to see how the edifice of identity, with its past and future, hopes and fears, paired with my striving to become someone, or to gain something, and my resistance to the inevitability of not being someone or losing something, had cut me off from the precious source of life—the dynamic, unitary flow of which we are all always a part but I had failed to recognize. Rather than being separated and pitted against life, I *was* life. The struggle to which I had resigned myself, indeed that had overwhelmed me since childhood, was revealed to be mostly a mental fabrication born of the delusion of separateness. For a moment, *in meditative absorption*, I thought I had entered a holy vortex, pierced through the veil of appearances, and accessed a sacred reality. Or had I?

That evening, in my conversation with Godwin, he put my eager, inner child at ease as he explained that while these breakthrough experiences were significant, they were by no means special. Many if not most meditators, as well as those using psychedelics or engaging in ritual actions such as Sufi whirling or drum circles or creative processes, taste the freedom of the dropping away of labels and separation. Godwin cautioned me not to confuse a glimmer of oneness with the radical transformation of awakening, and he reminded me that being present with pain, loneliness, and sadness offered profound opportunities for mindfulness, loving-kindness, and insight as experiences of beauty, the heavenly, or the Divine.

The goal of spiritual practice isn't to get outside oneself, beyond our tormented natures, but to come back to the self with more spacious clarity, unconditional love, and skillful creativity. It would take me many years of Gradual Path training to understand this vital teaching Godwin pointed to, but applying it is something that continues for me. That's why I begin this book as I'll end it—with the simple but radical truth that the goal of meditation is not the relief of escape but the compassion of relationality. In other words, transcendence isn't the destination but a necessary stop to unburden fixation, so we can return to ordinary life with open minds and warmer hearts. Or, as Godwin put it, "Breaking out is only as important as how we break back in."

Godwin was so skillful in helping me frame this early experience. He kept me from deifying oneness and venerating it as one might a sacred cow, thus sparing me years of misguided chasing, grasping, and suffering. As you join me on this Gradual Path odyssey, we'll circle back to this original insight, because it is the heart and purpose of the work, which is a journey to awaken gradually to an ultimate truth through which we return to a relative world with more compassion and the means to heal others.

My fortunate encounter with Godwin was the beginning of a succession of instrumental relationships with luminaries—giants among teachers. With each successive mentor I reached a new milestone in my process of maturity. Standing on their shoulders, relying on their years of experience, and building upon their accomplishments, I came to behold the horizon of infinite possibilities I would have been too limited to see on my own.

In the chapters that follow, it'll be my pleasure to introduce you to my heroes, including Dr. Joe Loizzo, my main role model and guide through life and the first American Buddhist scholar to translate the entire Lam Rim into neuropsychological language, making it clinically relevant and accessible to Westerners. You'll meet Joe's mentor Professor Robert Thurman, the first Westerner ordained as a Buddhist monk by His Holiness the Fourteenth Dalai Lama. Thurman is a champion of the Tibetan cause for freedom who challenged the elites of academia—their Eurocentric hubris, their colonialization of knowledge, and their disenfranchising paradigm of nihilism. I'll share the experience I had with Geshe Michael Roach, said to be the first Westerner to complete the arduous twenty-year course of study in a Tibetan monastery, and explore the painful but necessary lessons learned from a guru's fall from grace, stemming from his failure to deal with personal trauma. You'll also meet Lama Zopa Rinpoche, a far-out character who operates in what I call "Zopa Standard Time," has all the marks and signs of a fully realized master, and renewed my conviction that a complete awakening is possible. Along with Lama Zopa you'll meet his ever-devoted yet humble protégé Geshe Tenzin Zopa, a dynamic teacher who is my age. Raised on the wisdom of the Tibetan high lamas of Kopan Monastery since he was a toddler, Tenzin Zopa stole my heart, made me want to become a better man, and modeled the practice of guru devotion. Finally, you'll meet Lama Je Tsongkhapa himself, fifteenth-century scholar-sage, epitome of the Lam Rim, author of our sacred text, chief architect of this book's structure, and living exemplar for the whole succession of mentor beings who have blessed us and allowed us to access the reality of possibilities that exists beyond our immediate sense perception. On behalf of all my mentors and the lineage we uphold, it is to Tsongkhapa we pay our deepest salutations.

In every one of us is a child who hopes myths, mysteries, and dreams can come true. They can, and they have. May the pages that follow and the wisdom teachings I've gathered inspire you to walk the Gradual Path on your quest to become fully human. May any errors you find be solely attributed to my limitations, blind spots, and misunderstandings, allowing the legacy of the Lam Rim and its wisdom-keepers to progress unblemished. May this book and any benefit you derive from actualizing these sacred teachings fulfill the wishes of all mentors and all lineages of awakening, empowering us all to face the enormous challenges of our world with greater confidence, creativity, and collaboration. May all spiritual mentors live long and teach widely, and may we never be separated until samsara ends.

Thirty-Step Road Map

Because every hero needs a map before they set out on a journey, here is our Lam Rim Road Map of the Hero's Thirty Steps to Awakening:

1 Create a sacred space.

2 Set up an altar and make offerings.

3 Prepare your body and mind.

4 Evoke the mentor and the Jewel Tree refuge field.

5 Initiate the Seven-Step Mentor-Bonding Process:
    i Admire qualities
    ii Make offerings
    iii Disclose negativities
    iv Rejoice virtues
    v Request guidance
    vi Request presence
    vii Dedicate merits

6 Offer the mandala and final prayers.

7 Find a mentor.

8 Become a suitable student.

9 Preciousness of human life inspires appreciation.

10 Death inspires urgency.

11 Refuge offers evolutionary safe-direction.

12 Causality inspires agency.

13 Defects of samsara inspire distaste in compulsive existence.

14 Renunciation (aspiration to be free)—the milestone of evolutionary self-care.

15 Equanimity balances social reactivity.

16 Recognize all beings as kin—inspires solidarity.

17 Remember their kindness—inspires gratitude.

18 Resolve to repay their kindness—inspires reciprocity.

19 Equalize self and other—inspires empathy.

20 Contemplate disadvantages of self-preoccupation and take on suffering—inspires compassion.

21 Contemplate the benefits of altruism and give care—inspires love.

22 Take responsibility and aspire to save all beings—inspires purpose.

23 Bodhicitta (aspiration to free others)—the milestone of radical altruism.

24 Perfect generosity.

25 Perfect virtue.

26 Perfect patience.

27 Perfect effort.

28 Perfect concentration.

29 Perfect wisdom—the milestone of quantum view.

30 Manifestation (using MAPS):
     i **M**aturity
     ii **A**cceptance
     iii **P**ossibility
     iv **S**eeding

1 INITIATION

EMBARKING ON THE GRADUAL PATH

We have *not* even to risk the adventure alone, for the heroes of all time
have gone before us. The labyrinth is thoroughly known. We have only
to follow the thread of the hero path, and where we had thought to
find an abomination we shall find a god. And where we had thought to
slay another, we shall slay ourselves. Where we had thought to travel
outward, we will come to the center of our own existence. And where
we had thought to be alone, we shall be with all the world.

JOSEPH CAMPBELL, *The Power of Myth*

I am as much an enthusiast of all things Tibetan Buddhist as I am a
critic of modern, materialistic culture. I coined the term "McMindfulness" because I've grown uncomfortable with the ways we Westerners
exploit, capitalize on, and reinforce people's fantasies about happiness
and escaping pain by giving them watered-down spiritual practices in
sexy marketed packages. We've cherry-picked teachings from ancient,
mostly threatened, wisdom cultures and mass-marketed them as consumerist goods in the guise of a panacea, particularly now as we teeter
on the edge of evolutionary survival as a species. Yes, I understand
the argument that soft entry-points and bite-sized morsels welcome
people to explore and find the deeper dimensions of spirituality and
the rigorous contemplative science that underpins stripped-down versions of meditation and yoga practice. However, I also believe there
needs to be some pushback against our culture's appetite for the spectacular, for its Eurocentric hubris, shortsightedness, and hedonism. I
don't mind taking an unpopular, critical stance on how superficial,

misguided, and Kardashian we have become and how dangerous the capitalist agenda is. The short version: it's killing us.

I'll put my position as bluntly as I can here: *Any meditation practice that fails to address our culture's distorted worldview of scientific reductionism grounded in nihilism, and its equally misguided offshoots—materialism, hedonism, imperialism, neoliberal capitalism, and consumerism—that constitute the current zeitgeist, and fails to connect them directly to our society's mental health pandemic, general apathy, and the broader plight of our planet-in-peril is dangerous. Any such approach is the equivalent of encouraging people to rearrange the furniture when their house is on fire.*

Our distorted, impoverishing worldview—what I call our *sickness of paradigm*—is resistant to feel-good attempts to quiet the mind and relax the body, and it requires a *paradigm therapy* capable of uprooting the fundamental internal causes of human suffering while ushering in a global renaissance of science and spirit that can reestablish the sustainable well-being that we have lost touch with in industrial society. This book presents such a therapy—not a simple technique extracted from an exotic but "primitive" culture, not another mindfulness-based intervention fitting like a square peg in the square hole of our reductionist worldview, but a complete system unto itself. It's an in-depth, multidimensional exploration of what is called the Gradual Path to Enlightenment—the Lam Rim—that not only challenges our sickness of paradigm but could heal it completely.

In my estimation, combining Tibet's deep psychology, meditative techniques, and virtuous rituals offers far more transformational potential than merely sitting quietly following the breath. The chapters that follow serve as a practical training manual that will allow you to experiment with and actualize the benefits of role-modeling visualization, affirmations, contemplative themes, textual recitation, prayers, altars, offerings, and, of course, meditation. My teacher Geshe Tenzin Zopa defines meditation as a process of "familiarizing the mind with virtue," which I know isn't the way most people understand meditation in our mainstream Western culture, and that's my point. *We don't get it . . . yet.* We don't see the whole picture of what meditation is, where it comes from, how it works, and what it was designed to do. Meditation was developed for human liberation, not mere stress reduction or symptom relief. How mainstream Western culture approaches meditation is analogous to using a rocket launcher to light a candle.

This book is no more about converting anyone to Buddhism than a textbook on mathematics is about asking readers to believe in a higher, abstract power. You don't have to be "converted" in order for math's principles to be observable, to be applicable, and to cause an intended outcome. The same is true of this book. The world doesn't need more Buddhists vying for religious market share, but it does need radical healing and an accelerated global awakening of consciousness. Neither of these things can happen within dogmatic religion or equally rigid scientism, both of which discount our personal power. Nor can we hope to genuinely awaken ourselves through lightweight, pseudospiritual self-help that may be alluring but does not offer sustenance.

We'll need to level up and commit to something with substance and depth that can feed us, because a human being's complexity is only matched by the tenacity of our blindness and affliction, both of which inevitably withstand most attempts at change despite our sincere wish for transformation. The diluted and ungrounded dissemination of New Age teachings and DIY spirituality popular in the modern West can't compete with the refined and time-tested wisdom of ancient cultures. If you have found your way to the original teachings of Kabbalah, Sufism, Christianity, shamanism, the First Nations healers, or the way-finders of Polynesia, you have returned to a source of knowledge that still holds sacred insights and nourishing practices serving the same purpose as the ones I've compiled in this book. If you have found your way to basic mindfulness meditation or hatha yoga postures, then from there I'll take you to their source in Tibetan Buddhism and the contemplative science of India. If you've already dived into the vast ocean of Tibetan teachings, then perhaps my neuropsychological spin on things will help deepen your faith or nuance your understanding.

Reading this book may be the first step on *your* hero's journey, or it may serve to elucidate and help you navigate a path you have already embarked upon. For me, this book is many things—a gift, an invitation, and a practical manual among others. It represents the scars and breakthroughs I sustained during my odyssey toward personal healing and growth as a psychotherapist and Buddhist teacher. It's also a legacy I aspire to impart to my sons and perhaps your kids as well, so that they can all inherit a more sane and sustainable world and learn to be fully human again—wisdom-keepers of history's great spiritual lineages, altruistic warriors of love, and guardians of a planet that needs to be restored to balance.

Before you dismiss the thesis of this book, remember that the way we've been living in the West for several centuries, as if God is "dead," is directly connected to the fact that the ice caps are melting, lingering wars are now good business, and we ignore the vulnerable. I have made it my life's work to go beyond the superficialities of McMindfulness, to return to and revitalize the ancient, vast, and profound teachings of the Gradual Path's full-spectrum approach to contemplative practice. Using neuroscience as a bridge, we can return to "spirit" and integrate teachings and insights often disparaged and abandoned in favor of our culture's yearning for industrial progress. I hope you'll hang in with me long enough to consider how Lam Rim can play a part in the overall solution—not just for your life but for our world. I invite you to reconnect with an old-school science and set of practices in a relevant, meaningful, and fulfilling way.

The Hero: An Archetype for Our Time

Drawing from Buddhism and psychology—the traditions that have become the twin domains of my heart's passion—I'll begin by defining a key term in my teachings and this book: the hero. The archetype of the hero in Tibetan Buddhism is a Bodhisattva, an evolved being motivated by profound compassion for the suffering of others who vows to reach complete awakening. Bodhisattvas who pursue the Gradual Path follow a succession of training steps through stages of psychological development and reach specific milestones, or realizations, along the way to enlightenment. Both physicists discovering the ultimate nature of reality and poet-activists, Bodhisattvas generate love and compassion as practical and constructive forces to skillfully redesign the matrix of interdependence we all share.

I often refer to the great mythologist and American author Joseph Campbell (1904–1987) in this book. He used the designation of "hero" to describe individuals who embark on the monumental psychological task of expanding and evolving consciousness and famously charted this journey. This hero's journey begins in our inherent state of blindness, separation, and suffering and progresses on a circular (as opposed to linear) route made up of stages shared by myths and legends spanning all cultures and epochs. From Buddha to Christ, Arjuna to Alice in Wonderland, the hero's journey is one of passing through a set of trials and phases: seeking adventure, encountering mentors, slaying demons, finding treasure, and returning home to heal others.

Tibetan Buddhism's and Campbell's descriptions of the hero both offer a travel-tested road map of a meaningful life, a path to becoming fully human—we don't have to wander blindly, like college kids misguidedly hazed by a fraternity, or spiritual seekers abused in the thrall of a cult leader. The hero archetype is relevant to each of us, irrespective of our background, gender, temperament, or challenges, because we each have a hero gene within us capable of following the path, facing trials, and awakening for the benefit of others. Becoming a hero is what the Lam Rim describes as taking full advantage of our precious human embodiment. It's what Campbell saw as answering the call to adventure and following our bliss—not the hedonic bliss of chasing a high or acquiring more stuff, but the bliss of the individual soul, which, like a mountain stream, reaches and merges with the ocean of universal reality.

A Seismic Paradigm Shift

How did we get so fucked up? Why is the hero such an important archetype? Why is the journey of awakening, to heal others, so relevant? Western materialist culture was spawned in Europe less than three centuries ago during the age of reason, a reaction to fundamental and dogmatic Christianity, which stifled the individual's sense of self-determination and forced them to adhere through faith alone to hierarchical and often corrupt systems of centralized religious power. In the eighteenth century, reliance upon religion shifted in favor of logic. Freed from the mandates of the Church, educated individuals had the ability to pursue and manifest personal destiny, liberating the power of the intellect and the left brain. This movement produced radical and valuable breakthroughs in society and science—particularly the dissemination of information through the printing press. However, as we gained freedom with this seismic shift, we lost something vital to human identity and our survival as a species. Like a ship cut from its mooring, we began to drift too far from that which is beyond our five sense perceptions—the spirit.

Derived from the Latin word for breath, *spirit* is the ephemeral source, the energetic vitality that subsumes matter. It is the breath of life. Since the dawn of civilization, spiritual activities—the stuff of mystery, myth, communion, ritual, and dreams—have been the way people made sense of life's uncertainty and chaos, finding meaning and purpose when there appeared to be none, and consciously (and, as we now believe, epigenetically) driving evolution toward flourishing, beyond the instinctual imperatives for basic survival.

By reestablishing the individual and entirely displacing God with science, we risk erecting another false idol—scientism grounded in nihilism—with its own dogma and colonization of knowledge, ordaining scientists as new high priests. If we accept without further consideration the claims that Philip Morris, Pfizer, or Monsanto makes about its products, using only its own research as evidence, we're as naive as the pious who relied solely on the Church for guidance and information during the Middle Ages. Psychologist and author John Welwood summarizes well the cost of secular progress, particularly industrialization, as it relates to our neuropsychological attachment styles and ability to connect with others:

> In contrast to the indigenous cultures of traditional
> Asia . . . most of us suffer from an extreme degree of

alienation and disconnection that was unknown in earlier times—from society, community, family, older generations, nature, religion, tradition, our body, our feelings, and our humanity itself.[1]

Society's increasingly visible and abject suffering is the result of having abandoned its connection to the realm of spirit. If you're anything like me, you're angry about what's happening right now as our materialistic worldview and hedonic values are exported globally. The breakdown of the family and wider social bonds; the decline of ethics and morals rooted in our interconnection; the corruption and cronyism rampant in our financial and political institutions; the ever-growing divide between rich and poor; the shortsighted pillaging of finite resources and the militarization to secure what remains; the degradation of the biosphere; the extermination of species; the demise of indigenous cultures, languages, and the perennial wisdom they maintain; and the pandemic incidents of the so-called "diseases of civilization," including cancers, addiction, and depression, are all symptoms of our fragmentation and our disconnection from our bodies, emotions, values, communities, the natural world, and the spirit—*the breath of life.*

I am not naively recommending we return to a time before the age of reason—that's neither possible nor prudent given how technology, medicine, and the sciences can be forces of good. I am not opposed to science; as a Buddhist psychotherapist, I have feet in both worlds. Evolutionary neurobiology and quantum physics offer equally compelling maps of reality to complement Tibet's contemplative science and meditative methodologies. The challenge is to create a synthesis between views and methods to find the best solution. As greater interdisciplinary dialogue occurs—like the decades-long exploration among the Dalai Lama, scientists, and contemplatives of various traditions—we'll see an alternative paradigm emerge. Perhaps as we look more closely at how Tibetan Buddhism maintained both science and spirit for centuries without contradiction, we'll appreciate how they're compatible.

The irony is that today science is being used as a bridge back to spirit. More Westerners are interested in meditation today because of the mounting empirical research proving its brain and health benefits. We are being drawn back to spirit by reason. Perhaps further discoveries will reveal more about consciousness, subtle energies, and rituals that have been dismissed and abandoned as suspect metaphysics. Science as a method could then coexist with spirit within a new holistic worldview as we reintegrate the fragmented domains of analysis and contemplation, left and right brain, individual and collective well-being, the prosocial ethos of socialism and the individual liberty of capitalism, thereby marking a new epoch—the dawn of integration.

For Every Hero, an Initiation

As Campbell pointed out, in all spiritual traditions the hero must undergo initiation and testing. These rites of passage awaken and develop latent human capacities as they mark and safely ritualize the process of maturity, empowerment, and agency among members of a group. Initiation is a way adolescent naivete and dependency ends as we develop a sense of mastery, meaning, and purpose and are reborn as adults and active, contributing members of the tribe. Vision quests, shamanic journeys, sun dances, ordinations, Bar and Bat Mitzvahs, and confirmations offer access to a time-tested method steeped in a collective body of wisdom and community that mitigates risk and gives a reproducible outcome.

Regardless of time, place, or culture, the motifs and stages of every initiation are the same. Whether symbolic or actual they include leaving home or separating from the community, facing a symbolic or literal hardship that serves as a psychological catalyst for an altered state of consciousness, and awakening as the nascent hero. The process continues with integrating and embodying wisdom, sometimes with the help of elders, priests, or shamans, and returning to the community as a mature member, active contributor, or leader. Initiation hastens development so the latent hero nature can be realized.

Sadly, the modern industrialized world has commercialized most forms of sacred ritual and rites of passage. Even funerals and weddings can seem diluted and rote. What do we gain these days—other than the immediate gratification of ego and senses—with $50,000 weddings and Disneyland-like Bar and Bat Mitzvahs? We have lost meaningful ways of marking life-phase transitions and sacred portals through which we can pass to embrace and embody a perennial knowledge. As a result, we see the youth of Western industrialized societies struggling. They may have the latest gadgets and can drive themselves to the malls, yet they are deprived of the essential opportunity to be tested and transformed, from dependent child to capable adult, from neophyte to hero. By abandoning rites of passage, we have built a culture of immaturity and widespread juvenile entitlement. Look around. How many "adults" in their forties or fifties do you know who are as self-absorbed, dependent, disempowered, and purposeless as they were when they were twelve?

In *How Soon Is Now*, author Daniel Pinchbeck contends that the process of initiation activates the prefrontal cortex, the part of our brain associated with executive function, self-reflection, self-regulation, symbolic processing, insight, morality, intuition, and transpersonal perspective. He argues that the loss of rites is an evolutionary *digression*. Pinchbeck reframes our current global ecological crisis as an attempt by the collective unconscious to create the adventitious circumstance for the emergence of higher states of consciousness. To this I would add that the crisis also offers the opportunity to master the evolutionary self-care, altruism, and creativity in the Lam Rim. In other words, our collective psyches are self-sabotaging as if to recreate a new trial by fire that would transform us into heroes emboldened by crisis.

History of the Gradual Path

Before we embark on the Gradual Path, it's important to understand the historical context from which this stunning tradition and "pith" text emerged. The Buddhist teachings were first established in Tibet by the eighth-century master Padmasambhava, from Uddiyana (believed to be the modern-day Swat Valley in Pakistan), and the Indian abbot Shantarakshita of Nalanda University. They were championed by kings beginning with Trisong Detsen, whose patronage facilitated the transmission and translation campaign that helped establish Buddhism in Tibet. Two Buddhist philosophical viewpoints were vying for supremacy in the newly receptive Himalayan region. One, from the Northern school of Chan/Zen Buddhism, espoused *subitism*, or sudden enlightenment. Adherents believed that a complete transformative insight could be reached all at once. The other view, primarily from Indian adherents of middle-way philosophy, espoused *gradualism*, or the slow and steady progression toward enlightenment.

Beginning in 792 CE, at the Council in Lhasa at Samye Monastery, representatives of the two schools engaged in a series of great philosophical debates that lasted for several *years*. The Chinese meditation master Heshang Moheyan argued for a direct, nonconceptual, and instantaneous breakthrough, while the Indian scholar Kamalashila asserted the gradual approach to realization that begins with study at the conceptual level, moves toward critical reflection, and eventually blossoms as intuitive insight. Kamalashila was victorious. Gradualism emphasizes moral discipline, ardent study of wisdom texts, and the six impeccable activities (*paramitas*) of the Bodhisattva to facilitate progressive psychological development culminating in Buddhahood. King Trisong Detsen saw this approach as being more relevant and accessible for the people of Tibet.

Even after it was decided that gradualism was preferable, there was still a problem: sharing information. It was impossible (and remember, this was the eighth century) to distribute the vast corpus of Buddhist teachings in a coherent and organized manner north from India and throughout the Tibetan Plateau. The dharma teachings (and those who could teach them) traveled the treacherous terrain of the Himalayas—the size of Texas and Alaska combined—haphazardly in bits and pieces to disparate provinces. By the eleventh century, there was much confusion about the order and context of the many Buddhist doctrines and commentaries in circulation throughout Tibet. The fact that teachings appeared to contradict each other caused considerable but understandable doubt.

ATISHA (982–1054 CE)

As a result, there was a call—or plea—from an eleventh-century Tibetan king, Jangchub-Oe, to recruit one of the great sages from India to make some clarifications. Lama Atisha Dipamkara Srijnana, an Indian pandit (scholar) and abbot of the great Nalanda University, was asked to resolve contradictions found in themes from texts and commentaries that had been disseminated for centuries throughout the Tibetan Plateau. Atisha did something that had never been done before: he organized the many streams of Buddha's teachings and corresponding realizations sequentially, clarified common misunderstandings, and showed how Buddhist themes and practices interrelate and support (rather than contradict) one another in a cohesive progression. The result was The Lamp for the Path to Enlightenment, the original, quintessential Lam Rim text—the entire road map toward enlightenment via specific steps, stages, and milestones. This became an important and widespread method of instruction and literary genre, central to the curriculum for all schools of Tibetan Buddhism.

JE TSONGKHAPA (1357–1419 CE)

Many variations of Lam Rim literature inspired by Atisha's text emerged over the centuries, but the one I'll focus on is a version by fifteenth-century scholar and yogi Lama Je Tsongkhapa. Tsongkhapa's devoted students included Gendün Druppa—the first Dalai Lama—and thus the lineage of the Dalai Lamas is traced back to him. This makes the lineage via the current Dalai Lama a direct, mind-to-mind transmission reaching all the way back to Tsongkhapa himself.

Tsongkhapa is a revolutionary and renaissance figure in Tibetan history. As founder of the Gelugpa school of Tibetan Buddhism, the most modern of the five classical schools (the others being Nyingma, Kagyu, Sakya, and Jonang), he ushered in a new era of interest in classical Buddhist scholarship and emphasis on monastic discipline after a period of decline. He created and disseminated a more academic, scientific, morally grounded, and reproducible curriculum, making Tibetan monasteries places of spiritual learning akin to the Western university system. The teachings are academically rigorous and reproducible, rather than exclusively meditatively experiential and personal, and thus designed in the way modern universities might teach physics, mathematics, or geography.

From a mystical standpoint, it is said Tsongkhapa's purification practice and virtuous activities were exceptional and included hundreds of thousands, if not millions, of prostrations, mantras, prayers, and offerings, all of which contributed to him becoming an exceptionally realized being. He spent years in deep meditation, much of it in solitary retreat, and is said to have been in direct relationship with the Bodhisattva Manjushri, the embodiment of the Buddha's wisdom. It is through his meditation, his encounters with the subtle realms of reality, the wisdom transmission from Manjushri, and the ensuing revelations that Tsongkhapa's masterworks were written.

You may think this is all crazy fiction or indiscriminate folklore. Perhaps it is . . . *but* you may feel that way because our culture has lost a connection to magic and forgotten what humans are capable of. To be fair, the Tibetans, as well as the shamans of the Amazon and the First Nation elders, think Westerners are crazy too—so materialistic, believing only in what we perceive with our limited five senses while dismissing the rest. Some call us "orphans" because we've forsaken our connection to the Mother Earth, covering her in concrete and polluting rivers and airways the way we do our bodies. Tell me, who are the crazy ones?

REDEFINING OUR CULTURE'S ENDGAME

Think about this contextually: There was a time when we were hunter-gatherers. Life was about survival and we weren't as concerned with existential meaning and purpose. Then, during the Neolithic Era, as we became agrarians, culture and society evolved. Agriculture created surplus, and that surplus brought leisure time. We started exploring the outer world and studying the stars, and we started studying our internal universe—our minds. This led to profound self-discoveries and social developments, as well as spiritual inquiry culminating with the great sages of the Axial Age—Buddha, Homer, Zoroaster, and Lao Tzu—who offered humanity access to its own capacity for awakening and personal experiences of nature, the cosmos, the Divine.

Fast-forward to the present. What has happened in our postindustrial society is that we've cut ourselves off from our spiritual inclination, from inner exploration, and have become exclusively externally directed. All we're doing now is creating surplus for the sake of creating more surplus, with no inherent meaning or purpose. We're chasing money to make more, with no clear goals beyond acquisition and physical comfort. Instead of using these means for an altruistic end, the means have become the end. No wonder we're confused, starved, and apathetic.

The Tibetans may not have had sophisticated urban infrastructure and advanced technology, democracy, and allopathic medicine like we developed in Europe through science and the conquest of matter, but according to Robert Thurman[2] there was something profound and perhaps unparalleled in human history happening as an entire culture attempted to orient itself toward awakening, and thus supported the spiritual inclination of the individual to help make sense of and maximize their precious human life. In Tibet, no cataclysmic rift between science and spirit, logic and faith, has occurred. Tibetans maintain traditions of advanced ontology, epistemology, and debate that rival Western scientific methods, and yet they were taught in tandem with metaphysics, meditation, and ritual. Tibet offers an example of a paradigm in which science and spirituality, reason and faith, coexist.

Meditation is but a critical first-person inquiry into the nature of reality that follows the same logic as our scientific method of investigation, and yet its application goes beyond materialism to include the unseen world of consciousness, positive emotions, karmic causality, subtle energy, and even spiritual entities. I'm not idealizing Tibet—not every Tibetan was enlightened by any stretch of the imagination, and Tibetan society faced challenges like any other, in particular with its patriarchal, corruptible, authoritarian theocracy, as well as its share of wars, religious manipulation, and bloodshed. But what began to happen during those specific eras when the dharma was flourishing, such as during the fifteenth century under the leadership of Tsongkhapa, was remarkable, and it offers our postmodern society that's on the brink of self-destruction something of value to consider.

With their surplus and time, Tibetans created a cultural paradigm of introspection, which meant that within a generation a critical mass of people could go to monastic universities to study *inner*, or mind, science. Thurman calls the most adept among these fortunate ones "psychonauts," who explored inner—in contrast to outer—space. These monasteries were like universities, the Harvards or Stanfords of self-discovery. A large portion of the population could attend for free and devote themselves to understanding the nature of their own mind and how to be self-liberated. At the height of their golden age, Tibetans developed a way for most people to feel a part of something meaningful—those who couldn't take the monastic path or were too old or didn't have the predilection for spiritual endeavors still contributed, and they were gratified by their part in the meaningful process of sending someone off on a hero's journey. Can you imagine that happening in the United States now? What if we redirected most of our wealth, energy, and surplus away from defense and put it into education, creating technologies and institutions that feed the human soul and usher in a paradigm that values contemplation as much as we presently value consumerism?

As human beings, we are capable of greater things than the accumulation of wealth and fulfilling our sensory desires at the expense of others. We each deserve a chance to achieve our birthright of well-being, compassion, and creativity. We can *all* realize who we are and what we are here to do. Those realizations have a formula, which is elucidated in Tsongkhapa's Great Treatise, as well as our root text, the Three Principles of the Path. It's mind-blowing; there's a whole tradition and lineage available for the conscious evolutionary development of all human beings, revealing to them what their purpose is—not a solitary purpose, but one that connects them with *all life*.

The Great Treatise

Tsongkhapa composed several renditions of the Lam Rim and is best known for the extensive version called the Lam Rim Chen Mo, which is The Great Treatise on the Stages of the Path to Enlightenment. The Lam Rim Chen Mo is a phenomenal text—a crown jewel of world spiritual literature containing within its vast volumes everything, in perfect sequential order, that we'll ever need to become fully human if we are willing to commit to a slow but systematic, lifelong process. Everything.

The primary text in this book, the Three Principles of the Path, is a poetic distillation of Tsongkhapa's Great Treatise. It is composed as a letter to a friend and condensed into fourteen verses. Think about that: fourteen verses that hold the *entire* path to enlightenment, through which we can realize ultimate reality. It is the work of a fully realized master, a Buddha, generated for our practical benefit. Much like a codex, every word can be extrapolated and made into a teaching itself.

As a way of initiating you into the Gradual Path, I invite you to recite Tsongkhapa's text, artfully translated by my mentor Joe Loizzo. Please don't approach it with an analytical mind—that comes later as we unpack the verses. Instead, lead with the heart, see the text as a song or poem to chant aloud, and let the vibrations and evocations stimulate emotions, memories, and images.

Three Principles of the Path

Homage to all Spiritual Mentors!

[In this brief text] I'll explain as best I can   1
The quintessence of all Buddha's teachings—
The path revealed by his noble heirs,
As the crossing for fortunate freedom seekers.

Listen with open minds you lucky people   2
Who break the addiction to worldly pleasures,

And work to give leisure and opportunity meaning,
Trusting the path that satisfies Buddhas.

The drive to survive binds all embodied beings,   3
And no cure can stem the pleasure seeking
Tides of mere survival but real transcendence,
So first of all, work to renounce [mindless pleasure]!

Leisure and opportunity are hard to find,   4
And a lifespan leaves no time to waste—reflect on this
And you'll counter the obsessions of a worldly life.
Compulsive action and reaction inexorably cause
Future cycles of pain—repeatedly contemplate this
And you'll counter obsession with an afterlife.

With practice, your mind won't entertain   5
Even passing fantasies of mundane wealth or fame,
But will aim for freedom day and night—
Then you've developed transcendence!

Since transcendence without altruistic resolve   6
Can't yield the collective happiness
Of [a Buddha's] full enlightenment,
The wise conceive the spirit of altruism.

Swept away by the torrents of birth, illness,   7
    aging, and death,
Tightly bound by the chains of relentless compulsion,
Imprisoned in the iron cage of self-protectiveness,
All caught up in the blinding shroud of delusion,

Endlessly living and reliving the cycle of trauma,   8
Constantly suffering in body, speech, and mind,
Such is the state of beings, all dear as mothers—
So from your natural response build heroic resolve!

Even though you practice renunciation   9
And cultivate altruistic resolve,
Without the wisdom to realize reality,
You can't cut the root of traumatic life—
So, work at the art of seeing relativity.

Who sees the inexorable causation of everything   10
Whatsoever—mundane and transcendent—
And shreds any hint of reification,
So, enters the path that satisfies Buddhas.

Appearance is invariably relative   11
And emptiness is devoid of conviction—
So long as these two insights dawn separately,
You've not yet realized the Buddha's intent.

But when they appear simultaneously,   12
    without alternation,
From the slightest unbiased insight of relativity
Corrective knowledge breaks the reifying habit,
And your search for genuine insight is complete.

From then on, all appearance dispels absolutism,   13
And each emptiness eliminates nihilism—
Seeing how emptiness dawns as causation,
You're no longer blinded by biased views.

So once you realize the vital points   14
Of these three principles of the path,
Resort to solitude and persistent effort—
You'll quickly reach the timeless goal, child!

One of the beautiful things about this text is that it's for newcomers to Tibetan Buddhism and masters alike—the perfect first step on the complete path to enlightenment. My hope is that as you work your way through this book, you will return to Tsongkhapa's words regularly, like a daily recitation practice, until the verses become internalized, allowing the blessings of lineage and the wisdom to which these words point to kindle the spark of insight within you, revealing what was revealed to Tsongkhapa when he wrote it—ultimate reality itself.

Three Principles of the Lam Rim

In Tibetan, *rim* means "gradual," "staged," or "successive"—as in a terraced rice field, rungs on a ladder, or phases of development. *Lam* means "path" but also implies "realization." The text you've read contains all the realizations (lam), in stages (rim), for someone traversing the hero's path to enlightenment. These realizations and stages include preciousness of human life, inevitability of death, refuge, causality, defects of unconscious life, renunciation, altruistic intent, and so forth—a road map of thirty in all that I cover in this book. As we'll see, the intelligence of the sequencing is sublime. It's like a chord progression in music, or a posture sequence in Vinyasa yoga.

"Lam Rim" becomes the "Stages of the Path to Enlightenment" and suggests the progressive sequence of realizations that human beings undergo in an optimal evolution. The process of *awakening gradually*—that's what I'm presenting in this book: the Tibetan Buddhist psychology of human development, preserved for a thousand years in a university-style curriculum and passed in an unbroken lineage from teacher to student via close mentor bonds, mind to mind, from Tsongkhapa through a succession of masters to His Holiness the Dalai Lama, to Professor Robert Thurman, and, recently, to my mentor Dr. Joseph Loizzo.

In 1999, I met my main guide along the Lam Rim, Joe Loizzo, the contemplative psychiatrist and Buddhist scholar, at Columbia Presbyterian Hospital, where he was teaching a meditation-based clinical program inspired by Jon Kabat-Zinn's Eight-Week Mindfulness-Based Stress Reduction. Joe wore his signature black beret as he guided patients through a vibrant Tibetan-style visualization bookended by the sweet chimes of Tibetan bells. In his visionary brilliance, Joe had developed a protocol to include a full range of topics and meditative practices drawn from the wider Indo-Tibetan tradition. It covertly followed the Lam Rim style that progresses beyond simple mindfulness instruction and self-healing principles to compassion training, social psychology, and embodied practices associated with the subtle body science and power tools of the Tantras (Tibet's esoteric practices). This became the flagship protocol of the Center for Meditation and Healing at the Columbia University Medical Center's department of psychiatry. It is the world's first clinical protocol to incorporate the full array of Buddhist insights and skills forming the entire arc of awakening preserved and espoused in the Indo-Tibetan tradition, and it led to the founding of New York City's Nalanda Institute for Contemplative Science.

To my novice eyes, Joe's approach was elegant, sophisticated, and mesmerizing, and his method drew me in like an irresistible gravitational force. With each successive program Joe taught, I learned the stages of the path and saw how they anticipated and informed the trajectory of my development. Like a pianist practicing scales before a recital, I saw in my life, and in those of the patients Joe (and eventually I) worked with in the hospital setting, a sustainable progression from one contemplative theme to another, from one psychological breakthrough to another, along the hero's arpeggio of self-care, altruism, and insight (the structure of this book).

More valuable than what Joe taught through words was the living example and energetic presence he embodied. The themes he presented were accompanied by a subtle process of psychological internalization. Humans and other mammals do this naturally, maturing through proximity, mimicry, and role-modeling, absorbing qualities of their caregivers for better or worse. Joe became a new parent to my inner child, so I could disidentify from my damaged self-view and embrace new qualities of self-love and confidence. I owe him my life. Two decades later, not only am I the assistant director of Nalanda Institute, working with Joe to develop and offer a whole array of programs inspired by the Lam Rim, but also a more capable and flexible individual because of this mentoring relationship.

Joe has translated our primary Lam Rim text's title as the "Three Principles of the Path," but one could interpret it as "Three Principal

Realizations." That's because the idea behind the true lam is that it's an insight we're embodying, not merely a path we're walking. The three paths—renunciation, compassion, wisdom—are distinct yet inter-connected stages, embodied insights one actualizes *concurrently* on the way to enlightenment.

- The first realization is *renunciation*. I translate this as "self-love" or "evolutionary self-care." It is a mind-set on liberating oneself by abandoning perceptual distortions, emotional afflictions, and behavioral compulsions that create self-imposed suffering.

- The second realization is *compassion*, or Bodhicitta, translated as "awakened mind." It is a mind-set on liberating oneself for the benefit of others. It is the aspiration to evolve fully to help all beings awaken from the nightmare of their own self-imposed suffering. Due to its immense scope and lofty ideal, I call it "radical altruism."

- The third realization is *wisdom*. Often translated as "correct view" or "emptiness," it is a mind-set that nonconceptually, directly, and accurately perceives the subtlest nature of reality beyond superficial appearances. I call it "quantum view" because it pierces through any static, atomic, independent substrate of phenomena, breaks open the material world, and offers us a therapy for our sickness of paradigm.

Through the development of these realizations, Bodhisattvas, or altruistic heroes, turn their hearts inside out, radically shifting—from egocentric to other-centric—the axis on which their world rotates. Once we see—or taste the essence of—the three principal paths, we can spend our life unpacking them, understanding how they all fit together, and embodying them. Remember, enlightenment is not a race won by the fittest among us, but a process of slow and steady assimilation acces-sible to all. You and I, we get a shot at awakening too—it's incredible.

How to Use This Book

The Gradual Path is an ancient cookbook for enlightenment. Not an ad hoc, freestyle "add a pinch of this and a dash of that" approach that our modern spiritual materialism encourages, but more like the method prescribed in classical French cooking, wherein a dynamic master-apprentice interaction combined with years of training in technique, discipline, and protocol ensures the soufflé will rise no matter the kitchen or the era. Self-actualized masters with no formal training, like self-taught chefs, exist, but most of us, as we pursue awakening, must embark on and complete a well-thought-out and reproducible training program with proven effectiveness.

Tsongkhapa's Great Treatise and Atisha's Lamp categorize and delineate the Gradual Path steps according to the capacity and motivation of the practitioner—spanning from those of modest capacity, who simply want greater peace in their own life now or in the future, to those of greatest capacity, who seek liberation motivated by compassion for others. However, Tsongkhapa's text, the Three Principles of the Path, which we'll use in this book, explores the steps according to the major realizations, or milestones, practitioners develop in their appropriate sequence—evolutionary self-care, radical altruism, and quantum view.

This is not a simple book—*introductory* and *simple* are not interchangeable. We'll be overlapping multiple maps and traveling a lot of terrain together—there will be insights for your left brain, meditations for your right, and rituals that will unify them. How you relate to and best benefit from this material might depend on your predisposition and learning style, so know there are three approaches:

- The forest . . . *topical approach and theoretical aspect.* Using Tsongkhapa's fourteen-verse text as a scaffolding, I introduce and unpack the Three Principles of the Path, or the major milestones of renunciation, compassion, and wisdom, which constitute the arc of the hero's journey and parallel the foundations of Tibetan Buddhism. Those who are more theoretically inclined can recite the text daily, reflect on its meaning, and internalize these milestones.

- The trees . . . *practical approach and experiential aspect.* Within the three primary milestones are the thirty steps of our road map—each a discrete contemplation—that help build inner resources and allow you to efficiently actualize the deeper realizations.

- The landscape . . . *integrative approach and spiritual aspect.* This approach serves as a *paradigm therapy*, offering a complete spiritual context in which to practice the theoretical text and the thirty steps alongside prayers, altar offerings, inspiring mentor visualizations, and mandala offerings.

This is how the Tibetans meditate: they engage in study, discourse, debate, recitations of text, contemplations, and complex visualizations, along with focused bursts of meditation to holistically assimilate and become that which they focus on. They consider hearing or reading a sacred text to be a profound type of meditation, more profound than just relaxing the mind. This is because focusing and relaxing don't change the underlying psychic program—they only suspend it, like a vacation. We need mindfulness first, to harness clarity and power, but then we need to give ourselves a better program, something positive to take in, absorb, and structure psychic reconfiguration. Our bodies become what we eat, and so too do our minds become what we think. If you watch violent television or political propaganda, you're *meditating* on hostility, fear, and paranoia and habituating and reconfiguring your nervous system. Even the harmonics of song, prayer, and mantra are significant—more than simply pleasant acoustics, neuroscience and polyvagal theory suggest that singing, chanting, praying, and even dancing and yoga postures stimulate the vagus nerve (which regulates our entire autonomic nervous system), increasing stress resilience, secure attachment, and adaptive social bonding.

Take a moment to set your intention for the journey ahead. You've been initiated into a sacred, centuries-long stream—the Lam Rim, the Gradual Path, Tibet's crowning achievement, a realistic approach to psychological maturity and awakening!

2 PREPARATION

READYING SPACE, BODY, AND MIND FOR THE JOURNEY

You must have a room, or a certain hour or so a day, where
you don't know what was in the newspapers that morning, you
don't know who your friends are, you don't know what you owe
anybody, you don't know what anybody owes to you. This is a
place where you can simply experience and bring forth what you
are and what you might be. This is the place of creative incubation.
At first you may find that nothing happens there. But if you have a
sacred place and use it, something eventually will happen.

JOSEPH CAMPBELL, *The Power of Myth*

Clients often come to my office looking for techniques to alleviate
their depression, anxiety, grief, or physical pain. They've heard that I'm
a Buddhist psychotherapist and about the power of mindfulness meditation, and they want me to teach them something they can neatly
put in their pocket and take home to give them relief. While there
is compelling research showing that mindfulness-based approaches
have a positive outcome on physical and mental conditions, and basic
mindfulness is easy to learn, at the risk of disappointing them, I often
don't teach clients meditation . . . at least not at first. There are several
reasons for this, not the least of which is that no psychotherapeutic treatment can succeed without first building rapport, along with
establishing interpersonal safety, familiarity, and continuity.

Humans are more than the sum of their parts. We can't treat a
single organ in isolation from the entire organism any more than we
can treat an individual's irrational thoughts in isolation from their

history, relationships, lifestyle, ecology, culture, and genetics. Buddhism traces the root cause of suffering to misperception, sometimes translated as delusion, and affirms that the most dangerous worldview is the nihilistic one we have adopted during the centuries since spirit was thrown out with the bathwater of religion—our sickness of paradigm. Because everything is interconnected in an open life system, our nihilistic worldview has an adverse impact on how we feel, act, and relate to others. As a result, meditation training in the traditional Indo-Tibetan context is more holistic and comprehensive in addressing one's worldview, mental state, and lifestyle than the modern, secular mindfulness approach.

Six Conditions

Before we take up meditation, we must prepare to do so. There's a classic meditation manual written by the great eighth-century scholar Kamalashila—who was instrumental in disseminating the Gradual Path—that is surprisingly relevant today. His Stages of Meditation elucidates the Six Conditions, or advice, to be considered before beginning practice. It directs the secular meditator to consider "practice" in a more holistic context, wherein adjustments to one's worldview, attitude, and lifestyle are as important as the state of mind cultivated through practice and the technical instructions on how to meditate. Interestingly, with the onset of climate change, Kamalashila's advice for contemplation could be adopted by those hoping to live more sustainably on our planet.

1 Seek a conducive environment.

2 Live simply with few needs.

3 Be satisfied with what you have.

4 Avoid being too busy.

5　Live an ethical life.

6　Give up pleasure-driven pursuits.

1　SEEK A CONDUCIVE ENVIRONMENT

Anyone who thinks their external environment plays no part in internal well-being need only sit in a cathedral or temple, or gaze at a sunset. Kamalashila lists the elements of a suitable atmosphere for meditation as safety; food and clothing; freedom from disease, malevolent forces, and toxic people; access to friendship with like-minded, well-intentioned people; and quiet with few distractions.

Safety is primary—without it, the nervous system can never fully process information, learn, and evolve. It follows that we'd want to be physically comfortable and supported by a like-minded community. When it comes to finding a suitable place to meditate, it might not be possible to go on retreat, but whether it's your local dharma center or a corner of your bedroom, the environment influences the mind, so begin to envision and create a sacred space.

2　LIVE SIMPLY WITH FEW NEEDS

This is the heart of the dilemma between a contemplative culture, in which simplicity and minimalism are cornerstones of well-being, and our consumerist culture, in which we are addicted to chasing the high of accumulating but are suffocated by all our stuff. "Live simply" is not a recommendation to return to a hunter-gatherer society; that's neither realistic nor necessary, but modern life could be radically improved if we adopted an ethos of simplicity, particularly if we hope to benefit from meditation and proceed along the Gradual Path. Part of the shift asks us to discern between what we need versus what we want, and then to work with our impulses of greed, yearning, and fear that drive us to thoughtless consumption.

3 BE SATISFIED WITH WHAT YOU HAVE

Tibetan Buddhist teaching considers satisfaction to be more an active, karmic process and less a destination. In Western culture we're influenced by media and commercials that prey on our fantasies and insecurities, convincing us that if we buy the right car, go on vacation, or meet the right partner, we'll be happy. When it doesn't work out, we are offered new enticements. Conversely, Buddhist science sees inner satisfaction as a basic capacity or skill of the mind that can be developed through introspective practice independent of external circumstance. By systematically turning attention inward and cultivating emotional balance, we can consciously recalibrate the nervous system toward safety and gratitude and away from its negativity bias. As we exercise this shift, we become less preoccupied by what we lack and more focused on appreciating what we have, savoring while letting go, and can redirect our inner resources to meditative, eudaemonic (flourishing by way of pursuing virtue), altruistic pursuits.

4 AVOID BEING TOO BUSY

Digital overload, time-is-money multitasking, bigger-is-better culture, and how we've come to be ashamed of *not* being busy are ways we diminish our psychic inner space, distracting us at best and overwhelming us at worst. We stay busy as a pain-avoidance strategy, to tune out our inner doubts that we are worthless, unlovable, and alone, and that the world is unsafe. Busyness is an addiction like any other—an impulse of escape—yet it is prized, privileged, and reinforced in modern culture. The sickness of paradigm underpinning consumer capitalism, materialism, and nihilism keeps us in an orbit of self-perpetuating dissatisfaction and compulsive fear, robbing us of the inner space to access our inherent goodness, which can only be found when we shift from doing to being.

5 LIVE AN ETHICAL LIFE

The interrelationship between karmic causality, ethical actions, and psychological liberation will grow apparent as we progress on our hero's journey. Our actions—lifestyle—cannot be isolated from our life and how we feel, see, experience, and relate to the world and the people in it. We are all interconnected. When you enter a traditional ashram or meditation center, you are asked up-front to refrain from killing, stealing, lying, being sexually inappropriate, and clouding your mind with intoxicants. There is an assumption that the way we live either supports or contradicts our aspiration for well-being and liberation. As we become disciplined and restrain hedonic impulses, we grow sensitive and concerned about our actions, which has a positive effect on our state of mind, abating lethargy, restlessness, grasping, hostility, and self-doubt. As these afflictions subside, greater perceptual clarity becomes possible—like water in which the sediment settles when the glass is no longer agitated. That clarity fosters insight into the nature of things—or awakening—making ethics not only relevant to mental well-being but a critical foundation. From the Buddhist perspective, an ethical life is not about blind faith within the dogma of religion, rather it's the rational outgrowth of consequential thinking within a psychologically minded culture.

6 GIVE UP PLEASURE-DRIVEN PURSUITS

The ancient Greek Stoics distinguished between two orienting ambitions in life: hedonia and eudaemonia. *Hedonia* involves a life propelled by what Sigmund Freud named the "pleasure principle"—often involving indulgence and gratification of the five senses. *Eudaemonia* is the pursuit of virtue, meaning, and purpose, each for their own sake, which leads to a flourishing of the mind. Consider what it would look and feel like to be driven not by pleasure but purpose, finding meaning and satisfaction in living a good life for its inherent worth. During my trips to India I was humbled to meet people of limited finances—rickshaw drivers, cooks, and tailors—who derive satisfaction from treating their customers well and performing their service with dignity, in contrast to the wealthy and often miserable CEOs I've encountered in my therapy practice who have confused wealth with happiness. We must go beyond capitalism, scientism, and nihilism if we want to reconnect with spirit and pursue meditation the way it was intended—for the development and liberation of consciousness.

Professor Robert Thurman

In the eighth century, Kamalashila's Stages of Meditation detailed the prerequisites that allowed newly interested Tibetan Buddhists to develop their minds with the technology of meditation. Kamalashila's legacy endures in the twentieth century with a contemporary scholar-practitioner who facilitated the early transmission of Buddhism to America.

In 1999, Joe encouraged me to study with *his* mentor, Professor Robert Thurman, the first American ordained as a monk in the Tibetan tradition, holder of the first endowed chair of Indo-Tibetan studies at Columbia University, and lifelong friend of His Holiness the Dalai Lama. Affectionately known as Bob, or more impressively as the Thurmanator, he became the second-most influential mentor on my Lam Rim journey. His unbridled passion, dynamic teaching style, and use of intricate public discourse, along with his many books, including *Essential Tibetan Buddhism*, drew me deeper into the Tibetan tradition that had been ignited by Joe's interest and passion and informed by his clinical synthesis and adaptation.

I volunteered to fold chairs and collect coats at Tibet House—the US Cultural Center of His Holiness the Dalai Lama, founded in 1987 by Bob Thurman, among others—in exchange for access to Thurman's teachings, which were a fusion of enlightened wrath and creative articulation. I savored his words from the shadows of the last row of the room for two decades as my confidence grew and I became a faculty member at Tibet House. I now take the stage to teach with the teachers I admired from afar, thus fulfilling the true intent of the Lam Rim and the hero's journey—to become a mentor oneself and to bestow on others the life-affirming message and skills that Joe Loizzo, Bob Thurman, and, through him, His Holiness the Dalai Lama and the entire Gelugpa lineage of the Dalai Lamas imparted to me.

It was Bob Thurman's *The Jewel Tree of Tibet*, published in 2005, that blew my mind and stole my heart. In it, he writes:

> And it was not just the text and the teachings that
> affected me so deeply. It was the special context in which
> Tibetans meditate and use their teachings. I learned to
> look up with my inner eye, the third eye of imagination,
> which lies in the middle of our foreheads and opens
> a channel of vision into a subtle realm of reality. In
> this inner sky revealed by my third eye, I discovered
> mystical beings, buddhas, bodhisattvas . . . historical
> lama mentors, angels, deities mild and fierce, and all the
> saints and teachers and philosophers from all the world's
> spiritual traditions. I beheld the shining tree of jewels,
> decked with living jewel beings . . .
>
> The Jewel Tree opens its loving embrace to everyone
> and promotes happiness—which is our natural state and
> birthright.[1]

While Godwin reopened my heart and Joe Loizzo paved my career path as a therapist, Bob Thurman revealed the Jewel Tree—the structured, virtual-reality simulator in which Tibetans visualize—and illuminated the vast Lam Rim treasury for me, as did Atisha's The Lamp for the Path to Enlightenment for generations of scholars and practitioners in Tibet. Thurman insisted on maintaining the vibrancy and integrity of the Tibetan tradition, and he employed a new vernacular and teaching style to make these teachings accessible. While most Western teachers were content to extract and reduce meditation techniques from their original culture and philosophy, Thurman unapologetically and creatively drew students into the whole Tibetan paradigm. It is in this spirit of respect for the tradition that I'd like to share a classical Tibetan way of approaching visualization, nuanced by Thurman's creative flair and Loizzo's scientific rigor.

Six Preliminaries: A Comprehensive Visualization Practice

Once the Six Conditions have been established, both Kamalashila and Tsongkhapa present the Six Preliminaries—the context and basic structure for a comprehensive visualization practice. This preparatory system of initiation, ritual, and creative imagery is used by great teachers, such as the Dalai Lama, but it is so simple that any of us can employ it. No matter where you are on your path or what tradition—such as loving-kindness, centering prayer, shamanism, or yoga—you embrace, there's a natural way to build your daily practice within this scaffolding.

When I say "preliminaries," I mean the activities involved in preparing the mind for the three milestone realizations—evolutionary self-care, radical altruism, and quantum view—along the Lam Rim Road Map.[2] The Six Preliminaries compose a framework to support our psychological and spiritual development and parallel the first six steps on the road map. Everything we need is neatly packed into this complete system:

1 Create a sacred space.

2 Set up an altar and make offerings.

3 Prepare your body and mind.

4 Evoke the mentor and the Jewel Tree refuge field.

5 Initiate the Seven-Step Mentor-Bonding Process.

6 Offer the mandala and final prayers.

In this chapter, we'll focus on the first three preliminaries.

Create a Sacred Space

The first of the Six Preliminaries begins with creating a safe and sacred space by choosing, cleaning, and sanctifying a place for practice. Initially, this is a physical process—*clean up your mess*—but becomes a mental one, as in *clear your mind.* The starting point is finding a meditation place, and doing so is an act of reprioritization and a measure of your commitment to a spiritual life. That's what true transformation demands. If you are an athlete, part of your basement might be reserved for gym equipment, or if you are a musician, you might have a soundproofed room to rehearse in, so it follows that if you're interested in becoming a contemplative, you set aside an area in your home and make it meaningful and appealing for your spiritual practice. What that looks like depends on how you'd like to feel and express the virtue of contemplation and transformation.

Create and clear your meditation area and sanctify it in a way that feels authentic and meaningful to you. Outer clutter reflects inner clutter, so dignify this space as an extension of your mind: a laboratory where some of the most important discoveries of your life can occur. Thoughtfulness begins with our environment. There is an energetic circuitry between the external and internal, mind and motivation, that Asian cultures (particularly the Sino-Tibetans) appreciated, and which takes its full expression in Feng Shui.[3] When you get up in the morning and tidy the space, think of it as meditation in motion, not a chore. We bring meaning to life's activities, not the other way around.

Think about "cleaning up" your time as well. Do this by allotting a period for meditation each day, setting your intention to practice instead of doing things haphazardly. Consistency builds muscle memory, a biological set point like a regular sleep cycle.

Set Up an Altar and Make Offerings

Most of us come from secularized backgrounds from which spiritual forms, practices, and rituals have been scrubbed away, and we tend to have an aversion toward things like altars. However, most members of the world's religious population keep a personal altar or shrine in their home, where they connect with and perform rituals to ancestors, saints, and the Divine, even amid modern, urban lives. In Western secular culture, altars have morphed into man caves, home theaters, or packed closets where we worship the gods of fame, beauty, and success. Consider how much time, energy, and prioritization we give these. Sound judgmental? Would it be judgmental for me to say a crisp, fresh kale salad is healthier than a bucket of fried chicken, or a run in the park more vitalizing than a television binge? We've been trained to abandon discernment—some things *are* better for us than others. It's *not* all good.

If you can see an altar as psychological or emotional equipment—a bench press for the mind, augmentation for the heart—it might change your opinion. One of my teachers once said, "Clean your house as if the Dalai Lama was coming to visit for tea." *Now* imagine sitting down at your altar with the Dalai Lama. It makes for an incredibly different experience if you picture an inspiring person right there with you. This may *change your mind*, not because of anything magical or special that is *out there*, but because the visualization shifts the quality of your experience. *This altar is not for anybody else.* Whose mind improves if you look at your altar and see a real Buddha instead of a bronze statue of a Buddha? *Yours.*

When Tibetan Buddhists set up altars, they put many objects on them, but three are central:

- Buddha statue (symbolizing awakened body)

- scripture or other text (symbolizing awakened speech)

- stupa or other shrine (symbolizing awakened mind)

So when you sit facing an altar, you become familiar with transforming your own body, speech, and mind.

The body or form of a Buddha (*rupakaya*), particularly the aspects of compassion and engagement, is represented by a statue placed in the middle of the altar. Your Buddha might be a Tibetan *thangka* painting or a simple stone. It might be a photograph of the Dalai Lama or Pope Francis, an image of Pema Chödrön or Martin Luther King Jr. No matter who or what it is, imagine it's the embodiment of a real, living Buddha inviting you to practice, inspiring you to evolve.

1. **Statue**
   Awakened body
2. **Stupa**
   Awakened mind
3. **Text**
   Awakened speech
4. **Tangka Painting**
   Virtual archetype
5. **Water bowls**
   Sacred offerings
6. **Mentor**
   Real-world guide

Set up an altar and make offerings.

The expression, or awakened speech, and the teachings are represented by a sacred text, placed to the left of the Buddha when you're facing the altar, and by spoken mantras and chants that evoke the deity during one's liturgy (*sadhana*). A physical representation of a text can be anything that involves dharma—a correct understanding of reality expressed through words, which is the speech of the Buddha, or one who has awoken. It could be a book, such as Tsongkhapa's Great Treatise, Thurman's *The Jewel Tree of Tibet*, Zen Master Dogen's *Shobogenzo*, the Bhagavad Gita, the Bible, the Qur'an, Rumi poems, or books by Stephen Hawking or Mary Oliver—anything that directs your mind toward awakening. It doesn't have to be Buddhist. As Thurman says, we're not here to make Buddhists; we're here to guide society toward enlightenment by awakening its people . . . people who have the potential to evolve using whatever tradition they desire.

The *dharmakaya*, or mind of awakening, the actual realization of emptiness-interdependence, is represented by a miniature stupa, shrine, or small pagoda placed on the right side of the Buddha statue. A stupa or shrine is a repository for relics of great teachers, including the Buddha, to be housed, memorialized, and venerated. The stupa, a dome in India, Tibet, and Burma, evolved into a pagoda with a series of ascending levels representing consciousness for Buddhists further east in China, Korea, and Japan. You can select any object—a memento from a deceased parent, or an urn or box—and imbue it with meaning, allowing it to become a sacred portal to an ancestor, legacy, or lineage. Every time you see the shrine or container, associate it and its contents with awakening.

Once you've arranged the altar, the ritual of offering acts as a psychological antidote to our habits of fear-based attachment and clinging rooted in scarcity thinking. Making offerings is not limited to a single culture, and you might find that you are making them for reasons other than the ones described. One offers what and how one can. The importance is in the attitude, the sincerity with which we make the offering. The greater our intentions, the greater they resonate with the spirit of generosity.

WATER BOWL OFFERINGS

Once you understand the karmic significance of rituals, Buddhist or otherwise, they become a powerful psychological exercise sparking insights by circumventing the slower, verbal left brain, and by accessing, through symbols and gestures, the right brain's highway to the body, emotions, and intuition. If you understand karma (which for now we'll define as psychological causality) and meditation (as mental cultivation) the way I present them in this book, then you'll come to see how any ritual can be a complete psychological workout unto itself.

One of my favorite practices is the water bowl offering, based on a traditional Tibetan Buddhist ritual. While the practice involves offering water, it includes visualization and affirmation aspects as well, as we imagine that the water is transformed into delightful substances and symbolic gifts that we bless with purifying mantras. One thing about Tibetan Buddhism is that most ritual activities are ornate, multidimensional, and multisensory. That's important because we are completely involved and totally immersed in a process, not just at a cognitive or emotional level but in a sensory, behavioral, energetic, and verbal dimension as well. We're trying to rewire the totality of our being through ritual (behavior), mantra (speech), and active imagination (perception). This is a distinctive characteristic and advantage of the Tibetan approach, in contrast to simple mindfulness practice. It's the difference between cross-training—working many skills simultaneously—versus using only one piece of gym equipment to develop an isolated muscle. You can improvise and personalize this practice, but here is a basic form done in the Tibetan manner:

- Because one never puts an empty bowl on an altar, hold one of seven clean bowls, fill it with water, and place it on your altar in front of the Buddha. Repeat with each bowl, arranged in a line, separated one from the other by the length of a grain of rice.

- Pour water from the first to the second, from the second to the third, and so on. As you do, mentally transform the liquid into the sacred substances listed below by chanting the mantra Om Ah Hum. These three sacred syllables hold a resonance that purifies the body, speech, and mind.

1 Water to refresh
2 Water to bathe
3 Flowers to delight
4 Incense to perfume
5 Light to illuminate
6 Scented oil to ease
7 Food to nourish

• An eighth gift of music is represented by the sacred sound of your prayers, mantra, and chanting, or you can add a candle to stand for light.

The idea behind this practice is based on the science of karmic causality, not dogma or rote. The power of creative imagination to influence our neurobiology is well documented,[4] and so an ordinary act of giving water to a statue can be transformed into an extraordinary act of offering sacred substances to the actual Buddha and mentors themselves, as if they are there with us. The brain registers the potency whether the acts are real or imagined. The ritual then becomes a sacred exchange of empathic reciprocity and a skill training of openheartedness that optimally change your mind and affect future perception, leading you to behold abundance.

THREE PROSTRATIONS

We've purified and made offerings of sacred substances to evoke and delight the mentors; now we purify and offer ourselves. We do this by making three prostrations, or bows, at the altar.

On a physical level, bowing is an act of trust, because our gaze is turned down and our neck is exposed. Consider how much resistance an opportunity to bow stirs in you on a personal, transgenerational, and cultural level . . . and now, think of it like a yoga asana. The symbolic counterpart to bowing is the mental act of humility, reverence, and healthy reliance. By prostrating, we are surrendering egocentrism and unhealthy defensiveness. We are supplicating the Buddha, dharma, sangha (mentor, teaching, and community), as if saying, "The way I've lived my life, the way it is right now, has become unmanageable. I will humble myself . . . *surrender my delusion-driven will*, and symbolically place myself in the care of a greater force to have the opportunity to be free and happy."

Some form of bowing is important in most spiritual traditions. In Islam, the devout bow to Mecca five times a day. Catholics genuflect. The first steps of the 12-step program for recovery involve admitting one is powerless over addiction and turning will over to a higher power. That "greater force" to which we supplicate in Buddhism is none other than our innate wisdom of discernment that can perceive reality and choose to live well. Here is the way Tibetans make prostrations:

1 Place your thumbs together and cup your fingers in a prayer gesture around them so that your hands look like a candle flame within a lantern.

2 Touch four points on your body: crown, third eye at forehead, mouth, and heart.

3 Lower onto both knees and either touch your forehead to the ground from a kneeling position or do a full-length prostration, extending your entire body with five points of contact (two knees, chest, chin, and forehead) to the ground.

4 Extending both hands forward, raise your fingertips while visualizing yourself touching the feet (a gesture of respect) of the Buddha or your mentor, who is watching over you.

5 Bringing hands back together, raise the forearms in prayer gesture.

Repeat this process three times. As you do, pair the physical sequence with a verbal affirmation and visual cue to make the whole process multidimensional and integrated.

1 As you touch the top of your crown, chant silently, *I take refuge in my mentors*. Imagine your entire being is purified of karmic imprints that create suffering.

2 As you touch your forehead, say, "I take refuge in the Buddha." Imagine your body purified.

3 As you touch your mouth, say, "I take refuge in the dharma." Imagine your speech purified.

4 As you touch your heart, say, "I take refuge in the sangha." Imagine your mind purified.

Westerners can be weird about this stuff. I know I was. We are either critical and dismissive of cultural forms or blindly zealous. It helped me to remember I was bowing to "the Buddha within"—my own potential to transform and awaken, to loosen my fixation on a sense of self filled with pride, envy, and the rest that was making me unhappy. We have built up a lot of defense mechanisms because of trauma, and part of that defense is staying independent, disconnected, and seemingly in control. While these are understandable temporary reactions to pain and broken trust, over a lifetime these maladaptive strategies become hindrances to maturation, crutches that keep us hobbling on the path. Prostration practice is a good way to kick up painful memories and volatile emotions such as anger, fear, and shame related to power dynamics and vulnerability. It's when shit gets stirred that we have a chance to work through it; otherwise trauma stays dormant and can emerge when we least expect it, often with destabilizing outcomes.

If you go to some place in India where Tibetans in exile are still allowed to practice freely, such as Dharamsala or Ladakh, what do you think yogis and pious householders are doing? Three prostrations in front of the Buddha? No. *A hundred thousand prostrations!* And that's not an easy thing to do. It's a physical and emotional challenge. It's a full workout. It's *serious.* You get cuts, blisters, bruises, and spasms. It's hard to sleep, and it's hard to wake up. You may feel like you're eighty years old. That's the level of commitment it takes to erode our neuroses, to work through our bullshit, our pain, our entitlement, and the layer of defensiveness that Wilhelm Reich famously called "character armor." It's a way of letting go of who we think we are, clearing the field for planting what we can become on the Lam Rim journey. The process of maturity takes grace and grit. Especially grit. *No mud, no lotus.* Anyone who tells you otherwise may have an alternate agenda. Nothing truly spiritual is as pretty and manicured as the cover of *Yoga Journal* depicts.

The Tibetans call this a *purification.* I know that's another loaded word, but psychologically what we're doing is softening the rigidity of self-identification. Like alchemists heating an alloy so it can be transformed into gold, a hundred thousand repetitions kicks up the impurities and afflictions, stokes the fire to searing temperatures sufficient to melt defenses and penetrate and access the vulnerability of our tenuous sense of self, so we can evolve. Practices of purification abound in Tibetan Buddhism, and prostrating three times is a good place to start. "A little every day" characterizes the gradual approach.

Prepare Your Body and Mind   3 ROAD MAP

After you've created and cleaned a sacred environment, made offerings, and done prostrations, it's time to sit on your meditation seat. The iconic meditation pose is not mystical, but practical; an aligned and stable posture allows the body to become still so the mind can reach clarity, gathering virtues and insights. Think about a microscope looking at subatomic layers of reality, or a telescope focused on distant galaxies—the discovery of the ultimate beyond ordinary, subjective perceptions requires stability, focus, and vividness. That's what we're trying to replicate here in the laboratory of observing subjective experience.

SEVEN-POINT POSTURE

I like Tibetan teacher Mingyur Rinpoche's advice to keep one's back upright and body relaxed. With a general audience, he doesn't say any more than that about posture. The full lotus position, which is typical of a meditating Buddha, is ideal but not necessary. If you can't do it, that's okay, because comfort is important, especially for beginners. The Buddhist scriptures refer to four meditation positions: walking, standing, sitting, and lying down. The thing they all share is a straight spine, so if you have an injury or limitation, bear it in mind and do the best you can. Quality is the main thing to strive for; your posture should be balanced, alert, and fluid—not rigid or lax—and the quality of your mind should follow suit.

Traditionally, there are seven points to a steady meditation seat:

1 Legs crossed in full or half lotus

2 Hands in an intentional gesture, or mudra (for example, right hand underneath the left, with palms facing upward, or open palms facing down and resting on each knee)

3 Spine held like a stack of coins, upright but not rigid

4 Shoulders open evenly, floating and not stiff (be mindful of hunching or slouching)

5 Head level, with chin tilted down slightly to elongate spine

6 Mouth closed, with tongue lightly touching the front roof of the palate

7 Eyes half open, gently gazing about a foot in front of you, or closed, depending on your degree of restlessness

THREE LEVELS OF ASPIRATION

Just as Lam Rim can be divided into three paths—renunciation, compassion, and wisdom—it can also be parsed according to the three levels of practitioners' aspirations. A healthy and realistic self-assessment of aspiration without bias or criticism will lead to a pursuit that is authentic and will help you find your starting point on the Lam Rim map. What's more, inspirations change—we may start with one, and as we achieve realizations, come to adopt a more generous or greater aspiration as our capacity grows.

Aspirations correspond to our capacity for focus, our determination, our ability to tolerate difficulties, our level of compassion for others and ourselves, and how clear our view is. We can't fake aspiration. If we do, we may overlook our true stage on the Lam Rim and risk injury in the same way that overzealous or insecure martial artists rush toward a black belt before mastering basic skills and undergoing building-block experiences that have transformative potential. These are the three aspirations:

1 Humble aspiration for *well-being* in this life and beyond

2 Middling aspiration for complete *freedom* from self-imposed suffering

3 Great aspiration to awaken for the benefit of others, or *altruism*

Humble Aspiration

Let's start by contrasting the humble or modest aspiration for well-being within the predominant aspiration of our culture. What motivates most of us in the West? We strive for pleasure *now*. Immediate gratification, at any cost. That's why we are overweight, overstimulated, addicted, overmedicated, and self-destructive. Consumerism is all about having our cake and eating it, too, without considering the consequences. That's why I'm troubled by how self-help marketers co-opt and interpret spiritual teacher Ram Dass's seminal mantra "be here now"—playing into our culture's hedonic compulsion and making it all about "me." Who cares about the oceans, forests, and the people we leave behind? Sensory gratification, driven by what Freud called the pleasure principle, is the most pervasive, unconscious aspiration in our culture. The tragedy is that it has no endgame, no long-term purpose. You might wake up and go to work because it pays the bills, your morning muffin and soy latte giving you comfort on the way, and your evening yoga class making you unstressed or exhilarated so that you can go home tired, fall asleep, and do it all again. Not a single moment is spent asking what's it all for. Or maybe you have asked but didn't like or can't find the answer. Most of us are struggling to get by, so having a vision of something bigger might seem a luxury, but is it? An absence of aspiration is one reason why we see such apathy among those impacted by a capitalistic and consumerist agenda predicated on nihilism, leaving them disenfranchised with no intrinsic purpose to life, no encouragement to develop soul or mind, and no evolutionary gains to move toward.

In contrast, the Lam Rim offers several legitimate motivations for spiritual practice, which is to strive for some measure of inner well-being and contentment, to access and activate innate capacities for wisdom and compassion, and to see this as the arc of one's life ambition, so that daily activities—even mundane ones from lattes to email to yoga class—become part of a singular and meaningful pursuit. Ordinary life is not a distraction or dead end but a means to a higher purpose: the soul's development.

Two things differ between mundane and spiritual motivations: the shift from a hedonic orientation with an insistence on immediate gratification of the physical senses versus a eudaemonic orientation with an enduring patience for the gradual development of the soul. There is a qualitative difference to pursuing something you know will reap fruit years from now, versus striving for the immediate. Freud knew this, and he noted that it was a sign of maturity to be able to delay gratification rather than be a slave to impulses. From a Lam Rim perspective, blindly pursuing hedonic goals in the moment is a waste of inner resources such as energy and concentration, because those pursuits are short-lived. But if we harness energy and channel it toward creating something more sustainable, then our activities are more valuable.

Abating poverty, racism, climate change, and corruption requires a specific aspiration and maturity that directs energy toward a long-term solution of sustainable transformation and surpasses the temporary experience of gratification. That's a good description for how the humble aspiration works: we set our sights on a more peaceful and abundant future by curtailing impulses and karmically cultivating internal reward, both of which make us less dependent on the external environment. In the Tibetan tradition, this aspiration is called "eliminating vice and accumulating virtue" with the intention of redirecting energy toward a higher future purpose. It's still self-interested, but it's not hedonic. With such an aspiration, we recognize how to use principles of causality systematically (rather than haphazardly) to achieve the experiences we want, and we do so with an endgame in mind. However, this aspiration does not eradicate the root causes of the compulsive life cycle. (This will make more sense once we explore how karma works, which will happen in the next chapters. For now, practice delaying your gratification!)

Middling Aspiration

The second aspiration is for freedom. Here we expand the parameters from creating the causes and conditions for good fortune in the future to the complete elimination of suffering. Whereas the former keeps us bound within the unconscious cycles of compulsive life, trying to improve the quality of our experience and yet intermittently having to endure the residual effects of past negative actions, the latter aims to dismantle the trauma cycle so we no longer produce self-imposed suffering.

Whereas the humble aspiration asks us to appreciate karmic and ethical principles that create our experience of feast or famine, the second aspiration requires us to take refuge in the teachings, actualize renunciation, and achieve the wisdom of selflessness. It's important to know that the goal of being free is innately possible for us all. It is our birthright, and yet to be realistic, it is an exalted and rare accomplishment, requiring a full commitment of one's precious human resources. To commit one's entire life energy toward the pursuit of awakening might be an unreasonable or overly high bar for some, particularly in a culture where awakening isn't even part of our vernacular or paradigm, so start where you are, working with those perceived limitations, fears, and doubts rather than forcing it or abandoning the path altogether.

Great Aspiration

The third and final level of Lam Rim aspiration is the freedom to awaken for the benefit of others. In addition to karma, ethics, refuge, renunciation, and wisdom of selflessness, the aspirant seeking this needs the wisdom of interdependence and altruistic motivation, or the heart of universal compassion called Bodhicitta. This level of aspiration may seem lofty, because the scope of trying to awaken for all living beings is so expansive and grandiose, but from the Buddhist perspective, we all have the potential, just as we have the capacity as mammals to naturally care for our young, regardless of whether we choose to exercise it or not. In the optimistic cosmology of Tibetan Buddhism, all beings will evolve to see that there is no greater use of time and energy than to strive to awaken in order to help all living beings achieve freedom and sustainable happiness. This becomes the implicit thrust of the latter half of the Lam Rim progression of milestones. We'll all get there eventually, but it's best to show respect and "be here now" with humility and honesty. Do we feel ready to delay sensory gratification and work toward cultivating inner well-being in the future? Do we have an even more ambitious motivation to strive exclusively for complete freedom? Or do we have the most expansive ambition to awaken for all life?

Taking Refuge: Mastering Evolution

Before we begin meditating, it's important to set our intentions—for Lam Rim practice specifically, but it's a useful habit for any aspect of our life. All successful action off the cushion is predicated by clear intention. Just as one wouldn't run a marathon without preparation, I'd discourage you from coming to your meditation seat and starting haphazardly. Approach your practice in the way you would a session with a psychotherapist or doctor when you're urgently seeking relief: as an opportunity to discover and embody something that will set you free.

A prayer or chant is a way of creating an imprint in your mind to one day perceive and experience something favorable. It's a way of actively setting aspiration through a process of cultivation and familiarization. What you *think,* you *become.* If I take refuge in my unworthiness, I engender unworthiness, I stew on unworthiness, and I turn my attention toward and fill my lifestyle with actions that reinforce my unworthiness. However, if I take refuge in my basic goodness, I cultivate kind thoughts, I balance my emotions, and I practice a lifestyle consistent with healthy pride and mutual respect. In so doing, I remember (become mindful) that I'm fundamentally good, decent, and worthwhile. You can see why this mind-set would conflict with consumerism, which has a direct stake in disempowering us and making us feel bad and deficient about ourselves.

Aspirations or prayers are found in all lineages, schools, and cultures. A prayer is not a request to an external entity, it is a meditation, a mental exercise of reconditioning yourself with affirmative aspirations. As with the verses of the Three Principles of the Path, prayers work to prime the imagination so that our minds can absorb the nutrients meditation offers.

Let's start with Taking Refuge in Altruistic Resolve. Press "pause" on your analytical abilities for now and savor the beautiful sentiments here:

> From now until enlightenment, I take refuge
> In the Buddha, his Teaching, and Community—
> By virtue of practicing [transcendences] like generosity,
> May I reach enlightenment to benefit all!

Now, release that "pause" button—you don't have to rely on blind faith, although some faith is a wonderful complement to reason. Faith is undervalued in our culture, so if we are striving for balance and integration, we'll need to step up our faith game to match our reason. My job is to make these religious practices scientific enough for you to understand and appreciate, but not so watered down or rigidly scientific that they leave the soul hungry.

Let's start with the word *refuge. Reliance* is its synonym. When your ship is at sea in the middle of a storm, what do you look for? When you're in the desert and have run out of water, what then? At the end of the day, life is hard, and we are all looking for relief, a way to live that brings some measure of peace and satisfaction. Do your inventory. Where do you go for comfort? What do you do for some sense of satisfaction? And, the most challenging question: How's it working out for you?

So, what does it mean to *take refuge*? And, what is a reliable refuge? *Taking refuge* means trusting an institution, method, or person to help you through a predicament and deliver you to a more favorable outcome. For some of us, that has meant late night alcohol or TV binges. For others, it has meant a parent, therapist, or friend. For others, it's a notion of God, whose grace offers comfort. Relying on those who are more available, skilled, and trustworthy offers relief magnitudes beyond short-lived intoxicants and entertainments, but even still, are we staving off disaster only to find another one coming down the road? Are we putting out a series of fires that reignite in another spot? Is there anything in our culture that gives a lasting way to work with pain, directly amid confusion, and is worth investing the totality of our being? True *refuge* demands a complete and utter trust fall into the arms of reality.

The Buddha's deep realization under the Bodhi tree is encapsulated in his first teaching, The Four Noble Truths: suffering, its causes, freedom, and the path to freedom. These truths (particularly freedom) are the ultimate sources of refuge—not the Buddha himself but the nature of reality and our innate capacity to understand it directly. Realizing how our painful experiences are created, that we can consciously intervene in them and steer our developmental enfoldment away from suffering and toward contentment, may be the most reliable source of our conviction and investment. According to the Lam Rim, we can all wake up, free ourselves from the causes of future self-imposed suffering, and live completely free. This acknowledgment that everyone is suffering—compelled by afflictions and impulses—is not denial or reification of suffering. It's remembering that suffering is a temporary, universal circumstance, an impermanent condition, and it's *not our true nature*. If we were to see our true nature as open and exercised different muscles—wisdom and compassion—we would redirect our evolution and become radically different people. We can become the hero we were meant to be.

That is the gist of The Four Noble Truths. It is what you take refuge in when the shit hits the fan. It's what you invest your precious life energy in understanding completely. Those who are only praying to the Buddha to save themselves, hoping he'll intervene on their behalf, well . . . Unfortunately, I don't think they got his message about inner refuge. They are doing what many pious believers do, living in faith without the complement of analysis and hoping that Daddy will rescue them. True refuge is found within and is expressed not in subservience to external powers but in personal acts of truth and transformation.

Mahatma Gandhi made famous his nonviolent approach to conflict resolution called *satyagraha*, translated as "insistence" or "holding firmly to truth," which he embodied at all costs. The act of taking refuge similarly demands maturity and self-reliance, courage to face what appears to be insurmountable odds, and confidence in one's own capacity to eventually shape-shift specific outcomes and even direct one's entire evolution. Notice the word *eventually*. Once we understand that the challenges of our world are mostly coming from us, our "truth-act" is to courageously face our delusion-making and creatively manifest our destiny. If you want to feel different, if you want a new result, you take refuge in your innate ability to causally create a different outcome.

So, what are we taking refuge in? *Our power to create our circumstance.* You are the god of your life. Bold, right? You take refuge in the part of your mind that is naturally clear, knowing, and creative. Nobody can save you but you; however, you can't do it alone without a guide, a road map, and support. Interdependence helps us avoid extremes of isolation and external reliance.

Bodhicitta: Altruistic Aspiration and Action

From taking refuge, we transition into generating Bodhicitta. *Bodhi* means "awake" and *citta* means "mind," and together they refer to the "awakened mind." Thurman translates Bodhicitta as conceiving the "spirit of enlightenment." It is a mind-set on achieving awakening—motivated out of compassion—for the benefit of all sentient beings. With a goal that lofty and vast, I call it radical altruism. But Bodhicitta doesn't have to remain lofty and inaccessible—there's a seed of it in each of us that just needs to be cultivated. For example, if there was a moment in your life when you felt happy and yet were alone, you may have wished you had someone to share that joy with. Or when you see your loved one in pain, your spontaneous wish is that they would be free of suffering. We don't even have to think about it—it's so natural and innate. This points to what the Buddha and evolutionary neurobiology both say about our true nature: we are naturally connected through empathy, and we care for others' well-being. *We are made by love and designed to express it.* When we remember this, we can't pursue awakening solely for our own well-being. We can't enjoy our cake while everyone else is hungry. What food we have, what joy we have, even the highest accomplishment of liberation, we naturally and incrementally wish to share with others. That's the beginning of Bodhicitta.

As a father, I can say that it is natural and hardwired for me to wish that my kids be happy. It is a central preoccupation. But more than a wish, I would *do* anything in my power to make it possible for them to avoid pain and experience happiness. I would work longer hours, donate a kidney if needed, or die to save their life. That natural capacity in human beings and mammals is magnified and expanded to all beings in this level of motivation, and more than that, there is a specific way one can ensure their happiness that doesn't involve overtime or an organ!

Bodhicitta has two parts: aspiration and action. The *aspiration* is to pursue the full course of the spiritual path up to its conclusion, not solely motivated by evolutionary self-care for your own exclusive well-being but by radical altruism to benefit others. And, as we know, there are levels—humble, middling, and great. *Action* involves pursuing the Lam Rim training that will build the muscles required to benefit others. You must complement your aspiration with skills to bring the ideal down to earth and make good on your wish.

If you come from a Christian tradition, this should start to set off a lot of alarms. It's a big leap for someone to say, "Well, does that mean I've got to be Christ?" *The answer is yes.* Bodhicitta means you must become like Christ to rouse countless beings from their nightmare. It's not enough to stay a child and believe in Christ or Buddha and pray they will intervene before the ice caps melt and another child gets shot.

From a Buddhist point of view, we all can and must be Christlike. We must vow to help each other remember and actualize our Christ or Buddha nature.

All living beings without exception have this potential to awaken, and eventually we will feel compelled and capable of helping them actualize. From a Buddhist worldview, we've been living countless lives since beginningless time and have accumulated vast amounts of negative karma. To purify those karmic imprints, which are called *samskaras* in Indian philosophy, we must imagine saving an equivalent number of beings throughout space and time. Bodhicitta becomes an antidote lofty and vast enough to serve as the seed to purify our vast, past storehouse of self-centered intentions. We can use our empathy and concern for others as a rocket launcher to take us toward awakening, when we'll have the best psychophysical equipment for the job of awakening others. Bodhicitta is an amazing concept. The late, great Gelek Rinpoche, one of my teachers, once said to me, "When you imagine making offerings . . ." (and he was a big, robust guy, a big, hasn't-missed-a-meal guy) "imagine the whole room filled with offerings for all living beings. Not one sack of grain, but mountains of grains and fruits." The sheer volume, vastness, audacity, and radicalness of your altruistic intention is what counteracts the incalculability of your past self-centeredness and egoism.

Use your creative imagination to multiply the karmic effect of your aspiration. When you pass a beggar on the street and have nothing to give, imagine that for his entire life you'll feed him. Or, instead of feeling guilty that all you can offer is bread or five dollars, imagine and wish that one day you will lead him to enlightenment. Intentionality carries a residue on your consciousness. If you add imagination and *karmic* science into the mix of your aspirations, prayers, and visualizations, you can appreciate how quickly you will multiply the resultant imprints on your consciousness. And that's how you purify vast, countless lifetimes of the implicit scarcity bias, competition, and alienation we've accrued through evolution.

Because imagination can amplify karma, immediately following the taking of refuge and the generating of Bodhicitta, all Tibetan practices include the generous wish to extend positive intentions of love, care, joy, and peace to all beings—in all directions—who are included in the opening prayers. This amplification is called the Four Immeasurables, which Joe Loizzo translates as the Four Boundless Emotions.

> May all beings have happiness and its causes.
> May all beings be free from suffering and its causes.
> May all beings know pure joy untouched by suffering.
> May all beings live in peace untroubled by anger or clinging.

Ready for the Journey

You're in your sacred space, your altar is set up, and you've made water bowl offerings, performed three prostrations, sat down in the seven-point posture, clarified your motivation by taking refuge and generating Bodhicitta, and said your prayers. Hopefully as the process becomes more familiar it will all start to feel like a graceful sequence of yoga poses for the mind or the steps of a ballet, keeping you awake to the moment through meaning. If it ever starts to feel automatic or rote, pause and remind yourself what each part means and what it is designed to do.

Now that we have prepared our body and mind, we are ready to alchemically process our nascent hero into a master using the ancient flight-simulator technology of role-modeling visualization. You're ready to enter what Joseph Campbell calls the "space of creative incubation."[5]

STEPS 1-3   **Retracing Your Steps**

1 Create a sacred space.

2 Set up an altar and make offerings.

3 Prepare your body and mind.

3 VISUALIZATION

TRAINING IN THE FLIGHT SIMULATOR OF INSPIRATION

I am Shiva—this is the great meditation of the yogis in the Himalayas . . .
Heaven and hell are within us, and all the gods are within us . . .
All the gods, all the heavens, all the worlds, are within us.
JOSEPH CAMPBELL, *The Power of Myth*

Most of us recognize the classic meditation posture: cross-legged, spine erect, face serene, mind in transcendent equipoise. You may have found your way to a hatha yoga class and done some meditation after completing the physical postures and felt more relaxed, or maybe you've been to a meditation center and learned how to mindfully follow your breath, paying attention and quieting internal chatter. Perhaps your first encounter with meditation came via your therapist, health-care provider, school counselor, or workplace. It's a wonderful thing to see so many people practicing some aspect of the ancient art of meditation these days.

It's been more than a hundred years since Swami Vivekananda introduced Vedanta and yogic meditation and Venerable Soyen Shaku introduced Zen Buddhism to intellectuals in the West at the Parliament of the World's Religions in 1893. It's been more than fifty years since the Beats and the Beatles brought meditation into popular culture, and forty years since Herbert Benson and Jon Kabat-Zinn began the scientific study of relaxation and mindfulness, respectively, that led to the current "mindfulness revolution." As these secular and mainstream events unfolded, Western dharma communities—Insight, Zen, and Tibetan—developed to preserve and transmit the teachings of the Buddha. They included meditation practice in concert with a worldview based on interdependence and karma theory, incorporating prayers, textual recitation, and rituals, which are often marginalized and dismissed as culture-bound religious practice but all form the foundation for us to explore and appreciate—in ways designed for a wider Western audience—the complete way meditation is practiced within the traditional context of Tibetan Buddhism.

To do this exploration, we need to take a step back and recognize that there is so much more to meditation than sitting still and following the breath, and to do *that* we must ask about the thing meditation purports to develop and transform: the mind. From a Buddhist perspective, mind and body are related but separate phenomena. Body is made of matter, is conditioned, and is impermanent; mind is subtle, immaterial, indestructible, and without beginning or end. According to Buddhism, mind is neither a by-product of matter nor an epiphenomenon of the brain but an ongoing, mutable process—a mental continuum. When the body dies, it decays and energy transforms into another state according to the first law of thermal dynamics.[1] The mind's superficial layers of consciousness, along with coarse memories and associations, cease, but a subtle layer continues indefinitely, unimpeded by the deterioration of matter. This layer of mind is a repository for karmic imprints and tendencies that shift and progress across a dynamic, multilife evolution in much the same way that genes alter and transmit genetic information transgenerationally. Current thoughts, speech, and behavior leave an imprint, dormant in the soil of the subtle mind like a seed, until future conditions are conducive for ripening. According to the laws of karma, wholesome actions later ripen as favorable subjective experience, while unwholesome actions ripen as unfavorable experience; however, they all *will* ripen.

The classic Indo-Tibetan approach to practicing meditation relies on an appreciation for the continuity of consciousness and karmic causality. Let's start with a simple and short version drawn from Master Kamalashila, who articulates five elements or ingredients that compose a scaffolding for a complete, stand-alone meditation practice.

Five Elements of Meditation Practice

Kamalashila offers five essential elements that should form every meditation session. These may seem unfamiliar even to longtime practitioners because they are not rooted in a secular-scientific worldview but an Indo-Tibetan one sensitive to the paradigm of interdependence and psychological causality. These elements are taught at the outset of traditional Tibetan Buddhist education, are accessible to beginners, and can vitalize and deepen a more established practice.

1 Preparation

2 Contemplation

3 Meditation

4 Dedication

5 Application

1 PREPARATION

As a farmer prepares the soil for planting, we prepare the ground of mind for meditation. The first three Preliminaries—create a sacred space, set up an altar and make offerings, and prepare your body and mind—are the foundation of preparation. We create a comprehensive sequence of activities that purifies psychological hindrances, obstacles, and karmic imprints that might keep us from liberating insight or realization—the aim of meditation. At the same time, we cultivate positive energy or merit that will foster insight and the development of virtuous qualities, uplifting our practice with the blessings of our mentors and lineage.

Preparation also entails reciting prayers and scriptures largely abandoned in our scientific paradigm but essential to any spiritual culture. These are texts like the Three Principles of the Path and the Four Boundless Emotions and other prayers and verses from scriptures you'll find in this book. I encourage you to internalize and embody them, not just read *about* them—reading them is more than an intellectual activity.

2 CONTEMPLATION

Contemplation is the practice of focusing the mind on a theme, internalizing it, and actualizing it. A common misunderstanding about meditation is that it is exclusively a nondiscursive practice, but here we are using our analytic minds to focus on concepts, exploring them more deeply. Depending on the extent of the presentation, the Lam Rim can be made up of many themes, such as the preciousness of human life and the immediacy of death, each arranged in a well-curated sequence, thirty of which form the Thirty-Step Road Map presented at the beginning of this book. Our "practice" is to acquaint the mind with each theme systematically and repeatedly until they are all internalized in the depth of our being. Only from there can they rouse a realization, causing a transformational shift in consciousness.

In the monastic universities of India and Tibet, two devices foster the process of internalization: memorization and studying the related context, and reasoning. Westerners don't seem to memorize anything anymore (not even phone numbers) because we've become so reliant on technology, but if you think about it, memorization brings information in from the outside, making it internal and retrievable and us self-reliant. Those great Tibetan lamas such as Gelek Rinpoche, Lama Yeshe, and Lama Zopa, who were forced to leave their possessions and flee their homeland during the Chinese occupation, safeguarded their practices and the lineage because they had memorized much of the Tibetan Buddhist corpus of extant spiritual literature. By learning the points on the Thirty-Step Road Map (I think you can do it!) you will internalize them, and they will become part of your inner lexicon, retrievable as needed, and thus easier to metabolize at the soul level. In other words, the stages of the Lam Rim will become part of your spiritual DNA.

3 MEDITATION

After preparation and contemplation, we can begin what most of us associate with meditation—better described as nondiscursive, pinpointed concentration, or focal attention, on the resultant affective experience. For example, if upon contemplating the preciousness of human life, a feeling of gratitude and appreciation arises, that's when you transition to meditation, focusing your attention on the *feeling, not the theme*, to "seal it in." This shift in quality of attention is what deepens the process, fosters internalization, and ripens as realization. If, when we are meditating, the affective response fades, we can return to the theme, the commentary, and the lines of reasoning to reactivate the emotional response, and then return to focal attention. In this way, we vacilate between the activation of both brain hemispheres—the left is associated with linguistics, analysis, and attention, and the right with affective response and the scanning mindfulness that brings attention back to its object so that it can serve as a laser beam of internalization.

4 DEDICATION

Dedication occurs at the end of your practice and is a way of capitalizing on the karmic energy (momentum), affective response, and insight produced in your practice session. As you grow to understand how karma works, you'll appreciate why dedication is so central to the overall schematic of meditation and other ritual activities in Tibetan Buddhism. Think of it like this: When I can save a little extra money, I bank it in my kids' college fund. That ensures it won't be spent on something frivolous because it is "dedicated" toward a specific, meaningful goal, in a place where it can accrue interest over time. Likewise, karmic merit accrued as a result of virtuous activities can be earmarked for an ultimate goal: awakening for the benefit of others. Karmic investments need to be handled wisely or they will ripen for mundane reasons instead of altruistic ones. Thus, it's best to dedicate them for our highest spiritual aspirations.

There are many dedication prayers. I selected this one, translated by Joe Loizzo, to be the primary set of verses to close our seated practice and earmark our merit for life between sessions:

By virtue of this practice and all my efforts,
May I quickly become a mentor-archetype,
And lead all beings without exception
To the exalted state of full enlightenment!

May the supreme spirit of altruistic resolve
Be conceived wherever it has not yet spread,
And may that spirit already conceived not decline
But continue to flourish and spread ever more.

Although I and all beings are objectively empty,
By virtue of all the positivity I have acquired
Together with all enlightened beings through all time,
May I reach the state of perfect enlightenment,
And lead all beings, who are all equally empty,
As quickly as possible to that supreme state!

5 APPLICATION

The final step is to bring the skill, insight, emotional quality, and inspiration we have cultivated during practice to bear in our everyday life. The whole point of our meditation practice is to prepare us to live in the world with greater skill, yet often meditation practice feels confined to a specific time and space, and our skills do not transfer off the cushion. There is a real opportunity to create a fluid experience during and between meditation sessions. After dedication and before people end their practice session, I recommend they reflect and previsualize the ways they will apply what they experienced. Specifics are important. Practice becomes a soul contract to encourage yourself to think, speak, and act differently in daily activities. This contract becomes the blueprint for the new life we are designing using karmic causality, cultivating virtue, eliminating vice, and using mindful awareness, insight, and ethics to construct a new way of being. After we previsualize and leave our cushion, we seamlessly transfer mindfulness to the application of virtue and insight.

This is what a basic session might look like:

- Begin with preparatory activities. The simplest version is to clear your mind with a few rounds of breath meditation, take refuge, and generate the altruistic intention.

- Then, contemplate a theme, such as the preciousness of human life or the kindness of living beings.

- With this contemplation, a sense of appreciation or gratitude may arise, moving you to the next point. Now focus your mind on the sensate or visceral experience in your body, thereby sealing in the gratitude.

- If the visceral experience fades, you can return to the prior point of contemplation and review, or move to the next point. Dedicate the merits by directing your positive karmic momentum toward your original aspiration, such as self-healing, personal liberation, or the welfare of others.

- Before ending your meditation, previsualize how you will carry this sense of gratitude and purpose into your daily life. Perhaps you prime the mind for the next time you're disappointed, stuck in autopilot, or wondering what the hell it is we are doing on this planet. Autosuggest this to your mind: *the next time I feel that sense of loss, I will remember this sense of gratitude born of the reflection of the precious human life.*

- Remind yourself of the word *mindfulness*, which comes from *smirti*, "to remember," to bring the mind back to the storehouse of positive emotions gathered during meditation. We'll come back to this "construction effort" throughout the book, but particularly in the last chapter on manifestation.

PRACTICING THE FIVE ELEMENTS OF MEDITATION

The Five Elements of Meditation can be practiced in one of two ways: as a stand-alone system or strategically integrated within the Six Preliminaries. If practiced on their own, in each meditation session you'll go through all five points using one of the thirty Lam Rim themes on the Thirty-Step Road Map. You could do one theme daily, cycling through all thirty in a month and then beginning again, or stay with a single theme for about twelve days before moving to the next, creating a yearly cycle.

Taking the second approach constitutes a fuller visualization practice and requires understanding the next three activities in the Six Preliminaries (4, 5, 6 on the road map):

4   Evoke the mentor and the Jewel Tree refuge field.

5   Initiate the Seven-Step Mentor-Bonding Process.

6   Offer the mandala and final prayers.

ROAD MAP 4   **Evoke the Mentor and the Jewel Tree Refuge Field**

The fourth of the Six Preliminaries is a process of rewriting our life story, or narrative, as it's called in psychotherapy. Envision it like an onion, with neuroses characterized by afflictions, such as anxiety, and maladaptive compulsions, such as addictions, making up the outer layer. At the core of the onion, what is affecting us most fundamentally as human beings and preventing us from flourishing is a distorted self-image that grew out of the context of trauma across evolution and was reinforced in childhood development. From that distorted self-image arose our life story, a self-referencing explanation about who we are and why, which we believe to be fixed and true. It's *I was born to my parents, and certain terrible things happened to me when I was young, and they continued happening to me as an adult, and now no one understands me . . .* or *I'm all*

Tsongkhapa and the Jewel Tree Refuge Field

alone . . . or *I've missed out . . .* or *Nothing good will ever happen to me.* These are narratives. We identify with them. We think they are intrinsically and unchangeably who we are. I am alone. I am worthless. I am unsafe. I am unlovable. I am _____ . . . Fill in the blank.

Whether you like it or not, whether you are aware of it or not, your life is being framed by that story—about who you are, how you got here, and what's down the road. It feels like you're moving through space and time and things are coming *at* you and randomly happening *to* you, but if you slow down the film and look at each frame—and one way to do this is through meditation—you will realize that your life is *mostly* coming *from* you.

The idea within this Preliminary and this step of the Lam Rim sequence is to do our best to see through distorted appearances, access the unconscious software program that creates our tragic life story, and consciously rewrite it. As Joseph Campbell wrote,

> We must be willing to get rid of
> the life we've planned, so as to have
> the life that is waiting for us.[2]

In the Tibetan tradition, one of the most effective ways of doing this is through creative visualization, dissolving appearances, bonding with the mentor within the Jewel Tree refuge field, and being reborn anew. Creative visualization acts as a virtual-reality psychodrama to consciously reenact childhood development. With each session, we rehearse giving up the habitual narrative of ourselves and the world as they seem to appear—intractable and terrifying—and reconstruct them in more favorable ways so that the script is improved, the software updated, and our brain rewired.

First, we imagine dissolving the world and ourselves, like in a near-death experience or psychedelic trip, melting down rigid identifications and appearances through various levels of subtlety until we reunite with the ground of our being—what the Tibetans call our clear light or translucent, open nature. After letting go of the fixed sense of self, we re-arise from sheer quantum openness in the form of a hologram body made light. We are then reparented in the womb of the sacred mandala, the Jewel Tree refuge, with a mentor archetype as a new role model. Finally, we are reborn, reincarnated, or resurrected out into the world as heroes and heroines compelled by the bodhisattva vision and vow. These three classic phases of death, intermediary state, and rebirth occur naturally, though compulsively and haphazardly, for any organic living system, but uniquely in the Tibetan alchemical approach they are co-opted and consciously transformed into a process of enlightened reverse engineering.

We begin by dissolving the world picture. So many of us experience the world under severe and constant threat. We feel terrified, hopeless, and paralyzed with primordial fear. This karmically reinforces our threat narrative and self-protective instincts in a negatively reinforcing feedback loop. Fear is one of the strongest agents of perceptual calcification, solidifying self, other, and world into discrete atomic structures. This becomes a revolving door of self-imposed misery. "Imprisoned in the iron cage of self-protectiveness," as the seventh verse of the Three Principles of the Path says. So before we can release our subtle traumatic narrative and access our clear-light nature, we need to rehearse surrendering our fear-based projection of the world and re-envision it as a safe and healing paradise with the power to positively reinforce our sense of being protected and uplifted.

Next we dissolve our sense of self, letting it melt just like the world, into quantum openness. From there we re-arise as a hologram body made of breath energy and pure awareness. You see yourself taking on this ethereal form, also known as a dream body because it is no longer made of matter; it's made of *mind*, like a body in a dream. You're no longer weighed down or concretized by any inner monologue. You simulate being reacquainted with the felt sense of your natural fluidity. This is a way of emptying ourselves of the neurotic identity and traumatic narrative to make space for new heroic identity and optimal life-narrative, which is much more adaptive and capable.

This is the point where people get defensive and even indignant and say, "You're fostering denial! You're indulging a fantasy! The world is dangerous, and by dreaming up a healing bubble aren't you proposing that we make ourselves even more vulnerable?" Reenvisioning the world as part of our meditation practice is a way to retrain perception, balance energy, and prime for effective engagement by replacing fear with love, and recklessness with skillful action (even if imagined). Once our practice session ends, we *do* have to face the so-called reality, but hopefully we'll be coming from a more constructive place because we have reconnected with confidence, optimism, and love, the most proactive and creative qualities to solve the problems that exist.

If you *still* think visualization is a useless fantasy, don't just take the Tibetan masters' word for it; examine the mounting evidence in cognitive neuroscience[3] and quantum theory,[4] which suggests we visualize all the time, that there is little difference between the dream and waking states, and that the brain is actively creating a virtual reality we mistake to be externally real.

According to current neuroscience, our brains don't know the difference between what is real and what is imagined. When we're visualizing our mentor in a sublime setting, we're in a *flight simulator of love*. Airplane pilots learn much of what they need to know working with a flight simulator. The targets aren't there, the enemy aircrafts aren't real, the emergency scenarios aren't happening, but it doesn't matter because the brain registers the information and learns from experience regardless if it is fabricated or not. And this occurs at no risk or cost to the pilot's life or the billion-dollar piece of equipment. Cool, right?

Tibetan Buddhist tradition challenges the notion of a fixed reality. In other words, what we see as the world is more like a virtual reality or a dream—we are consciously constructing appearances. In "real" life we forget that we coconstruct reality by fusing bits of external data with past associations, expectations, emotions, and environmental cues, unconsciously fabricating our experience of reality. In other words, we assume things are more real than they are, and we overreact in destructive ways that karmically determine our future experience. Just as we might react to a nightmare, scaring ourselves awake only to find it was a dream, most of the time we react to real events as if they are life-threatening, only to realize they are not what they appeared to be.

JEWEL TREE REFUGE FIELD

Once we've tapped the ground of possibility and reemerge, in a simulated hologram body of openness, we imagine ourselves within a more sacred, uplifting environment, which can further facilitate learning and development. Thurman has creatively called this the Jewel Tree visualization based on what is known in the Tibetan tradition as a field of merit or a refuge field—a place to gather virtue, to accumulate positive experience. Think of an apple orchard as a place to collect fruit, and visualize a field of mentors and living beings as a place where you can exercise your mental muscles, or skills for prosocial emotions such as devotion, love, care, joy, and compassion. As you cultivate these skills, you accumulate karmic energy, momentum, or force called merit that ripens in the future as a transformative realization. By visualizing a place filled with sentient life—awakened and ordinary beings—we create an interdependent matrix from which we can simulate the skills needed to evolve, without all the hang-ups, obstacles, fears, and doubts. It's an imagined alternative universe (Thurman calls it "Buddhaverse"), but there is still neurological and psychological benefit to be gained in an optimal virtual reality that encourages the best qualities in us, such as creativity and compassion, to thrive.

The language or template of the Jewel Tree visualization is Thurman's adaptation of a Lam Rim text called the Lama Chopa (Guru Puja in Sanskrit), translated as Mentor Devotion. In his eloquent synthesis of the text, we are guided through visualizations of our mentors in a sublime setting as we take them into our hearts and minds and merge with them. Although Thurman translated and adapted this practice, the science and psychological lens I'll share was developed and focused by Joe Loizzo. Both my mentors employ creative license to skillfully make this ancient science and art applicable to us in the West. It's the devotional offering of two people who spent nearly a century between them studying and internalizing these traditional practices until they were confident enough to know that once we've mastered something we can play with it—like jazz, once you perfect the scales. In fact, Thurman likes to compare the way the Lam Rim moves gracefully from one theme to the next, and the way the visualization moves from one phase to the next, to an arpeggio.

Here are steps to follow as you dissolve the world and arise as a hologram:

- Get out of your left brain for a moment—your literal, rational mind—and relax into the right brain of creativity, dreams, and emotion, into the awe and wonder of a child.

- Dissolve "ordinary appearances," including your neurotic sense of self and the fear-based world, by picturing yourself within an imagined, sacred environment that's safe, meaningful, and uplifting—your Jewel Tree sanctuary, which may be an ancestral pagoda, a safe place, or a natural setting.

- Invite and fill your sanctuary with a host of mentor beings. They can be real people, archetypes of the world's perennial philosophy, or a confluence of both. Their purpose is to guide you through an alchemical, transformational process. If you have an affinity with another spiritual tradition, you don't have to use Buddhist iconography. Choose any inspiring beings—Gandhi or Jesus, the black Madonna or Yoda, or your rabbi, grandmother, or fourth-grade teacher who deeply blessed your life.

- Find an affirmation that echoes from your heart, the harmonic resonance evoked by the Jewel Tree circuitry, custom-designed to amplify your greatest wish and hasten your evolutionary unfoldment. My personal one, bequeathed by Joe, is *Everything is possible; love heals.*

Every little thing in this meditation process has meaning. You can envision the Jewel Tree refuge and your exalted mentor gazing at you with love and care, and let the meditative process move from your left brain into your right and down into your body, into your heart, and, further still, into the soul you've forgotten you have. This is a way of accessing another part of our brain to download a new, more inspirational software about who we are and how we should live.

Some people will experience creative imagination and guided imagery as pure fantasy, while others will come to appreciate it as a metaphor for a truth that's deeper and more profound than splitting the atom. When you envision mentor beings, try not to freak out, or at least understand that initially you might have to process some of your adverse reactions to come to appreciate their value. If you have trouble imagining a mentor being (and many people do), try exploring archetypes from the world's mythical traditions, and let one of them speak to you. Also, try not to be so analytical that you lose your creative vision, your soul's third eye of innate intuition. Open your heart. Be willing to be foolish, even if it means straying from the mainstream agenda and risking ridicule. I think we all sense that the world is ready for us to think outside the box, because that box of limited, conventional, rational thinking is destroying us.

REPARENTING: MENTOR AS AN EVOLUTIONARY SURROGATE

A powerful aspect of Jewel Tree visualization and meditating on and with our mentors is the opportunity to reparent ourselves, to retroactively rewrite our childhood with greater insight and love. According to Joe Loizzo's neuropsychological interpretation, the visualization, structured within the Six Preliminaries, involves a type of depth psychotherapy with an alchemical twist that's thousands of years old. That mentor being is looking right into you with the love and care you've always yearned for. They don't have resentments. They don't have neurotic hang-ups. They don't judge. They don't have conditional needs or insecurities. They don't need to recruit you for their own narcissistic validation. They don't need anything from you, except for you to wake up, and even that is held within the tender embrace of compassion and patience. They're completely there *for* you. They love you and see directly into your true nature of radical openness and universal compassion. Unconditional love, the most valuable resource on the planet, has been available in abundance the entire time, deep within our psyche like a fluid, diamond elixir, but buried and made inaccessible because of our lack of imagination. Commercialism, competition, and scarcity have further drowned it out. In the visualization we use an imagined, surrogate protoparent as a magnet to pull from within us the well-being that has been there all along.

The other part of working with a role model or a mentor is that, as mammals, we learn from *mind to mind*, through mimicry. If you want to become proficient at something, you find a master. If you want to learn to be a carpenter, you study with the best goddamn carpenter around. If you want to be a pianist, you don't download a book on it (that's what Amazon wants you to do!); you go to Juilliard and study with the best. If you want to be a basketball player, you emulate Michael Jordan. If you want to learn French or Farsi, you seek out someone who is fluent. You dedicate yourself with body, speech, and mind. Depending on how badly you want something, you turn your whole life over to it. You'll do whatever it takes, which is a necessary, external act of taking refuge.

When I first met Joe Loizzo, I was in my early twenties and had come back from my second pilgrimage in India. I had a meditative breakthrough with Godwin in the Garden of Eden, but didn't have a profession or career path yet, and I was a little lost in that regard. Seeing both desperation and hunger in my eyes, Joe graciously offered me an internship. I got up and busted my ass to get into the city, which was several hours roundtrip, with a few bucks in my pocket. I got Joe tea, set up his teaching space, fetched his patient folders, and prepped the meditation tapes for his clients. I ran around doing whatever he needed so I could sit in his office for an hour and study how a master therapist works. I did that for fifteen years. And those experiences far exceeded anything I learned during my expensive three-degree academic education. And in a way, my apprenticeship with Joe hasn't stopped. It will never stop. He'll always be my mentor, and the learning never ends. The only reason I'm writing and sharing this book now is because I got some good downloading time with that guy and other evolved mentors like him.

This process of modeling already happened once in our lives. Most of us had two role models from birth. We unwittingly apprenticed ourselves to our neurotic parents, and, well . . . this isn't about blame. It's no one's fault human beings are evolutionarily designed to be sensitive and are, as an unfortunate result, often broken by life. The good news is that we get a second chance to do childhood better, more consciously, and with realized human beings as surrogates who found credible, well-traveled paths of self-transformation and can help us heal and evolve. We get to redo childhood with them in the virtual reality or flight simulator of our active imagination. (There is good science behind this gathered and presented systematically in Joe Loizzo's book *Sustainable Happiness*.)

Even though some of us cringe at the idea, as a therapist, I assure you most of us become like our parents because our original software came from them. All our ways of being, thinking, and acting, how we interpret and respond to experience, were learned because we are an open system available for new impressions and coding. We are not encrypted hard drives but unlocked ones, with the most significant downloading having occurred during childhood, when we didn't have filters for discernment and choice. Along with their good qualities and interests, we may have inherited our parents' anxious traits or temper or scarcity thinking. We got it all. We had no choice. There was no spam filter.

It's up to us to find better models and use the ancient virtual-reality technology of the Jewel Tree visualization to consciously override and update the program. We all want version 2.0. Here's the good news: our brains are flexible and designed for learning and adaptation in a phenomenon known as neuroplasticity, so we can reprogram at any time in the life span and make genuine, radical changes. With the right tools, a human being can travel the Lam Rim, from ordinary neurotic to extraordinary hero . . . all the way to a Buddha.

Initiate the Seven-Step Mentor-Bonding Process 5 ROAD MAP

The fifth Preliminary is classically referred to as eliminating nega-tivities and accumulating virtue, which we accomplish using what the Tibetans call the Seven-Limb Prayer and Joe Loizzo calls the

Seven-Step Mentor-Bonding Process. In this book I use Joe's name for the actual method of transformation when discussing this Preliminary. I consider this Preliminary the engine that propels the evolution of consciousness. It is the phase in the Lam Rim that reprograms our software, and it is the heart of the visualization practice—using another human being to help us abandon what doesn't serve us while cultivating the qualities, views, and skills that do. Here is Joe's translation of the process through a neuropsychological lens:

> I honor you, Buddha, in body, speech, and mind.
> I offer you all that is dear to me, real and imagined.
> I regret all faults I've acquired in this life and throughout evolution.
> Gratefully I enjoy the virtues of all beings, mundane and transcendent.
> Buddha, please shower me with your guidance and blessings,
> And please stay in my heart until I break the cycle of trauma.
> By virtue of this may I reach enlightenment to benefit all!

We can break it down to be more accessible so that the poetry becomes a virtual therapy—a scaffolding within our Thirty-Step Road Map:

1 Admire qualities.

2 Make offerings.

3 Disclose negativities.

4 Rejoice virtues.

5 Request guidance.

6 Request presence.

7 Dedicate merits.

These seven steps can transform your life. In his book *Sustainable Happiness*, Joe Loizzo applied childhood-development concepts introduced by the psychoanalyst Heinz Kohut to describe how those embarking on the Lam Rim use their relationship to the mentor to progress from idealization to identification to internalization to the integration of these latent qualities. It's an amazing, novel synthesis incorporating a powerful technology and ancient tradition, while spelling out the psychological mechanisms behind this process in a language modern readers can understand. Using science to dispel the mystery while not sacrificing the mysticism involved in visualization and guru devotion is an art, and through it Westerners like us receive a critical justification to engage in something we might normally dismiss with skepticism.

BONDING STEP 1 ADMIRE QUALITIES

I honor you, Buddha, in body, speech, and mind.

The first step in our inner therapy is admiring the qualities of the mentor. Think about all the things that draw you to the person, that make them inspirational and influential. What do you want to cultivate in your life? Be specific. Is it their kindness or passion? Their peace or wisdom?

Whatever it is, let yourself be filled with awe. Then, think about how amazing it would be if you could be more like them. This idealization is the mental equivalent of a prostration, of bowing down, of making ourselves available. Awe and reverence help to harness neuroplasticity, our brain's natural capacity to learn, grow, and change through new, enriching experiences.

BONDING STEP 2 MAKE OFFERINGS

I offer you all that is dear to me, real and imagined.

In the Jewel Tree visualization, we rehearse giving our mentor something as simple as a flower, moving all the way up to our body, mind, and even the fruits of our dharma practice. We imagine our mentor accepting these gifts with great delight. They are so honored, are so happy to share with us, and are moved to teach us. They couldn't be prouder. The offerings act as a seal, an epoxy that binds, so that after repeated practice we feel close, safe, and connected with the mentor. The act of giving also empowers us to ask for their support and evolutionarily harkens back to an ancient sense of reciprocity—how human culture was built on the exchange of care and community.

By offering, we purify scarcity thinking—that we don't have enough to give, or that we are somehow essentially not good enough to receive. Through the act of giving generously we cultivate a sense of proximity and warmth with the mentor, which creates a healthy entitlement for human exchange and lubricates the circuitry for energy transaction. This safety, warmth, and closeness of interpersonal interaction provides a crucible or container for our development.

BONDING STEP 3 DISCLOSE NEGATIVITIES

> I regret all faults I've acquired in this life
> and throughout evolution.

Next, we make a confession. If this language bothers you, Joe Loizzo recommends the word *disclosure*, which is often used in therapy. Either way, the point is that our minds are afflicted with habits ensnared and reinforced by guilt and shame. We need to let these go without overlooking or suppressing them. To do this, our so-called "dirty secrets" need to be brought into the light from the dark cavern of the unconscious. What Joe Loizzo beautifully calls the "warmth and moisture" of human intimacy, developed in the making of offerings, now allows us to surrender defensiveness and armoring in order to access the frozen pain of past traumas, including the reified distortions of self-image and narrative. Shame, a calcifying force in our evolution, can then be dissolved and purified in the warmth, acceptance, and validation of the mentor's unconditional love. Virtual, healthy reliance on the mentor is established over time, just as in real-world therapy, and can equally cultivate a renewed sense of trust and refuge that may have been broken in the actual past but is necessary for the organic process of maturation to resume and continue.

It's not simply disclosure that heals. We need to constructively learn from our limits, missteps, and blind spots. There's an important distinction between shame and healthy remorse. Shame is "I'm a bad person." It's self-identifying with an action or thought and leaves no room for learning. Remorse is "That action or statement was tactless. I was caught in angry emotion and could have done better." Dan Siegel says we must "name it to tame it."[5] Imagine disclosing to your mentor any real or fantasized limits, blocks, or failures. Coming from a place of basic goodness rather than original sin allows a realistic inventory and evaluation of our actions of body, speech, and mind. That evaluation is necessary for self-correction.

At this point in meditating on the Seven-Step Process, take a moment to scan your recent intentions, words, and actions. Try to pinpoint a moment, an exchange, a tendency that was unskillful or hurtful toward yourself or another. Then use the power of the mentor—the safety and unconditional positive regard they provide—to let go of the shackles of guilt or shame so that you can reencode and rewire better tendencies, affirmations, and perspectives. It's not punishment that helps us grow, but love, learning, and better choices.

As we take this moral inventory, our mentor sees through our transgressions as mere wrinkles in the cloth of our evolution. Our mentor has an expansive vision of us and the confidence that these habits can be ironed out because they are not who we are. The mentor sees us at our ultimate level, actualizing our potential and becoming a mentor Buddha ourselves. Can you imagine vicariously getting a glimpse of that in the mirror of your mentor's caring eyes?

After we've done our inventory and glimpsed that our activities don't define us, we vow sincerely to watch and correct these transgressions, for a period that is manageable to us—a week, a day, or an hour when we vow not to think, say, or do those things again. We use the mentor as leverage to help us become more accountable to ourselves. Confession isn't for God, but for you—the karmic recipient of your current actions. You vow to be more mindful, restrained, and disciplined. That's how you shift your neural circuitry and mental continuum—one action at a time.

Rather than simply being mindful of our breath, we become mindful of our vows—the voluntary commitment to steer evolutionary activity in a better direction. This is how mindfulness is best applied. Next time you're about to say something nasty, pause, then apply recognition that resists the gravitational pull of past negative tendencies that have never served you, and apply choice to adopt skillful actions that will fulfill your aspiration. Within the context of karmic causality, this is the biggest favor you can do for yourself and others. If you employ mindfulness as leverage to help you change your behavior, words, and intentions, you'll see your life transform incrementally and sustainably. Using mindfulness to resist vice and recruit virtue steers the ship of consciousness toward awakening. This is the real secret of the Gradual Path; guard it well.

BONDING STEP 4 REJOICE VIRTUES

> Gratefully I enjoy the virtues of all beings,
> mundane and transcendent.

After we've taken an honest look at our shortcomings, we allow ourselves to see and rejoice in our spiritual accomplishments. According to Joe Loizzo, this positive reinforcement marks the hero's stage of identification, as the young apprentice identifies with the possibility of being an equal partner or collaborator with the mentor. Celebration is such a beautiful thing, yet we rarely do it, so take some healthy pride here in the effort you have made to change your life for the better. Acknowledge all the good things that we all do, and rather than being jealous of other people, enjoy their virtues and merits, and by proxy, share in their success.

There's a neurological benefit to this endeavor. Neuropsychologist Rick Hanson has a catchy phrase for it: "taking in the good"—savoring the positive emotions that lead to happiness and resilience. Taking in the good means counterbalancing the so-called negativity bias—a leftover, hardwired strategy of our brain to focus on the negative—that originated to ensure survival throughout evolution. While it's important to consider the negative so we don't repeat failures or missteps that lead to pain, we need to consciously focus on positive actions and experiences, take them into our body, savor them, and rewire our brains around them so we can feel safe, good enough, and efficient, rather than unsafe, bad, and incapable. Rejoicing is an important neural and psychological reinforcement contingency for virtuous intentions, words, and deeds, and it places our psychological development in a more positive cycle or homeostatic setting. The more we do good and *acknowledge* it, the more we feel good about ourselves, displacing the conviction that we are sinners, failures, or rejects.

Not only does rejoicing reset our negativity bias, it can have an impact on others. We underestimate the radical reverberations that being joyful and gracious can have. We can't know the consequences of one smile, one act of kindness, one moment of acknowledging someone, but in our meditation we can take a moment to rehearse noticing and validating the good we and others are doing. We habituate constructive tendencies. When the delivery guy rides through the rain and brings you the white rice instead of the brown rice you ordered with your meal, give him a ten-spot for a tip, not a five! Haven't you been there? Don't you know what it's like to be that person worrying about your billable hours or your tips or your health insurance and how you're going to pay rent? That's you. Every single one of those living beings out there *is you*! How would you like to be treated? Look them in the eyes, see them, and acknowledge their effort and kindness to do things like deliver food to you. Acknowledge them as human beings and respect them because they're doing their best. That is rejoicing.

It feels good to rejoice, to give thanks, rather than to find fault, criticize, and complain. It feels good to acknowledge the kindness of living beings who make everything in life possible. There's a remarkable talk and contemplation by Thich Nhat Hanh called "The Universe Is a Single Flower"[6] in which he analyzes what appears to be a discrete object and exposes how everything in the universe is utterly interconnected. This process evokes wonder and deep appreciation. Think about a single button on your shirt. *See* how many infinite beings went into making it possible, how many people gave time and energy in the process of causes and conditions for that button to hold your shirt together. Amazing. Every single accomplishment you've ever had, right down to your body and breath, has only ever been possible because of the kindness and effort of others. Give thanks. Rejoice. Life is a miracle.

BONDING STEP 5 REQUEST GUIDANCE

> Buddha, please shower me with your guidance
> and blessings . . .

We've confessed and rejoiced, and now we request. This step marks the hero's stage of internalization, as now we experience the mentor and their attributes within us as our own budding qualities. Ask the Buddha or your mentor for the guidance you need to heal and evolve. Nobody can do it alone, especially mammals. This is when we ask, "Please, mentor, give me the teachings that I need to learn, the blessings to be inspired, the modeling to become competent. Teach me how to be like you, how to be a life-artist, how to live well."

Once we've made our requests, we imagine that our mentor smiles and sends us a wonderful rainbow light from their heart that represents their experience, the blessings of the lineage, and the intuitions of the awakened, and fills our hologram body as a flame does a lantern. Simultaneously this affirmation emanates from the mentor's heart in a harmonic resonance, and like tuning forks, you both are bathed in the sonic frequency of affirmative speech. I tend to suggest chanting Om Ah Hum (the purification mantra we used during the water bowl offering) silently or aloud while visualizing nectar lights dripping down the crown, throat, and heart, purifying body, speech, and mind. But you can select any affirmation that is meaningful, such as "Everything is possible; love heals." As you receive the waves of rainbow blessing, imagine giving up on grief and pain for the past and receiving everything you've ever needed.

This is when we begin to see the inner therapy—we can now get everything we need to transition from surviving to thriving. In his seminal treatise on interpersonal neurobiology, *The Developing Mind*, Dan Siegel uses neuroscientific research[7] to show how we can revise traumatic memories if we revisit them from flow states—safe places of real-time abundance and nurturance. The concept that our brains are flexible, adaptable, and even our worst memories are revisable is not new; for millennia Tibetans Buddhists have dedicated themselves to developing an art and science of psychological rewiring.

BONDING STEP 6   REQUEST PRESENCE

And please stay in my heart until I break the cycle of trauma.

After having imagined ourselves downloading the blessings and the new way of being that our heart desires, we recognize this is a virtual simulation and that the actual process of waking up and of metabolizing and realizing those blessings takes time. With deep sincerity, we request that the wisdom the mentors and lineage represent remain with us always so that we can progress with them for however long it takes to awaken. We ask that they dissolve into and become one with us, remaining ever accessible, until we fully realize our potential and become the loving, capable altruist we are meant to be.

We imagine our mentor is delighted to be asked. They have infinite love for us. They will never abandon us. A reliable guide will stick with you. At this stage in the visualization, our mentor and the entire refuge field of awakened beings, and even the Jewel Tree itself, dissolve into rainbow light, enter our crown, and slip past our throat and heart, anointing us and merging with our inner mentor and the inner Jewel Tree sanctuary at the center of our being. Two become one, and we are consecrated as the mentor. Whereas in step five we received and refracted the blessings from the mentor as their emissary, in this step we become the mentor, a full-fledged Buddha. We assume the role of master, trying on for size a future-capable identity and allowing our brain to prime itself for that inevitability. We've moved from internalization to integration, when our best qualities ripen as our own, and the maturation process is completed when we recognize ourselves with confidence as mentors in our own right.

I've thought a lot about why this point falls here, what it's designed for, and what its psychological import might be. One explanation is the concept of "object constancy" proposed in child development theory and particularly in psychoanalysis, suggesting that in healthy development, a vital capacity grows in infants and children to feel their parents are available and are protecting them even when out of sight. Their developing brains need to internalize a sense of parental continuity over time and space that allows them to survive being alone and prevents them from succumbing to a sense of peril or perceived abandonment. Another point of consideration is that everyone will lose their parents and mentors to death, and so as a species, there is a legacy of abandonment fear within our psyches. As a result, our ability to attach or bond as adults is limited or inhibited, and so to counteract the latent anguish or anticipation of the disappearance of our mentors, we rehearse reconnecting with their buoyant presence that transcends lapses of time—between meditation sessions, and even between lives . . . until samsara ends.

BONDING STEP 7 DEDICATE MERITS

By virtue of this may I reach enlightenment to benefit all!

The final step is dedication. We can't understand dedication without karma. Remember that karma refers to psychological causality, or intentions that drive actions, and those actions create specific subjective results. During the visualization practice (and in all our practices, from the opening prayers to the Seven-Step Mentor-Bonding Process), we are purifying negativities, planting seeds of virtue, and creating tremendous amounts of positive energy. Like steam in a kettle, it must be released, and good karma is certain to ripen as pleasant subjective experiences in the future. Left undedicated, that merit or force previously generated could ripen as another pleasurable mundane experience, such as the subjective sense of satisfaction from a good meal, wonderful sex, or an exotic vacation. There's nothing wrong with pleasant sensual experiences like these, but from a spiritual point of view, we know they are short-lived and leave us hungry for more.

Remember, karma is not a boomerang; the meme "What goes around comes around" is misleading. While what we put out comes back at us, karmic results aren't external events; they are perceptions and interpretations of events that produce subjective experience. They happen in our minds and bodies. It's not what happens *to* you, it's how you experience what happens to you that is your karma: *you are* your karma. Current actions change our perception and brain wiring. Karma is not magic. It's not a moral justification for why good and bad things happen to people. It is a science of causality that explains how past actions affect future perceptions in a cycle of psychological feedback.

What's more useful than haphazardly letting past merits ripen as pleasurable experience is to consciously direct karmic energy toward a specific spiritual goal, such as an insight or realization, or the next steps on the stages of the Lam Rim. This can have more lasting impact on our psyche, accruing merit that results as spiritual realization rather than a single pleasure. The delight of a good meal fades, while an insight that life is fleeting, and the resulting sense of urgency, endures because it compounds itself in a favorable reinforcement contingency. Directing karmic merit toward our spiritual aspirations is a wise way to reinvest in our spiritual journey. It has a profound return on investment (ROI).

Achieving this noble goal requires fuel, known in the Buddhist tradition as merit, which is generated on the basis of virtuous activity. Dedicated merit is consciously directed back toward our original motivation, well-being, and liberation, or the aim of awakening for the benefit of others. As we progress and collect more merit, realizations happen with greater ease and frequency, and, with these, virtuous activity becomes more spontaneous and consistent, securing a reinforcement contingency until the final goal of awakening is achieved. For this reason, during the spiritual journey, Buddhists amass merit and wisdom: the former rebuilds a Buddha's body, or neural circuitry, made of pure compassion, and the latter rebuilds a Buddha's mind of radical openness. Radical openness makes quantum view our default setting so we can abide in and have direct access to possibility, whereas the body of pure compassion is what keeps us grounded in the mission of awakening living beings.

Not understanding the value of merit may be one reason why many Westerners work tirelessly at their secular meditation practice without deepening realization. All guts, no glory. Much of our culture's approach to meditation has been either watered-down or secularized, and we aren't taught about the accumulation of merit by way of ethics and virtue; thus we don't include merit-making rituals such as prayers, altar offerings, or imagined interactions with the Jewel Tree beings—the field of merit—in our practice. By stripping away karmic activities from our practice because we misconstrue them as hollow religious rituals, we deprive ourselves of the opportunity to accumulate spiritual power that greases the tracks of realization. I call merit the secret sauce, that extra variable that makes the whole enterprise of spiritual practice so tasty! That's why Lam Rim is practical, revolutionary, timeless, and timely.

If we do virtuous activities, such as prayers and offerings, enough, we will start to see our world differently. Not *the* world, objectively out there, but your piece of the world, the only one there is for you. If we start to behave more skillfully, the perceptual filters change. It's not what you see out there, it's what you see from here—through the doors of perception. What you're experiencing now is conditioned and determined by your past; what you're doing now conditions and determines what you'll see in your future. When you can take responsibility for that causal process, you are on the first stage of the hero's path. You change your piece of the world by changing your body and mind from that of an ordinary, deluded, sleepwalking, and afflicted human to that of a hero and eventually a Buddha—one who is utterly awake. Then you inspire others, until everyone's piece of the world is utterly, collectively transformed.

Offer the Mandala and Final Prayers   6 ROAD MAP

At the end of the Seven-Step Mentor-Bonding Process, we close our meditation with a mandala offering and request blessings. In Buddhism, a *mandala* is a two- or three-dimensional representation of a celestial palace or an abode of a deity. More than a decoration, a mandala is a symbolic, visualized environment—the architecture of enlightenment, if you will—in which we imagine ourselves as a deity presiding over a perfected world. That exalted vision can be offered at the beginning and conclusion of meditation practice to honor the mentor and the Jewel Tree refuge, and to request blessings and hastened evolution. Remember, psychologically and in terms of karma, the practice of gratitude, of

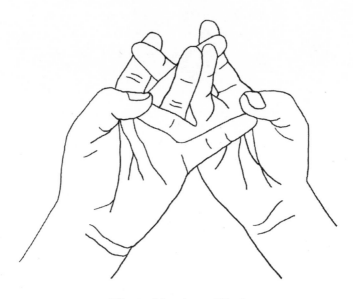

Offer mandala and request blessings.

offering, primes the mind to perceive abundance. So imagine making a final gesture of gratitude to your mentor and the lineage of mentor beings who have realized, preserved, and spread the methods of awakening for the benefit of all who approach them. Also, imagine giving them all you are and have, including your flaws, and say to the mentors, "I offer this mess of my life to you. Can you help me make it into something extraordinary?" This is another example of karma and emptiness, because everything is workable. Even our foibles can be compost for awakening. We can make this life of misery into a paradise by offering it to the Buddhas in a simulation, asking that they help us reverse engineer the world and ourselves.

Feeling grateful, we place our hands in a specific gesture (mudra) representing a purified world, with its central axis surrounded by four continents literally and figuratively in the palms of our hands.

The purified universe is in your hands . . . Get it? We offer it to the mentors and ask for their blessings to help us actualize that pure vision. While doing so, in karmic exchange for their help, we imagine giving away four objects with four successive levels of meaning:

1 The outer mandala is one's visualized environment, conceptualized as a purified universe, healing space, or divine palace that has been constructed out of the transmutation of the three afflictions of greed, hatred, and delusion.

2 The inner mandala is one's virtues, merits, and positive activities: past, present, and future.

3 The secret mandala is one's own happiness and biochemistry of bliss.

4 The suchness mandala is one's intuitive realization of reality itself, bliss indivisible with emptiness.

By enacting the giving away of each mandala at the end of our meditation practice, we seal in a potent emotional charge and direct that collection of energy toward the fulfillment of our altruistic intention. As we do so, we recite the Paradise Offering:

> This gemlike earth filled with sweet smells and wildflowers,
> Adorned with mountains and continents, sun, moon, and stars,
> I envision as Buddha's paradise and offer you—
> So all beings may inhabit so perfect a world.
> Mentors, please accept this precious environment!

Add your personal dedications and final prayers to seal in your practice.

Minding Your Maps: A Convergence of Scaffoldings

If you're housing your meditation practice within the Six Preliminaries, at this point the process becomes more extensive and complex than the Five Elements of Meditation alone. The table on the next page illustrates the convergence.

Here's one way to look at it:

1 Preliminary one (Create a sacred environment).
Five Elements number one (preparation) includes
Preliminaries one through four.

2 Preliminary two (Set up an altar and make offerings).

3 Preliminary three (Prepare your body and mind).

4 Preliminary four (Evoke the mentor and
the Jewel Tree refuge field).

5 Preliminary five (Initiate the Seven-Step Mentor-Bonding
Process) and Five Elements number two (contemplation).

- bonding step one (admire qualities)

A CONVERGENCE OF SCAFFOLDINGS

Six Preliminaries	Seven-Step Mentor-Bonding Process	Five Elements of Meditation*
1. Create a sacred space 2. Set up an altar and make offerings 3. Prepare body and mind 4. Evoke mentor and Jewel Tree refuge field		1. Preparation
5. Initiate Seven-Step Mentor-Bonding Process:	i. Admire qualities ii. Make offerings iii. Disclose negativities iv. Rejoice virtues v. Request guidance	2. Contemplation (e.g., death**)
		3. Meditation (e.g., urgency**)
	vi. Request presence	(Contemplation)
6. Offer mandala and final prayers	vii. Dedicate merits	4. Dedication
		5. Application

*Shading corresponds with the steps in the Five Elements of Meditation
**Example: Road Map Step 10—Death inspires urgency

- bonding step two (make offerings)

- bonding step three (disclose negativities)

- bonding step four (rejoice virtues)

- bonding step five (request guidance), including Five Elements number three (meditation on affective response)

- bonding step six (request presence) and return to Five Elements number two (contemplation)

- bonding step seven (dedicate merits) and Five Elements number four (dedication)

6 Preliminary six (Offer the mandala and final prayers).

- Five Elements number five (application)

We're using a lot of lists and maps, and this organization may seem confusing at first because we are converging the Six Preliminaries, the Seven-Step Mentor-Bonding Process, and the Five Elements of Meditation—the first two processes augmenting and amplifying the experience of the third. In other words, you might be contemplating the theme of the preciousness of human life within the contexts of an ancient ritual practice (meant to act like a karmic turbo boost) and an imagined psychotherapy (with an ideal figure meant to speed psychological development).

Find a Mentor 7 ROAD MAP

The short answer to the question you may be asking is, yes, you still need a real-life mentor. The virtual mentor and inner therapy contained in the visualization are powerful, but combining them with an actual relationship is considered essential in the Tibetan approach. Karmic activities in both worlds, virtual and real, become mutually reinforcing until the distinction between realities on and off the cushion, within and between sessions, is indiscernible. The shift from virtual to real marks our first steps away from our meditation cushion toward the first Lam Rim milestone of renunciation. If you are going to apprentice yourself, mold your mind upon someone, and aspire to be them, your choice can't be random—the relationship shouldn't be based on some fuzzy feeling in your heart. Not everyone with a robe or a chain of retreat centers or an impressive Instagram following is a suitable guide on the Lam Rim. Mentors must meet certain requirements and have specific qualities. If they don't, keep looking. The guru is like a safety harness when you're skydiving: you need to check your equipment regularly or you could be in danger. Scandals abound, and as I share in chapter 6, the fallout can be tragic.

Fortunately, there is a method for finding a qualified teacher and being a good student. In *Liberation in the Palm of Your Hand*,[8] by Pabongka Rinpoche, in Ashvagosha's *Fifty Stanzas on the Spiritual Teacher*,[9] and other texts and commentaries, we find a comprehensive examination of the ten qualities we should look for in a teacher:

1 **Discipline**   Well established in virtue and keeping ethical vows

2 **Quiescence**   Well established in meditation and sustaining focal attention

3 **Wisdom**   Well established in correct view of reality and diminished self-grasping

4 **More knowledge than student**   Has insights and realizations the student has yet to achieve

5 **Enthusiasm**   Never tires and is happy to do whatever it takes to ripen the student

6 **Scriptural knowledge**   Firm foundation of sacred texts, commentaries, and their meaning

7 **Insight into emptiness**   Has at least a correct conceptual understanding of ultimate reality

8 **Skill in teaching**   Knows how to adapt a teaching to effectively reach students

9 **Great compassion**   Thought, speech, and conduct are motivated by Bodhicitta

10 **Readiness to teach**   Always well prepared to share appropriate dharma instruction

It may be a challenge to find someone so thoroughly transformed and qualified, so you do the best you can. Even if we find a teacher with half of these qualities, we also must consider how karma works. What we see in the spiritual teacher is also a reflection of our minds—a projection—formed and framed by our past. If you met my teachers Gelek Rinpoche or Lama Zopa, you might have a different response to them than the awe they inspire in me. We all have different perceptions about who are moral, tranquil, and wise teachers, and how skillfully they interpret and teach the dharma. Do they conduct themselves responsibly and make the teachings accessible? Do they move or repel us? Some of the qualities might be easily recognizable, whereas others may be more subjective and interpretable.

Ashvagosha tells us what to look for in the teachers out there, but what we see depends on where we look from and who is doing the looking. Our pasts color the mind and influence how we perceive the world. When I'm asked how one should find a teacher, I advise three things: First, recognize the importance and repeatedly generate the intention to meet a qualified master. Second, do a lot of shopping, testing the waters according to these guidelines and qualities. Third, work on purifying your mind, making offerings and creating the causes and conditions for an inevitable ripening.

ROAD MAP 8   Become a Suitable Student

If our perception also matters, then in addition to asking "How do I find a qualified teacher?" we should simultaneously inquire "How do I become a good student?" According to Ashvagosha, there are three qualities to develop: open-mindedness, pure motivation, and utter sense of urgency. This goes back to karma, because if we want to see certain qualities in a teacher, we must overcome unfavorable qualities in our mind. The Tibetan Buddhists illustrate the desired qualities using a metaphor of three kinds of cups: upside-down, contaminated, and leaky.

- You can't pour liquid into an upside-down cup, so a student should be open-minded, impartial, unbiased, and able to receive.

- Secondly, if a cup is contaminated or dirty, no matter how pure the liquid you pour into it, it will be tainted. A good student is well-intentioned. Their impetus for receiving a teaching is tied to one of the Three Levels of Aspiration: well-being, freedom, and altruism.

- Finally, the leaky cup can't hold liquid. A student who doesn't retain information may not be bringing the necessary concentration, energy, or determination to their practice—thus disrespecting themselves, the mentor, and the dharma the mentor imparts—or they might not have found the right teacher. The idea is to study with vigor and passion and to wholeheartedly apply the teaching to our life with as much unhindered attention and determination as we would to finding a way out of a burning building.

A qualified student is receptive, well-intentioned, and determined. Is that you?

From Virtual to Reality

We're starting to see that we need to relinquish our hubris in order to stand on the shoulders of giants and benefit from both virtual mentors and an actual mentor, the so-called root of all virtues. Meanwhile, we understand that our state of mind as a student is critical for selecting and following a good mentor if we're going to progress on the path. Beyond the meditative session, the first eight Lam Rim steps on the road map direct us toward our first milestone: renunciation, or evolutionary self-care. Just as a snake sheds its skin, so too do we relinquish actions, words, and views that compose our current life of misery and longing so we can be reborn as a Bodhisattva hero, a child of the Buddhas. Are you ready to let go?

Retracing Your Steps   4-8 STEPS

4 Evoke the mentor and the Jewel Tree refuge field.

5 Initiate the Seven-Step Mentor-Bonding Process:
   i Admire qualities
  ii Make offerings
 iii Disclose negativities
  iv Rejoice virtues
   v Request guidance
  vi Request presence
 vii Dedicate merits

6 Offer the mandala and final prayers.

7 Find a mentor.

8 Become a suitable student.

4 RENUNCIATION

REACHING THE MILESTONE OF EVOLUTIONARY SELF-CARE

When the Buddha declares there is escape from sorrow, the escape
is Nirvana, which is not a place, like heaven, but a psychological
state of mind in which you are released from desire and fear . . .
It is right here, in the midst of the turmoil of life. It is the state
you find when you are no longer driven to live by compelling
desires, fears, and social commitments, when you have found
your center of freedom and can act by choice out of that.

JOSEPH CAMPBELL, *The Power of Myth*

I grew up in an affluent family. We had it all. My father was a successful businessman and my mother an interior designer. My brother
and I were educated in the best schools. I did exactly what everybody
in our culture expected: got a degree, went for the advanced degree,
pursued a profession, got married. Yet, from the time I was sixteen, I
felt an underlying discontent. It didn't take me long to figure out that
no matter how much money we accumulated, how many vacations
we took, all the nice stuff we had, it *wasn't enough*. More wasn't better.
Something was missing.

I was fortunate to find an alternative, to make it all the way to
India, to a tiny town called Bodhgaya I couldn't even find in the family
atlas, and discover in that Burmese monastery that there are other ways
to live and other aspirations to follow; other ways to imbue life with
meaning and purpose; paradigms other than those that reduce us to
robots stuck on a treadmill of production and consumption in a world
where God is dead. The moment you hit that existential crossroads,

you have two choices: surrender and let your soul shrivel, or relinquish the bullshit worldview our culture sold us and allow your soul to thrive. This crossroads is where we can turn to renunciation, by giving up on hedonic pursuits grounded in a worldview that fails to acknowledge the spirit. Renunciation is what Joe Loizzo calls transcendence in the Three Principles of the Path and what I call evolutionary self-care.

Renunciation is about finding the true purpose of life and not accepting the lies our culture tells us about who we are, why we're here, and what we're here to do. Our materialistic, often nihilistic culture assumes we're a randomly occurring set of neurons in a sack of meat that climbed out of the Precambrian slime solely to compete, procreate, and consume. If we buy what they're selling, we feel dissatisfied, apathetic, and lost. Not right away, but we *will* realize that there will never be enough. Look around: lives aimed solely toward economic accumulation result in social alienation, ecological degradation, and existential purposelessness.

The nascent hero within us begins to wonder, Who am I and what is the true purpose of life?

To be a little confused and dissatisfied with our current condition is understandable from the spiritual point of view. To be a little concerned or pissed-off about what you've been told—about how to live and why you're here—would be completely appropriate. Healthy, in fact. In an aphorism often attributed to the philosopher Jiddu Krishnamurti, "It is no measure of health to be well adjusted to a profoundly sick society." Our distaste with ordinary life and our willingness to renounce and rebel is the ray of our Buddha nature piercing the veil of delusion, and it is instrumental in guiding us to the Lam Rim. Rebelling is what Campbell described as the hero answering the call to adventure—leaving the comfort of home and embarking on a path, not knowing exactly where we're going or what we'll find along the way, but motivated by the recognition that we can no longer stay where we are.

Think about your life right now, all the busyness and energy you're putting into projects and goals. Where does it all lead? Where do they end? Follow the trajectory for six months, or a year, or five years, or ten years. It all leads to the same place: death! As I've often heard

American Tibetan teacher Lama Marut say, "You either lose everything one by one, or all at once." "One by one" means that everything incrementally falls apart, dies off, or leaves you. "All at once" means *you* die. Think about your partner—the person you go to bed with at night. Think about your parents. Think about your kids. You will lose them. All of them.

Our culture is designed in such a way that we don't have to look. We've stopped considering where our meat comes from, where our elders go once they're no longer useful, how the homeless guy on the corner survives, or who funds and profits from war. We've stopped analyzing. "Bread and circuses" is an expression that means if we have enough deep-dish pizza and Jets football, we won't complain about the crappy economy and the lies about weapons of mass destruction in Iraq. We'll be temporarily satiated but utterly disempowered—zombified.

The whole idea of renunciation is that the way we have been living—the way we have been conditioned to live—is what the ancients called an illusion; I'm calling it a lie. Living this way won't work out for us. It won't result in lasting happiness. There's a carrot dangling and we keep going for it. And we don't even like carrots! We have a voice in our head that says, *Maybe next time . . . if I try a little harder . . . if I get that promotion . . . if I marry that person and have a kid, then it will all make sense. It'll all be okay. I'll be okay.*

We're also motivated by pain avoidance. All living creatures have a habituated response to suffering: we recoil. We use all available energy to avoid pain. The minute we suffer, we reach for the Advil, the television remote, the glass of wine, the shoulder to cry on, God's grace, or even meditation. The disadvantage of our modern infrastructure—science and technology—is that we're so damn good at distracting and numbing ourselves, at getting away from our pain, that we hardly experience it anymore. Getting better at avoiding pain has compromised our ability to deal with the inevitable discomfort that is part of embodied human existence, because pain finds a way to us. No one is exempt.

Here's where what the Buddha called *samsara*—or compulsive existence—comes in, what Tsongkhapa called the "samsaric ocean." The literal translation from Sanskrit means "to wander aimlessly" and implies a cyclic existence, a meandering through life again and again. From the Tibetan multilife perspective, samsara is to cycle through states of compulsive grasping and avoiding and to experience the same result of suffering or dissatisfaction infinitely. In our conversations, Joe Loizzo has translated it as "the repeated cycle of suffering conditioned by a mind and body contaminated by stress instincts and traumatic imprints." Samsara is a state of being unconsciously and perpetually driven by our evolutionary stress instincts and our traumatic memories and narrative from childhood.

Samsara is a way of talking about what's causing our chronic state of existential dissatisfaction and turmoil. It's not the world outside us with its unfortunate events and unpredictable circumstances, it's the way we mentally process those things. Samsara is inside us. It's a state of mind. It developed from past trauma, calcified through our narration and interpretation of that trauma, and became hardwired in our behavior by our reactions. Samsara is inside us and always there; it's what Jon Kabat-Zinn is talking about with the phrase "Wherever you go, there you are." Samsara is also synonymous with what Buddhists call all-pervasive suffering. From the Buddhist perspective, it is the current existential predicament of all life, a conditioned state that self-perpetuates its own misery, a faulty program stuck on autorepeat. Pretty bleak.

Remember what Godwin told me? "Breaking out is only as important as how we break back in." Spiritual practice is not about distraction or avoidance or getting numb, it's about being with pain in a different way. It's about the learning and insight that can develop by getting close to the things we try to avoid. That's where renunciation comes in.

Renunciation doesn't mean giving up something material. It may have meant that in pre-Buddhist Vedic culture, but the renunciation the Buddha proposed wasn't about avoiding worldly life, or transcending the material realm, or giving up our savings account, our relationships, or even pizza and football. We're not expected to wear a loincloth and live a celibate life in a cave. However, we do have to give up on delusions that trigger afflictions, drive compulsions, and create suffering. Like a heavy wagon wheel spinning in the mud, creating an even deeper groove from which the likelihood of escape decreases with every rotation, the unconscious chain reaction in our mind is what we're renouncing. That means renunciation also involves a reorientation toward waking up here and now in the world, forming new relationships with our bodies, people, our work, and the environment based on a realistic understanding and ethical sensitivity. It means staying in the world, breaking back in, being present with discomforts and habits, and working through them. Renunciation is the doorway to liberation. The only way out of the fire is to let go of the coals.

When you've found that space of despair and confusion, that crossroads where you're staring despondently into a void of meaninglessness, you can use the doorway to wake up your innate genius and discover what you can accomplish with this amazing life. That's transcendent renunciation, which is a form of love: caring enough about life, recognizing your innate power and potential, and being motivated to do something about your predicament before it's too late. It's also self-care. People use the term *self-care* a lot these days, and that's a good thing. Self-care means getting plenty of rest and exercise, eating well, and putting up healthy boundaries regarding work and toxic people, but what I mean here is *evolutionary self-care*—care for your psychological development and evolution over countless lives. Kale smoothies won't lead to liberation, but caring deeply enough about your soul to eliminate fundamental delusion will.

Lama Je Tsongkhapa put this succinctly in the Three Principles of the Path:

> [In this brief text] I'll explain as best I can   1
> The quintessence of all Buddha's teachings—
> The path revealed by his noble heirs,
> As the crossing for fortunate freedom seekers.

Tsongkhapa begins with an expression of humility and desire to teach, to the best of his ability, the entire path to enlightenment. It's like asking, "How can I, as best as I'm able, express quantum physics in fourteen verses?" and then having the courage and skill to pull it off.

He then refers to the Buddha and his heirs—all those who have conquered their inner afflictions and delusions, traversed the path, and become enlightened. You could say the Buddhas have arrived at a final enlightened state, while the noble heirs, or Bodhisattvas, are still on their hero's journey. One becomes noble not by birth, status, or wealth in Buddhism, but by seeing reality, by achieving a direct perception of emptiness. Additionally, Bodhisattvas have taken a vow: the aspiration to gain enlightenment for the benefit of all beings. Their altruistic intent is coupled with altruistic conduct. Since the Lam Rim journey is a continuum, any of us who vow to cultivate this extraordinary intention as we progress along the path would be considered Bodhisattvas-in-training.

Also, it's noteworthy that the path is revealed as a *crossing* rather than a gateway in Joe Loizzo's translation. This word emphasizes the gradual nature of developing from samsaric misery to complete awakening. It's a progression, like crossing an ocean, rather than opening a door, as one might do in the sudden-enlightenment approach.

> Listen with open minds you lucky people 2
> Who break the addiction to worldly pleasures,
> And work to give leisure and opportunity meaning,
> Trusting the path that satisfies Buddhas.

Tsongkhapa urges us "lucky people," who already have everything we need to be liberated, to "listen with open minds." Here is the encouragement for how we should receive and practice dharma. Break your addiction to hedonic pursuits with urgency! Trust and pursue the spiritual path as if your life depended on it, like following the exit signs in a burning building. We can think about this in terms of the three qualities of the good student (open-mindedness, pure motivation, and utter sense of urgency or determination), as well as in dedicating our aspiration to reading a text like this. Avoid the complacent attitude you may bring to other mundane tasks in life, because the Gradual Path could set you free!

> The drive to survive binds all embodied beings, 3
> And no cure can stem the pleasure-seeking

Tides of mere survival but real transcendence,
So first of all work to renounce [mindless pleasure]!

Tsongkhapa encourages us to recognize that there is no lasting satisfaction to be gained on the hedonic treadmill of pleasure seeking.
Renunciation is compassionate, as Tsongkhapa is clarifying, so there is
no further doubt that there is only one cure for the existential hankering and angst we share with all embodied beings. Real transcendence
is necessary, a complete reorientation from hedonism and neurotic
self-preoccupation to sustainable well-being and evolutionary self-care.
In the next stanza, Tsongkhapa begins to provide the specific ways to
reorient our soul's GPS toward renunciation.

> Leisure and opportunity are hard to find,   4
> And a lifespan leaves no time to waste—reflect on this
> And you'll counter the obsessions of a worldly life.
> Compulsive action and reaction inexorably cause
> Future cycles of pain—repeatedly contemplate this
> And you'll counter obsession with an afterlife.

This verse contains the seeds for what Tibetan Buddhists call the Four
Thoughts That Turn the Mind toward the dharma, or away from samsara.
They can also be called the "four mind turnings" or the "four reminders"
because they redirect our attention from misguided pursuits of gratification toward the contentment of awakening. Contemplating each of these
thoughts that turn the mind (with a pause at the halfway point for taking
refuge) produces a psychological outcome or realization and brings us to
the evolutionary milestone of renunciation. Here are the four thoughts:

- **Thought one**   Preciousness of human life inspires
  appreciation (road map step nine).

- **Thought two**   Death inspires urgency (road map step ten)
  and refuge offers evolutionary safe-direction (road map
  step eleven).

- **Thought three**   Causality inspires agency (road map step twelve).

- **Thought four**   Defects of samsara inspire distaste in compulsive existence (road map step thirteen).

Let's return to the Lam Rim.

ROAD MAP 9   **Preciousness of Human Life . . .**

Thought One: Inspires Appreciation   Tsongkhapa writes, "Leisure and opportunity are hard to find." I associate this with winning the lottery. If you're reading this book, you're a winner! Not because this book is special, but because you are. The contemplation on the preciousness of human life is a reflection on gratitude that allows us to appreciate that we have everything we need now to liberate ourselves. There's nothing else to hanker for. That is not the case for countless living beings. Whenever we watch the news, we see people who are deprived of the necessities of life. It hits the heart hard.

We are fortunate to be free of major physical and mental illnesses that obscure the natural capacity of the mind to learn, grow, and transform through realization. Fortunate to be free of having bombs drop on our neighborhoods. Free from breaking our backs working in rice fields or diamond mines. Free of being tormented by oppressive governments and fundamentalist regimes. The list goes on, but when we look at the world, we see there are countless people in conditions so harsh they could never even imagine doing what we are doing right now. They might never have an opportunity to contemplate and practice the life-bestowing teachings of the dharma, to sit quietly and meditate in safety. They might never be able to admit how vast and valuable their life is because their circumstances are restricted or worse.

Not only do we have mental and physical freedom, we have opportunity, inclination, and choice to pursue something spiritual. Many of us don't think twice about women being in a classroom, but in other countries they would be segregated, or their presence forbidden. We live without fear of the military police busting in and arresting us for congregating, contemplating, and discussing how to empower ourselves. Think about the staggering situations in Syria or North Korea, and even communities in Los Angeles or New York that the Trump administration labeled "target rich" for ICE raids.

We have the rich legacy of thousands of years of texts and information at our disposal. We have access to vast libraries at the click of a mouse. We have Tsongkhapa's Great Treatise on the Stages of the Path to Enlightenment translated into a language we can read! You can have this awakened being's cookbook for how to get enlightened delivered to your door the next day by Amazon for fifteen bucks! People in ancient India died traveling to places where they might have access to such marvelous teachings. They might have had one opportunity in a lifetime to hear one teaching from an awakened master. We have the leisure of going to a bookstore and choosing from an infinite variety of spiritual texts. It's not that way in Afghanistan. Thankfully, a few Tibetans memorized texts or chose to carry them, instead of food and water, and to keep them safe on their arduous passage over the Himalayas, from Tibet to India, while escaping the Chinese, and so many others committed their lives to preserving all the knowledge one needs to awaken—to get off this wheel of compulsive living. How fortunate we are.

The traditional Buddhist list of our great fortune is called the Ten Endowments:

1 Born a functioning human being, the human life-form is optimal because there is enough suffering to motivate the hero's journey, and it possesses all the attributes necessary to wake up.

2 Intact senses, specifically all five sense faculties, plus the mental faculty that permits reflection and realization.

3 Born in a spiritually tolerant country, because if we weren't we couldn't study, reflect, and practice.

4   Faith in or inclination toward the dharma, because if
    we didn't have this we wouldn't prioritize our study of
    contemplative practice and life.

5   Having not committed any of the five egregious
    acts—hurting a Buddha, killing one's mother, killing
    one's father, killing a saint, or causing division in the
    sangha—because these create a karmic result in which
    realization becomes nearly impossible.

6   Born in a time when a Buddha appeared. This is auspicious
    because there are said to be eons between appearances
    of fully awakened beings and dark ages when there is no
    access to teachings.

7   Born when a Buddha taught the dharma. This is significant,
    because even when a Buddha finally appears in the world
    after eons of darkness, some awakened beings don't teach.

8   Born when the dharma still flourishes, instead of a time of
    utter dharma darkness after a Buddha has died and the
    residue of their legacy is faint or diminished.

9   Born when there are realized beings and great masters to
    uphold the teachings and serve as ambassadors and guides
    in the Buddha's absences.

10 Born when there is a community of spiritually like-minded
    individuals to support our practice, because we all know
    how challenging it is to practice alone.

We also list our great fortune in the Eight Freedoms. I have translated them using the language of clinical psychology. These reflections
help us appreciate the myriad variations of adverse temperament we
are free from, thus enabling us to evolve:

1 Not being born tormented, schizophrenic, or delusional (traditionally called a "hell being" in Tibetan Buddhist cosmology).

2 Not being born or compelled by severe addiction (hungry ghost realm).

3 Not being born severely anxious or preoccupied with securing basic needs for survival (animal realm).

4 Not being pathologically narcissistic and self-absorbed in one's fame, power, or privilege (god realm).

5 Not being born at a time where there is no Buddha (the inverse of the endowments).

6 Not being born where there is no dharma.

7 Being born free from defective senses—our abilities to think, reflect, and communicate are intact.

8 Being born free from disempowering beliefs in an omnipotent creator controlling one's fate, or nihilism (believing that life is meaningless).

Death . . .   10 ROAD MAP

Thought Two: Inspires Urgency Tsongkhapa writes, "a lifespan leaves no time to waste." The only certainty of life is death. When we visit someone in the hospital who is dying, and they're sucking air out of a tube, surrounded by weeping family, we have the audacity to think, *These poor people*. No way—that's you lying in bed. Death is coming for us all, and it's rarely pretty. It's miserable, painful, and sometimes drawn out. I'm not trying to be dramatic, but how many of us get to pass away peacefully in our sleep? Without spiritual training, we leave like we came in—flailing and screaming.

You aren't going to have the luxury of waking up early to study and meditate when you're on a respirator. All the wasted hours shopping on the internet, gossiping, or binge-watching TV—you don't get them back. Given how precious life is, it's sobering to calculate how much time we waste. We will lose everything—it's not *if,* but *when.*

Think about the urgency of death the next time you argue with your partner or you react unskillfully when your teenager talks back to you. It will change your whole perspective on how you live—to know that it will all be gone. All the petty little disagreements, all the tiffs and fights, all the inconsequential pursuits and preoccupations fly out the window when you look at life from this perspective of death and dying.

However, don't let it paralyze you. Let this reflection motivate you. A sincere and thorough reflection on death should light a fire under your ass to radically reprioritize how your precious life resources will be used. There are three related reflections: death is inevitable; the time of death is uncertain; and the things that can help you at that time are your dharma practice and mental preparation. So, prepare now! You have the winning lottery ticket but could lose it at any time!

ROAD MAP 11   Refuge Offers . . .

Thought Two: Evolutionary Safe-Direction   Tsongkhapa writes, "reflect on this . . ." The first two of the Four Thoughts That Turn the Mind—preciousness of human life and death inspires urgency—turn the mind away from reckless, hedonic pursuits, but then what? After we've been tossed in the waves of compulsive existence, seeking a safe harbor to rebuild our ship, reset our compass, and refuel for the ongoing voyage is vital. That's what is meant by taking refuge. Refuge is the act of assuming your innate power to master and direct evolution.

The Buddhist scholar Alex Berzin uniquely translates refuge as "safe direction."[1] I like that because it suggests a revolutionary reorientation of consciousness—using the outer and inner Buddha, dharma, and sangha as a compass heading. The outer Buddha is the role model for best evolution, the dharma the teachings on how to achieve it, and the sangha the like-minded community that supports the hero's journey. The inner Buddha is the mind's innate potential to awaken; inner dharma is our direct realization of reality as it is, when we actualize our wisdom potential; and sangha is the love that connects us to living beings. Makes for a good hashtag: #awakenwisdomlove.

Causality . . .   12 ROAD MAP

Thought Three: Inspires Agency   Tsongkhapa writes, "Compulsive action and reaction inexorably cause / Future cycles of pain." The third thought that turns the mind is karma. It's my favorite because it presents a reasonable explanation for personal experience without resorting to a theistic position such as "God's will," or a nihilistic one of random meaninglessness. Both are equally disempowering and neither ever satisfied my skepticism.

The first two mind turnings—*preciousness of human life* and *death*—are said to stop us from screwing things up in this life and lead to refuge, which offers our soul, or mental continuum, safety to prevent it from devolving into more tormented states of consciousness. The final two reflections, *karma* and *samsara*, are said to help us stop screwing up our *future lives* and lead to evolutionary self-care (renunciation), which further refines states of consciousness, directing it toward complete liberation.

The entire pursuit of liberation depends on this most essential yet misunderstood insight: that karma, or intentional action, is the primary force shaping human development. In my estimation, any understanding and application of mindfulness meditation without karma theory is limited at best. However, apart from Joe Loizzo, to date, no one has thoroughly translated karma theory into scientific parlance, and so it remains an obscure concept prone to dogmatic, religious mythologizing, blind faith, or misuse. In traditional Buddhist cultures, as in the popular imagination of the West, karma is often taken to mean an impersonal, cosmic law of reward or retribution that explains how our past actions, like an external boomerang effect, create either negative or positive consequences in the future. For example, if we get a promotion, we consider it "good karma"—a result of positive past acts—but if we break up with a partner, it's "bad karma"—the result of negative past acts.

According to his extensive interdisciplinary research[2] on the subject, Joe Loizzo proposes an alternate, scientifically critical interpretation (one I subscribe to) of karma theory as accounting not for external events, but how we perceive what happens to us based on past actions. Karma derives from the Sanskrit root word *kri*, meaning "action," and assumes a reaction—a cause and its effect. Karma involves four subphases of action and reaction: the imprinting of past actions called the "past causal seed"; the "current ripening effect" of past actions that distorts present perceptions; the "current causal seed" planted because of compulsive reactions triggered by those perceptions; and the "future ripening effect" of those current actions on perceptual interpretations of future moments. The future ripening effect can manifest in one of four ways: as a pervasive psychological state,[3] as a mental tendency (e.g., often generous or stingy), as a subjective experience (e.g., feelings of abundance or scarcity), or as a perception of the environment (e.g., supportive or hostile). This slight shift of emphasis removes karma from the realm of speculative metaphysics and places it in the domain of human perception. It's not that environmental, organic, or interpersonal phenomena and experiences don't follow a principle of causality—of course they all do—it's that their primary causes are not necessarily an individual's intention-driven action. So, while it is true, as the Buddhists say, that *everything is karma* in the sense that everything follows a principle of causality, it's not the case that everything in the world is solipsistic (caused by one's mind). In Indic science, nonliving matter such as environmental forces and weather patterns operate according to their own classification of causality, as do living organisms such as plants and biological processes such as developing cancer cells. When the mind is purified of delusion and affliction and there is no longer malintent or egoic identification—as with a Buddha—there is a third type of causation. What we are discussing here using the term *karma* is a fourth category, psychological causation, representing an ordinary human's actions compelled by benevolent or malevolent intentions and their results on the psyche.

How do we untangle the vast web of interrelationships from the fact that multiple domains of life experiences, each with their own karmic causalities, might be at play in any given moment? We focus on what we can—and where we can—have agency over: our minds, intentions, and actions. For example, infant mortality, epidemics, and tsunamis are all results of specific causal processes, but are not necessarily the direct result of one's past intentions. The result of one's past actions determine how one perceives, interprets, and reacts to a baby's death, a crop failure, a Zika outbreak, a stranger punching you, or the devastating impact of a tsunami.

Past actions create current perceptions, triggering emotions and responses that influence future perceptions. The boomerang effect is happening internally as a psychological cause-and-effect process over time. For those of us indoctrinated by a materialistic worldview, we think these habitual reactions are where the causal chain of events ends—actions have no consequences and evaporate into the ether, and so we don't care much about what we think, do, or say. But there is a growing appreciation emerging in neuroscience for subtle mind-body processes that has some resemblance to karma theory. For example, the uncontrollable activation of implicit, traumatic memory based on the neural net of association, operating according to the Hebbian axiom ("Neurons that fire together, wire together"), parallels the activation of latent karmic deposits. Over time, our cycle of perception, emotion, and reaction becomes neurologically wired, establishing a neurotic personality or ingrained way of being that would be consistent with the Buddha's notion of how we unconsciously create a compulsive life (samsara). It is possible that a job promotion could be perceived as threatening and stressful, just as it might be seen as validating, or that a divorce could be perceived as liberating as much as it could be experienced as traumatizing. Thus, karma theory entails a science that accounts for the variation by which individuals perceive and experience the same events differently, based on their conditioned development, as well as how they can actively shift future perceptions through present learning and behavior change.

Within the karmic worldview, no single moment of human experience exists in isolation, self-arising out of nowhere. Each moment is accounted for by a cyclic loop of causation that resembles a domino effect. This causal loop works at many levels simultaneously: within a single moment of experience, over a single lifetime, and through the mental continuum over the course of multiple lives. As a result, we are not completely free to experience anything fully in the moment because our current perceptions are filtered by latent associations from our past. Nor are we able to act with full freedom due to the force of habituated involuntary reactions that shape future perceptions. Because we're often stuck in a revolving door of unconscious, self-perpetuated misery, reflecting on this principle of karmic causality inspires agency and empowers us to skillfully intervene, arrest, and reverse the cycle.

According to Buddhist mind science, karma, like gravity, is governed by four specific principles, or characteristics. Acquainting ourselves with these characteristics can help us direct the process and power of intentional actions to our evolutionary advantage.

KARMA IS DEFINITE

The first characteristic of karma is that it is definitive; it's certain. Take karma out of the mystical realms. Take it out of the boomerang idea of what goes around comes around. If you act out of aggression by hurting other people or yourself, you are reinforcing hate and a perception of lack of safety. If you're acting out of shame, you are imprinting feelings of inadequacy. Every action produces a result like its cause.

If we plant a lemon seed, we will get a lemon tree, not a cherry tree. The nature of the motivating force, the intention, whether it's malevolent or benevolent, creates a similar result. It's definite. It's not random. If we act violently or self-interestedly, we will get an unpleasant result. If we act with compassion and wisdom, we will get a pleasant result. The relationship breakup is not the result; rather it's your experience of being devastated or relieved, abandoned or grateful for the time you spent together—that experience is the ripening effect of past non-virtuous or wholesome activities.

This is where Tibetan mind science gets mind-blowing: every action we take creates our future experience.

KARMA GROWS

The second characteristic is that karma grows. The analogy is of a tiny seed becoming a tree. Don't be deceived by thinking that seemingly inconsequential intentions can't have far-reaching implications—good or bad. From the classical Buddhist point of view, the potential force of small intentions accumulates and magnifies over time. When the conditions are present, the seed ripens as experience, converting into a massive kinetic release of either misery or joy, depending on the nature of the original action. One analogy is of a bank account in which deposits increase with compound interest over time. This is relevant to our practice of dedicating the merit at the conclusion of each practice. Another analogy of the wheel in the mud is also a helpful illustration: that heavy wheel spins in a circle in the mud once, twice, three times, and the groove gets deeper until it becomes a nearly inescapable rut. Current neuroscience reflects this analogy in how the brain forms and develops new connections (neural pathways) based on repeated experience. These pathways strengthen with repeated experience, and habits grow more robust. With more mental activity in certain areas of the brain, that region grows, while with less or no mental activity, those connections or brain regions atrophy. We're changing brain structure here—in both directions, positive and negative—so little things count. The more we lie, the more lying becomes an automatic part of us, and the more consistently we have paranoid perceptions of being deceived. Over time, through small actions, we create an unconscious perception of a nefarious world. It's the same if we repeatedly tell the truth, which grows to become part of us, and we consequently engender trust and reliance among our peers. So, small acts of virtue can deliver huge internal rewards, rewire your brain, and change your outlook. What you do you become, and the world treats you in turn.

Karma can also grow interpersonally as a ripple effect, which we sometimes call the butterfly effect. If you say something sincere and kind, it can make a difference in someone's whole day. If the barista gives you a smile with your latte, can't it change things? And if your day is a little better, then you treat the people around you with a little more decency, and that smile can expand like a ripple in a pond. One smile, one word, one seemingly inconsequential moment of validation can affect humanity through a harmonic resonance. An argument between two people can cause a war, but slavery can be outlawed, the Berlin Wall can fall, and apartheid can end because of the motivations and actions of a few people.

KARMA IS NEVER LOST*

This is classically the fourth characteristic of karma that I've swapped with the third, because it works more logically to speak about them in this order. Essentially, you can't get rid of the seeds you've already planted. You can't erase the impression. Those seeds that you planted in the past must ripen, and so there is no avoiding the consequences, both negative and positive, of your actions. I call this the "no clemency" principle. The years you spent criticizing yourself or others; the countless times you lied or spoke divisively; the repeated acts of subtle or overt violence, cheating, or stealing—whatever it was, these activities will create an unpleasant effect on your perception. There's no way around it. For example, stealing in the past could ripen as a pervasive anxious personality, the tendency to be miserly, the subjective chronic experience of scarcity, or the perception that the environment is hostile, barren, and unforgiving. You will be responsible for those moments when the outer circumstance appears ideal, but internally you're miserable because the seeds of greed and violence you planted in a prior moment are now ripening and coloring your current perception of a perfectly good circumstance. Past negativity contaminates that "perfect" moment, not as a boomerang circumstance but as a perceptual ripening.

This is where the work and the real opportunity for freedom lies. All the external conditions are right, but because of past deeds, misperception triggers afflictive emotions and unpleasantness is experienced. That was inevitable because it's the ripening effect of a causal seed that was already planted. It has little to do with the immediate situation. The immediate situation or event is merely the delivery mechanism, the conduit, for the activation of latent seeds. This is where past, present, and future are all meeting in a quantum window of opportunity that we are usually too asleep or ill-prepared to take advantage of. That current experience is mostly conditioned by the past, triggered by a real-time association. In that moment, there is nothing you can do. It must ripen. No clemency; no escape. So be a brave warrior, and take *your* ripening effects on the chin with acceptance.

Did you notice the asterisk in the subhead for this section? There is a caveat. Causal seeds can be processed with specific purification practices, such as the diamond hero (*vajrasattva*) visualization and recitation. This powerful practice involves a method called the Four Opponent Powers[4] that can't neutralize karmic effects but can mitigate them. These four powers can also be built into the disclosure in step three of the Seven-Step Mentor-Bonding Process. The most committed yogis follow four prescriptions: with moral discipline, they refrain from planting further negative seeds; with purification practices, they mitigate negative seeds already planted; with virtuous acts, they plant favorable seeds; and with prayers and dedication, they enhance virtuous seeds already planted.

KARMA IS SPECIFIC

We won't get a desired outcome without initiating the specific cause. We'll never feel loved or secure without first planting the right causal seed. God, Buddha, your partner, or your boss won't hand you the life you've always wanted. Positive thinking and praying alone won't help much. It's time to grow up. For the life you want to emerge, you must build it, seed by seed, act by act.

According to karmic science, we can consciously plant and cultivate the seeds for all the things we've always wanted in our life. This is where ethics come in, and they are indispensable. Prescriptive moral guidelines are recommended in every major perennial philosophy and legitimate spiritual culture, although they're often misinterpreted as dogmatic injunctions. In Indic cultures these guidelines are based not on blind faith and subservience but on reason, on understanding that the psychological laws of causality indeed govern ethical actions.

Since karma is the fuel that runs our ship to enlightenment, it's worth spending a little extra time unpacking the point and highlighting the specific cause-and-effect relationship. Here is Joe Loizzo's[5] encapsulation of the standard Buddhist ethical recommendations called the Ten Modes of Virtuous Conduct:

1 Violent actions lead to traumatic injury; nonviolence leads to peace.

2 Compulsive acquisition (stealing) leads to scarcity; generosity leads to abundance.

3 Perverse sexuality leads to frustration; sublimation leads to satisfaction.

4 False speech (lying) engenders mistrust; honesty engenders trust.

5 Slander engenders mistrust; tactful speech engenders respect.

6 Abusive speech engenders isolation; caring speech engenders leadership.

7 Idle speech engenders contempt; meaningful speech engenders authority.

8 Covetous intent results in dissatisfaction; philanthropic intent results in contentment.

9 Malicious intent results in insecurity; nonviolent intent results in confidence.

10 Unrealistic views result in confusion; realistic views result in clarity.

The modern materialistic world wants us to believe that we get the things we desire based on animalistic impulses of competition and self-interest. That's why it never works out. By following karmic science and ethical action, we're influencing how we will perceive and experience everything we have ever wanted. We do not experience the result of actions not taken. Isn't that beautiful? Start planting noble seeds and watch your life grow.

Defects of Samsara . . .   13 ROAD MAP

Thought 4: Inspire Distaste in Compulsive Existence Tsongkhapa adds, "And you'll counter obsession with an afterlife." The final of the Four Thoughts That Turn the Mind is the contemplation on the deficits of samsara. I call this the "chicken nugget" reflection. Do you remember the day you discovered what was inside a chicken nugget? Up until then, you'd been eating and enjoying them. (You know who you are—twelve-pack with all three sauces.) Then one day you learned that chicken nuggets aren't made of chicken meat but a sickening sludge of chicken parts—feet and beaks, sinew and tissue, and other unspeakable synthetic stuff. That was the last day you ate a chicken nugget: you saw their true nature and never wanted one again.

The fourth mind turning works the same way. It's formed from a reflection on six aspects of an unconsciously lived life, or samsara. These qualities don't reflect reality as it is, rather they characterize life bound to mistaken self-identifications and the need to defend and secure what is considered "me" and "mine":

1 *Uncertainty of life.* We never know when that karmic bomb will explode. We never know what to predict in the next moment, never mind tomorrow. We can't control anything, and that creates enormous anxiety.

2 *Dissatisfaction.* Even the good things in life don't last. Hedonic or "worldly" pursuits of fame, praise, pleasure, and possessions are short-lived and leave us wanting more. We can work hard and save for a fantastic beach vacation and it could rain, or we could work our whole life to build a reputation that is smeared in an instant.

3 *Death.* We grow old, get sick, and wind up in the hospital on morphine, totally unprepared and terrified. From the multilife perspective this doesn't happen only once, but repeatedly. Whether we adopt the multilife perspective that our consciousness continues or simply see things from the perspective of a single life span, it feels arduous and disheartening to build an entire career or establish a sense of stable identity only to have all we've worked for dissolve instantly at death or gradually in a series of near-death crises. It's painful to realize the inevitable demise of everything we identify with as I, me, and mine.

4 *Rebirth.* Being reborn is as painful as death. Coming back into a body is as difficult as shucking one off. It's hard to be a naive, helpless child and struggle to learn again. Who wants to repeat those awkward preteen years filled with insecurity and social dread? Birth, whether it's across lifetimes or having to reinvent

oneself after a disaster in a single lifetime, is like crawling out of the primordial sludge each time; it creates a drag on the process of evolution and is considered an impediment.

5 *Vicissitudes.* The constant highs and lows. We want things to even out, yet the minute it's calm, the tornado hits. The minute we get the job, we lose the girlfriend. The minute we find a boyfriend, we receive a cancer diagnosis. The sea change of life is exhausting if we are ill-prepared to ride its natural ebb and flow.

6 *We feel so chronically alone.* New York City is a classic example: we can be surrounded by so many people, in such proximity, and yet feel so separate. Even when we are surrounded by loved ones, they never truly know our thoughts and inner world. So many of us go through life feeling different, alien, and other.

These contemplations form the final mind-turning reflection. Contemplate each theme in succession, make them personal, let them generate the feeling of disgust, and then meditate on that to let it convincingly permeate your being. And, finally, remember that feeling the next time you are compelled on a hedonic pursuit for the new iPhone, job, or hookup, hoping it will lead to lasting satisfaction. Realistically thinking about these defects engenders disgust in samsara and results in turning away from compulsive existence and turning toward a contemplative life. Remember, that doesn't mean no iPhones; it means no more compulsive hankering governed by mistaken ascriptions.

Renunciation (Aspiration to Be Free)— The Milestone of Evolutionary Self-Care
14 ROAD MAP

After a significant process of habituating one's mind to the inevitable defects of samsara, and as a result having the repeated experience of disgust and disappointment, eventually a firm conviction in its futility arises, and a desire to be free subsumes the pursuit of mere pleasure. We have reached the first major Lam Rim milestone, which is also the first of the three paths: renunciation.

We awaken to the truth that running in circles and achieving nothing is not only a complete waste of time but extremely disheartening. Through evolution we have been driven by the pleasure principle of instant gratification, pain avoidance, greed, and fear, and it takes an epic moment in the development of consciousness to say, "I'm no longer going to be compelled by these unconscious instincts when I can finally see there is no endgame." Abandoning instant and temporary gratification leaves an opportunity to pursue a path that provides an inner contentment despite the external circumstance, but more importantly, it can culminate in a direct realization of the true nature of reality, which is what we are here to achieve. That is what transcendent renunciation affords: a gateway to eventual liberation. It is the sine qua non of Buddhism, the essential condition without which awakening is not possible.

This brings us to Tsongkhapa's final verse on renunciation:

> With practice, your mind won't entertain   5
> Even passing fantasies of mundane wealth or fame,
> But will aim for freedom day and night—
> Then you've developed transcendence!

Doesn't that send chills down your spine? Every time I read it, I freak out. When we realize we have achieved renunciation, we can say, "I can't do this anymore. I can't live like this, sleepwalking through a shit storm of my creation. I have everything I need and must pursue freedom now. I must go for full awakening. It's not enough even to have a nicer samsara, intelligently working my karma so I can reposition deck chairs for a better sunset view from the *Titanic*. This life, this precious life, is set up not just for me to be happy, but to be free. I'm perfectly content with what I have. If I'm not, I'll work my karma so that I will be, but once I arrive at a more contented place, I must strive for lasting freedom."

Renunciation means giving up on the samsara-making program, purifying our minds and bodies that have been contaminated and compelled by stress instincts and traumatic imprints. When the wish for liberation from self-imposed suffering arises with consistency, displacing the hedonic orientation, that's when you know you have arrived at the Lam Rim milestone of transcendent renunciation. Renunciation is about changing your priorities; it's about working your karma and redirecting consciousness toward a more liberated, less encumbered way of being. The Four Thoughts That Turn the Mind help by engendering appreciation for what we have, urgency to take advantage of it while we can, agency to direct consciousness optimally, and distaste so we can let go of what has never served. This phase of the journey is about self-mastery of the soul with a long-range view—evolutionary self-care. It's not about quinoa or kale smoothies to be healthy in the moment but protecting and directing consciousness toward liberation.

Retracing Your Steps 9–14 STEPS

9   Preciousness of human life inspires appreciation.

10   Death inspires urgency.

11   Refuge offers evolutionary safe-direction.

12   Causality inspires agency.

13   Defects of samsara inspire distaste in compulsive existence.

14   Renunciation (aspiration to be free)—the milestone of evolutionary self-care.

5 COMPASSION

ACTUALIZING THE MILESTONE OF RADICAL ALTRUISM

A hero is someone who has given his or her life
to something bigger than oneself.
JOSEPH CAMPBELL, *The Power of Myth*

Thus far our hero's journey has focused on self-mastery, redirecting our precious life energies and resources away from unconscious, hedonic pursuits toward consciously breaking the cycle of self-imposed suffering to achieve personal liberation. Making this our central preoccupation and orientation, we arrive at the milestone of renunciation, a mind-set of evolutionary self-care. For those with this humble or modest aspiration, renunciation can be a meaningful and revolutionary goal, or it might be a way station, a transit point for the next milestone up ahead on the spiritual path: compassion.

When the motivation for spiritual practice is not exclusively for your own liberation but awakening for the benefit of others as well, you naturally transition to the next stage of the Thirty-Step Road Map—moving toward Bodhicitta. Since it's a lofty pledge that includes all life-forms and is envisioned across a vast evolutionary continuity, I like to translate it as a mind-set on radical altruism.

Essential to understanding this critical transition from renunciation to altruism is the recognition that the goal of liberation (nirvana) isn't elsewhere; it's not a destination set apart from the world of suffering (samsara). If we were to reach enlightenment right now, we would realize that we are still completely embedded with all of life. It's the wisdom of no escape: we can get untangled from our karmic web, but we cannot extract ourselves from the larger matrix of interdependence with others, so seeing that freedom is possible doesn't free us from our interconnectivity; it only frees us from our compulsions. Liberation is thus reconceived as the release of what Bob Thurman calls the "heart-clamp," freeing our natural sensitivity from self-armoring and allowing the natural flow of care to connect us with others.

Historically speaking, Nikaya Buddhism, or Individual Vehicle Buddhism—the classical teachings of the Buddha, preserved and prevalent in Southeast Asia—is based on what is called dualism. When we see two distinct worlds and do our best to renounce one (samsara) and achieve the other (nirvana), we are operating on the premise of dualism. Our motivation is to free ourselves, and as we do so, we become an integrated and virtuous being, someone who has mastered their mind and karmic activity. Dualists—typified by the soloist virtuoso archetype of the arhat, or saint—are motivated by renunciation and seek individual liberation from the world of suffering.

Mahayana Buddhism, or Universal Vehicle Buddhism, upholds a set of teachings and practices that evolved five hundred years after the Buddha. It is prevalent in Tibet and East Asia and is based on non-dualism. From a Mahayana perspective, we are a little further along the Lam Rim of psychological development, and looking back, we recognize that the milestone reached by saints isn't the end of the line. If we see the world from a nondualistic perspective, we realize we can never escape interconnectivity with others, and we can only temporarily enjoy the victory of personal freedom until the suffering world pulls on our heartstrings and draws us back into relationship, into embeddedness.

This is where radical altruism comes in. Recognizing our inescapable interconnectivity, we choose to upgrade our aspiration from middling to great—to develop a new, specific skill set grounded in renunciation but combined with wisdom and compassion—thus returning to the ordinary world, to everyday life, and to relationships to effectively wake others up and transform the interconnected web of life. We vow to return home with the medicine or elixir, as Joseph Campbell might say. Bodhisattvas, altruistic heroes—the new, prosocial virtuoso archetype of the Universal Vehicle—understand nondualism and aspire to awaken the world. Bodhisattvas are thus motivated by great compassion that is inseparable from the nondual realization of interconnectivity.

Neuropsychology of Attachment

To ground these ancient philosophical principles, I'd like to connect them with recent developments in the field of interpersonal neurobiology pioneered by Dr. Dan Siegel.[1] Using an interdisciplinary approach combining attachment theory, neuroscience, psychotherapy, and contemplative studies, Siegel articulates how the intersection of mind, brain, and relationships tangibly creates what the ancients called the "web of interconnectivity" that links living beings. Mammal brains have evolved to be hardwired to connect with one another in what we call a neural circuitry. Our minds and brains receive, register, regulate, and emit the flow of energy and information intrapsychically (within ourselves) and interpersonally (between individuals and groups). Brains are like antennae that tap and channel the invisible force, or energy exchange, among all life-forms. This is crucial in an infant's prolonged period of dependency, when the parent's brain acts as an auxiliary nervous system to allow for the healthy development of the infant's brain. If the parent is available, consistent, reliable, and attuned to the flow of energy and information, what D. W. Winnicott called the "good enough parent," the infant internalizes what is called a safe base—the ability to self-regulate through states of distress while exploring the unknown—and the ability to connect and regulate with others.

If, on the other hand, a parent's neural circuitry has been damaged by their own childhood trauma, causing insecure attachment, their ability to self-regulate and appropriately send and receive energy and information is compromised. Inevitably, this influences the development of the infant's brain, thus hindering psychological progress and their ability to self-regulate, leading to insecure relationship attachment styles in adulthood. As a result, some individuals present as more rigid and shut down emotionally, and aloof and uninterested interpersonally, in what's called avoidant attachment. Others present as more chaotic and overwhelmed emotionally, and needy and preoccupied interpersonally, because of anxious attachment. In the case of severe early trauma, an extreme combination of both can occur, sending individuals on a rollercoaster of intrapsychic extremes of emotional rigidity and chaos, and interpersonal extremes of dissociation and preoccupation in what is called disorganized attachment. Current science suggests we are inherently and intimately interconnected, and that the way we relate can improve or damage the life experience of others. Thankfully, for those of us coping with transgenerational trauma, emotional deregulation, and insecure attachment, there is hope.

Dr. Siegel discovered that the region of the brain known as the mid-prefrontal cortex—responsible for such vital functions as affect regulation, attuned communication with others through the neural circuitry, insight (perception), empathy (emotion), and response flexibility (behavior)—can be voluntarily accessed and activated, thus enhancing each of these domains. Furthermore, two methods correlated with the activation and development of the prefrontal cortex include psychotherapy and mindfulness meditation. The neuroplasticity of the brain can be recruited in the service of healing and restoring secure attachment, and this can occur intrapsychically by developing focal attention with meditation skills, and interpersonally through an attuned relationship with another secure person.

As we go through this chapter, we can examine the Lam Rim map through a neuropsychological lens, seeing the Bodhisattva as an altruistic hero as well as a protoparent who first uses evolutionary self-care to reestablish self-mastery and secure attachment and, in the current leg of our journey, makes effective use of the neural circuitry to reparent others so they can achieve secure attachment. The endgame is when all beings are securely attached and linked in the biosphere, able to regulate the flow of energy and information in ever-expanding circles—from individuals to families, societies to cultures, and species to environment—resulting in a collective harmony and state of integration. Don't confuse this achievement with enlightenment, but consider it as a precursor or corollary.

As our altruistic hero Tsongkhapa put it:

> Since transcendence without altruistic resolve   6
> Can't yield the collective happiness
> Of [a Buddha's] full enlightenment,
> The wise conceive the spirit of altruism.

Tsongkhapa is reminding us that renunciation isn't the destination on the Lam Rim—we must still find the treasures of unconditional love and universal compassion and return home to help others. Transcendence without altruistic resolve can't produce collective happiness for all beings; only a Buddha's full enlightenment can do that. Therefore, we—the wise ones—should conceive the spirit of altruism.

If we ascribe to nondualism, we can't just hang out with our treasure in a separate reality, so what good is it? It may be a profound and rare evolutionary accomplishment, but how can we enjoy our freedom when everyone around us is suffering? Think about it; when you're having a good day and your partner whom you love isn't, what happens? Your enjoyment is short-lived, and your attention turns to improving their situation so you can enjoy life together.

For that return journey to face the collective, altruistic heroes not only need to generate the compassionate aspiration, or awakened mind, they need to complement it with a unique set of altruistic skills—generosity, virtue, patience, effort, concentration, and wisdom—called paramitas. First responders on the frontlines of human affliction require more than goodwill; they need the right emotional tools for the job. The next two verses paint a picture of what exactly we're about to face and the courageous resolve we'll call on:

> Swept away by the torrents of birth, illness,   7
>   aging, and death,
> Tightly bound by the chains of relentless compulsion,
> Imprisoned in the iron cage of self-protectiveness,
> All caught up in the blinding shroud of delusion,

Endlessly living and reliving the cycle of trauma,   8
Constantly suffering in body, speech, and mind,
Such is the state of beings, all dear as mothers—
So from your natural response build heroic resolve!

This is the pivot from transcendent renunciation, or evolutionary self-care, to generating an altruistic mind, when we shift from the archetype of the saint to that of a protoparent for others who is motivated by Bodhicitta. It is compassion that will propel us through to the final stages of Buddhahood via the final milestone of quantum view. The development of compassion is easy when we are talking about someone familiar or pleasant, but how about when the person is a stranger or even a jerk? How about the corrupt and diabolical politicians who disenfranchise their citizens, or worse? Can you generate Bodhicitta with Kim Jong-un, Bashar al-Assad, or Joseph Kony as the basis? That is far more difficult, bordering on impossible. But for a mere civilian, entering a burning building to rescue people seems equally impossible. The difference is training and experience.

So, how do altruistic heroes train?

ROAD MAP 15-23   **Examining the Three Training Methods of Altruism**

At this point on our road map, we synthesize a succession of steps:

15   Equanimity balances social reactivity.

16   Recognize all beings as kin—inspires solidarity.

17   Remember their kindness—inspires gratitude.

18   Resolve to repay their kindness—inspires reciprocity.

19   Equalize self and other—inspires empathy.

20 Contemplate disadvantages of self-preoccupation and take on suffering—inspires compassion.

21 Contemplate the benefits of altruism and give care— inspires love.

22 Take responsibility and aspire to save all beings— inspires purpose.

Instead of racing through the steps, engage them systematically and repeatedly to finally reach the aspiration to awaken in order to benefit others:

23 Bodhicitta (aspiration to free others)—the milestone of radical altruism.

There are three traditional methodologies synthesized in steps fifteen through twenty-two that arrive at step twenty-three—Bodhicitta. They can also be practiced as stand-alone trainings:

- the Seven-Point Cause-and-Effect Method, attributed to Asanga (fourth century)

- the Four-Point Exchange of Self and Other, attributed to Shantideva (eighth century)

- a fusion of these, which is the Eleven-Point Method, attributed to Tsongkhapa (fifteenth century)

As the Four Thoughts That Turn the Mind engender renunciation, the reflections in these methods engender radical altruism. Each method is apt and appropriate for different types of people in different contexts, yet they all arrive at the same milestone: Bodhicitta.

The Seven-Point Cause-and-Effect Method can be more challenging for Westerners because it assumes a multilife cosmology of infinite relationality. It tends to be characterized as affective and emotional, whereas the Four-Point Exchange of Self and Other is more analytical and critical. Because of this, I have found the latter easier to teach Western students who are coming from a scientific worldview and tend to be more cerebral. Nevertheless, one could argue that teaching the seven-point method to Westerners is more radical and necessary, not only to open their minds to the quantum matrix of reality, but to reengage their hearts and the compassionate warmth of interconnectivity. That's why teaching both methods is more comprehensive and balanced, something Tsongkhapa's Eleven-Point Method embodies.

Pedagogically speaking, you should study the seven- and four-point approaches separately, to accurately lay the foundations and lines of reasoning at the outset. Then, when it comes to practice or application, it is recommended that you combine both approaches according to Tsongkhapa's eleven-point synthesis, which is said to be more powerful than the sum of its parts. Practicing this method activates and synchronizes reason (through critical analysis) and the heart (through affective response) in an integrative and neurologically coherent manner.

To do this, we need to work these points of contemplation in a thematic sequence, like a series of musical scales or yoga postures that soften the mind and revitalize the neural circuitry. They call it Lojong in Tibetan, which translates as "mind training," but I call it an attitude adjustment or heart opening. These reflections sensitize you to the plight of others organically, not by mandate. If you rehearse and repeat these deep, philosophical examinations into the nature of things, they will open your heart in the same way a Fox News binge closes it.

ASANGA'S SEVEN-POINT CAUSE-AND-EFFECT METHOD

The Seven-Point Cause-and-Effect Method has six causal links that yield the seventh, which is the effect—the milestone of Bodhicitta.

Asanga One of Seven: Remember All Living Beings Are Our Mothers

Remember that all living beings are our mothers? I know, this is a challenge right out of the gate.

The cosmology of the Buddhist worldview is one of an infinite life perspective . . . multiple lives spanning infinite time without beginning or end—truly quantum, beyond space-time, infinite interconnectivity. Therefore, we were, are, and will be reborn in infinite interconnection with all living beings—we're perpetually recycling our roles and changing our relationships. Following that reasoning, all beings have given birth to us at one time or another. So, Asanga's first reflection is to recognize all living beings have been as intimate as a mother and her infant. Do they look like your mother now? Of course not. But they have occupied that role, and now they're wearing different clothes, and we have all forgotten our past relationship. One of the ways that Joe Loizzo likes to translate this, to get to the spirit of the reflection and not get stuck on the infinite-life cosmology, is to recognize all living beings as kin—we're genetically and evolutionarily related. This is a relevant message in our era of increasing racism, classism, sexism, and nationalism.

Flex your mind to get to what Asanga is pointing at. Use evolutionary biology or whatever reasoning necessary to arrive at a place where you are resensitized to your affinity with others across arbitrary, imagined boundaries. All the divisions of the mind are learned; they're not innate. We create false distinctions and then act with preference for some, hatred for others, and indifference for the rest. By recognizing that all beings are mother, we see that we are one family, designed to share an expansive neural circuitry, and are capable of regulating the flow of energy and information for each other. The person next to you could easily be a sibling. The goal here is to equalize or harmonize our karmic relations with people by clarifying our view of them, because views, roles, identity, and relations are all contextually constructed.

It is essential, from the standpoint of the development of wise compassion, to recognize our commonality and solidarity with all beings. As a result, we can relate to them more creatively and effectively. That serves you, me, and them. When I think of this point, I recall something John F. Kennedy said in his 1963 speech at American University: "For, in the final analysis, our most basic common link is that we all inhabit this small planet. We all breathe the same air. We all cherish our children's future. And we are all mortal."[2]

Asanga Two of Seven: Remember Their Kindness

Having established equanimity and impartiality, the next point is to reflect on the kindness of all mother beings. The traditional method is to meditate on everyone having been our mother, and then to reflect on how much sacrifice these mothers endured to birth us, nurture us, and give us everything we needed to survive and thrive. We take our insight into maternal sacrifice and kindness and universalize it. When we do this, we discover that every living being is sustaining life and is making everything possible for us.

If you want to take this reflection out of the Tibetan multilife cosmology, think about the complex social-global matrix of interdependence. Alison Luterman puts it like this: "It hit her then that every strawberry she had ever eaten—every piece of fruit—had been picked by calloused human hands. Every piece of toast with jelly represented someone's knees, someone's aching back and hips, someone with a bandanna on her wrist to wipe away the sweat."[3] The farmers, teachers, cooks, nurses, printers, electricians, birds in the trees, and the trees themselves—there is no end and no beginning to account for the interconnectivity of independent beings—are our mothers. Everything in your life is possible because of the kindness of other living beings.

I know what you're thinking: *Kindness?* "They weren't so kind this morning during rush hour." *Kindness* here means the human exchange of the flow of energy and information.

As you reflect on this, remember, as with the Four Thoughts That Turn the Mind reflections, each point is designed to elicit an emotional response that you can meditate on, seal in, and evoke as insight, or realizations (lam). String these insights together between each milestone in a process of integration.

Asanga Three of Seven: Vow to Repay Their Kindness

Thank your mother beings for birthing and sustaining your life! Vow to repay them all. This reflection isn't a dogmatic insistence from some moral imperative, it's a natural outgrowth of a personal understanding. If you're grateful, you want to reciprocate. We start where it's natural and train in ever-expanding and all-encompassing circles.

We want to keep the currency of kindness in circulation rather than hoard it. Repeatedly generating gratitude will lead to the dawning of the motivation to reciprocate. You will organically want to give back, to pay it forward, to make your life an offering, to make something possible for other living beings who have nurtured and supported you. Although taking without giving feeds our longing and desire temporarily, it stops the circulation with others in the web of life, so it's only a matter of time until the supply truck stops coming by for delivery. In terms of karma, paying it forward is the engine for a sense of contentment and abundance; plus, it has the added social value of delighting others, firing their dopamine deposits, and keeping the currency of exchange vibrant within the social matrix.

What happens when others dump toxic waste such as anger and greed into the shared stream of our social circuitry? Every spiritual tradition advocates the high road, and Buddhism is no different. However, it relies on reason as much as faith and has a psychological way to justify its principles: we should be kind to people who are unkind because they obviously need kindness most of all, and because we are forever bound to one another, their welfare becomes part of our self-interest. In a world of interdependence, everyone has contributed to making things possible for each other. A few bad apples might spoil the barrel, but they aren't inherently bad. We can't get rid of them anyway, so why not try to improve our collective circumstance? In the long view, it's all for one and one for all.

Asanga Four of Seven: Lovely Love
The fourth point is generating love. Thurman describes it as "lovely love." I love lovely love! *Love* in the Tibetan Buddhist perspective is not sentimental or romantic love. It has a clear definition: the wish for others to be genuinely happy. It's not romanticized, it's not sexualized, nor is it personalized. It is simply the aspiration that every living being deserves to be as happy as your family and friends who have been kind to you. If you're the protoparent, you start to see all living beings as your children, or at least psychologically as having a wounded child within them who deserves the secure attachment that results from love and attunement.

As we saw in point one earlier, the lines between family and others are arbitrary, so it's possible to grow our natural affection more expansively depending on how we identify with people. It is because you feel close to people that you have affection for them, and it is from that affection that the wish for them to be happy naturally arises. Identification leads to affection, and affection leads to lovely love. For example, look at your iPhone and imagine where it comes from. What are the working conditions in that sweatshop in China? Who died to obtain the natural resources in Africa that went into the phone? What torturous environment did those people survive to produce the thing that you put in your pocket and take completely for granted? Wouldn't it be nice if they had a safe home, a decent wage? Wouldn't it be nice if they could come home at a decent hour and watch their children grow up and thrive? What if every single living being across this entire planet could be safe, valued, healthy, and happy?

Most of us are too afraid to love so generously, because love has always been associated with disappointment or pain; but it's likely that our experience of love was a conditional one, tainted by insecurities and prejudices, and so we have come to form an association based on a distortion. If we all had secure attachments, then love would flow more naturally and effortlessly; we'd trust that we could each produce enough for ourselves with more to spare and share with others. If love is the wish for beings to be happy, then lovely love is the wish that they know the unsurpassed happiness of liberation. Imagine that. Through your care, every single being could come to know who they are to dispel their delusion of separateness.

Asanga Five of Seven: Great Compassion

Seeing all beings as kin generates commonality, solidarity. Reflecting on their kindness generates gratitude. Vowing to repay their kindness generates a sense of reciprocity. Lovely love kindles the affection that wishes all beings happiness. The fifth point is to generate great compassion, but before we can, we need to know what this means. According to Joe Loizzo's translations,[4] there are four kinds of compassion, originally referenced by Tsongkhapa: sentimental, technical, evolutionary, and spontaneous.

1 *Sentimental compassion* is the one we first think of as "real" compassion. It is the least useful because it is laden with human yearnings and cross-contaminates the neural flow of love with shame, guilt, and fear, and is rooted in the delusion of separation between self and others. It is of little benefit because it reinforces difference, as we care about others without seeing ourselves in them or them in ourselves. We can call this "idiot compassion."

2 *Technical compassion* is genuine because it is grounded in the understanding of interconnectivity, an empathic clarity or knowing. Specifically, it's being able to see someone's karmic propensity and to skillfully intervene in their cycles. An example is how a therapist might gain insight into a client's transference dynamic and help bring it to their awareness.

3 *Evolutionary compassion* is also genuine, based in the empathic understanding that sees another's suffering in a more general context, such as their survival instincts, particularly when they are acting like a threatened animal or a scared child. This understanding helps us to not take their toxicity and reactivity personally, in the same way that a parent impartially responds to their child's tantrum because they know it's rooted in fear.

4 *Spontaneous compassion* is nondual wisdom and love. It is a response without conception to alleviate the pain of another without subject/object distinction, just as we'd pull a thorn from our foot without thought or wish for reward, but out of necessity to alleviate pain. It's when someone else's kid falls off the monkey bars at the playground and you spontaneously respond as you would to your child—without intellectual calculation.

Compassion is specifically defined in the same manner that love is. Love is the wish that all beings have happiness; compassion is the wish that all living beings be free from suffering. Love recognizes the value of others being happy; compassion recognizes that they deserve to be free from suffering—and not just ordinary suffering, such as long hours in a sweatshop, but the all-pervasive suffering of samsara, that condition of being compelled by stress instincts and traumatic imprints in a self-imposed, revolving door of suffering. All living beings are stuck in the web of their own delusion and karma. They are all held captive by fundamental ignorance. It's a gross case of mistaken identity. Compassion starts with the heart of evolutionary self-care, but then the heart radiates outward, sending that same care through the neural circuitry toward others. There's no ultimate difference between self and other, so why reserve the care for only a few?

Asanga Six of Seven: Extraordinary Intention

The sixth point generates the wish that we help free all beings from suffering. You want to be the one to save your mother beings from drowning in the vast ocean of samsara. We are approaching Bodhicitta—you can see it up ahead. So, on the heels of compassion comes the wish—the extraordinary intention—that we do something about the unfortunate predicament of living beings.

We need a certain amount of denial to even get up and walk through a world filled with as much suffering as there is on this planet; otherwise we might collapse under the weight of it. The other day, I was eating my breakfast and watching the news when it flashed to a scene of babies starving in Somalia. I couldn't take another bite. Horrific misery! I was crying into my oatmeal as if these were my children, but ten minutes later I'd finished eating and was on my way to work. There are times when we feel we must close our eyes, self-anesthetize, to function. The reason for the shutdown is a sense of hopelessness. Hopelessness is tied to a lack of agency and confidence. We will see our mother beings whom we love in so much pain, and we have only two choices: become overwhelmed and paralyzed by the monumental challenges of the world, or be prompted to do something to alleviate the situation. If we know we have the skill, we'll enter the burning building; otherwise we'll run or freeze in place.

By reflecting on this theme repeatedly, we come to acquaint the mind with the wish that we will eventually be the one to do something about it. "I'll be the capable, secure parent to help ripen all these children who have been arrested in their development due to trauma. I won't wait for someone else—I will do it." Does it sound crazy? In a way, it is. It's borderline delusional thinking. In psychology, they would call it a messianic complex and prescribe lithium! But tempered with the wisdom of emptiness and intact reality testing, it's the natural higher calling and true purpose of every living being. Sure, we're not prepared for something like that right now—firefighters run into burning buildings, not me—but the Lam Rim offers an altruistic bootcamp to help us rehearse and strengthen our Bodhicitta muscle, to embrace the inner hero. This process helps us get over the inadequacy we feel from childhood, the learned helplessness of trauma, and the self-image of incapability, and it strengthens the extraordinary agency and resilience within us. The sixth point is crazy and radical, which is why it's called the extraordinary *intention*.

Look at history. There are all kinds of people doing radical, unbelievable, superhuman things. Terrorists strap on suicide vests in the name of Jihad; Japanese kamikaze pilots flew their planes into US naval ships in the Pacific Campaign during World War II. These examples show the power that a distorted worldview, systematic training, and a sense of mission can have to galvanize individuals toward unthinkable violence. The opposite is also true: we can sacrifice ourselves in order to save lives, to spread messages of freedom, hope, and dignity. That is our Buddha nature, our Christ nature—people who have embodied the principles of love and compassion and have taken extraordinary measures to change the world for the better. We call them heroes and heroines—for example, Gandhi, Martin Luther King Jr., Nelson Mandela, and Malala Yousafzai, along with the nameless aid workers, neonatal surgeons, and ordinary parents who make extraordinary choices in life-threatening circumstances. And we admire them. Those are the people who we want to occupy our Jewel Tree, letting their nectar rain down upon us in a shower of blessing and inspiration. They are the people who have discovered interdependence, wisdom, and compassion, have seen through the illusion of separation and come out the other side with the hero's elixir for the welfare of others.

If we don't believe we can do it, if we don't have the confidence, that's the last hurdle. We believe there is something special about the hero and something deficient about us, but the only difference is that the Bodhisattva has training, has walked the Lam Rim, has reached the various milestones that each contemplation is designed to evoke, and collectively those experiences have brought confidence.

Our natures are the same. It's in your DNA to become a hero. As heretical as it may sound to some, there is no inherent specialness to His Holiness the Dalai Lama. He is not inherently different from you. If you had his modeling, training, support, and devotional refuge, you too could be a paragon of hope and goodwill. Now, hopefully you will recognize how critical it is for you to embrace your training, so that we can shape-shift civilization through the neural circuitry of living beings.

Asanga Seven of Seven: Bodhicitta

The difference between points six and seven is that six is the intention to help free others, whereas seven is the vow to take action to manifest it. Six is "I will be the one to do something about this," whereas seven is "To effectively help, I must achieve full enlightenment. I will give my life over to this sole intention." We can only be of benefit to others, in the ultimate sense of helping them eliminate fundamental delusion, if we are free of that delusion ourselves. The only way to lead living beings through the jungle, or samsara, is to have successfully traversed the terrain ourselves. Only then will you know how to help navigate the thicket of confusion. You can only take someone along the path as far as you have ventured.

How do we do this? We should give others shelter and safety, food and medicine, emotional support and skills, and business loans and supportive infrastructure for them to thrive. We should do all those things, and that would improve life, making samsara more inhabitable. However, freeing people from self-imposed suffering requires an education and a self-reflective and inner healing process. Teaching is the most effective way the Buddha and his lineage learned to help other beings wake up from their nightmare. Buddhism, at its core, isn't on a mission to indoctrinate and convert; rather it is an educational movement based on an ancient inner science. It teaches spiritual quantum physics and universal compassion with an evolutionary health benefit. That is why, late in his seventies, His Holiness the Dalai Lama keeps a rock-star-like teaching schedule, offering his erudition to sold-out stadiums. Getting free requires an educational process of hearing, reading, studying, and meditating to make use of this precious human life, to see the causes of suffering and eliminate them.

This doesn't mean you must go to a monastery or transcend the world. You can arrive at renunciation here and now as you release the heart-clamp of self-enclosure that cripples the neural circuitry. Motivated by Bodhicitta, unleash your love and care to manifest in the relational field of living beings.

What does that look like? Lama Zopa lives with a mind-set completely oriented to radical compassion. His every single activity is perfumed by Bodhicitta. The distinction between spiritual and mundane activities has dissolved, and with the heart-clamp removed, love and compassion ripple through all his intentions, words, and actions. Lama Zopa's way of life and being in the world have become their own nuclear reactor, karmic fusion spinning in a virtuous direction, increasing his merit and deepening his realization exponentially. When he eats his meal, he doesn't do it compulsively out of self-interest; he reframes it as an opportunity to nourish his body to serve living beings. From the highest spiritual ritual to the most mundane activity, such as taking a shower, everything can be transformed by the altruistic aspiration and directed toward the benefit of others. That means nothing must be sacrificed, but the orientation must change, the attitude must be adjusted, and the direction of the flow of energy and information must be reversed. I call this living inside out. Rather than grasping out at the world for the things we need and drawing them back inside us, we tap the ever-flowing fountain of abundance within and channel it outward to those who are thirsty. "There is enough for all" is an excellent mantra.

SHANTIDEVA'S FOUR-POINT EXCHANGE OF SELF AND OTHER

The second method for arriving at the milestone of Bodhicitta is Shantideva's Four-Point Exchange of Self and Other. There are similarities to Asanga's seven points because both lead to the same place, but in my estimation, Shantideva takes a more rational or scientific approach.

Shantideva One of Four: Equalize Self and Other

The first point is to equalize self and other. When he teaches publicly, His Holiness the Dalai Lama often simplifies this connection perfectly, conveying that all human beings by nature want happiness and do not want to suffer. That is how we are all the same, all equal at a fundamental level. When you are thirsty, you want water. When you are in pain, you want relief. Everybody on the planet, every sentient creature, is like you in these ways. They want to avoid suffering and secure happiness.

Much of our culture emphasizes that there is something unique and different about each of us, highlighting the individual at the expense of the collective, and once we make a distinction between self and other, we create group identification and exclusion. That is why it's important to equalize self and other, which is what all the most inspiring figures on the planet have done—Saint Teresa of Ávila, Gandhi, Martin Luther King Jr. What was every one of them saying? "We are all the same. Live in peace, united as one."

Differences exist and are important, but beneath them we are all fundamentally the same. Race, religion, gender, ability, and nationality play a role in our daily lives, to be sure, but aren't fixed realities. Furthermore, they don't represent who and what we are on an ultimate level. If we can see both the ultimate and conventional levels of reality simultaneously, we'll be able to tolerate and resolve the dissonance between relative distinction and ultimate oneness and not collapse into either extreme.

Equalizing self and other is the same as recognizing all beings as mother, as kin, but instead of using a universal interrelationality based on a multilife cosmology, Shantideva employs a more critical perspective that dismantles arbitrary notions of difference based on intergroup identification. It is another way to arrive at the same necessary foundational perspective of identifying with a more collective sense of self—"we" instead of "me."

Our relationships are divided into three categories: friends, strangers, and enemies. Why do we like our friends? Why do we have no interest in strangers? Why do we hate our enemies? The main criterion is how we experience these people in relation to us. It's a subtle narcissism, our life oriented around self-interest. We tend to think this way without taking responsibility for how we are interacting and cocreating those relationships. They appear like fixed entities, as if they are coming at us, but they're not. A friend can become an enemy if they disrespect us. A neutral person can become a friend overnight if they show us spontaneous kindness. These arbitrary designations shift constantly, mostly guided by delusion and karma. This is where we can take responsibility for the way we unconsciously construct and react to people based on self-centered delusion, attachment, and aversion, because every division we have created between us and another being is a construction of mind.

To karmically construct more allies and fewer enemies, we should purify our projections of difference, clinging, and repulsion. Consciousness is our greatest tool in working through these evolutionary instincts. As we equalize self and other, we train to see beyond appearances, recognize that all are equal in being open systems, and avoid collapsing into moral relativism. We respect that we all want and deserve happiness and are capable of being scared and triggered and angry in our own way. Depths of suffering are vast and varied, yet we all have potential for awakening and transformation.

The Dalai Lama is fond of saying that to equalize self and other is to recognize we all have the same inherent value. We tend to exaggerate our importance and worth compared to countless living beings, but our significance is relatively minor. Without falling into masochism, we should invest less time on our narcissistic self-concerns, and without falling into codependency or self-denial, we should advance our concern and care for others.

Shantideva Two of Four: Contemplate the Limitations of Self-Preoccupation

Reflect on the deficits of living life rooted in self-involvement. This point is sometimes translated as "self-cherishing," but I don't like the term because genuine self-cherishing is a good thing; rather than self-deprecate or fall into self-denial, appreciate your precious human life. Self-preoccupation means being myopically invested in "I," "me," "mine" until your life becomes an egocentric bubble: *imprisoned in the iron cage of self-protectiveness, all caught up in the blinding shroud of delusion.* Self-preoccupation creates justifications like "There is only so much oil on the planet, so we need to control it," which leads to fear of scarcity, which leads to wars and fractured societies and ecosystems. When we overinvest in self, when we separate from our interconnection with others, ill intentions and destructive acts follow. Violence, lying, grasping, and all our negative karmic constructions follow from the delusion of self-preoccupation that mistakes "me" as more important than "you" or "us" and defends what is considered "mine."

This contemplation is an analytic reality check on our neuroses. Consider the matter, not from a faith-dogma perspective but using objective reason. Trace all your misery to its source and you'll find it arises from self-preoccupation and self-protectiveness within the hallucination of separateness. This reveals the delusion, the root affliction that is driving everything else. As we contemplate the limits and repercussions of self-preoccupation, we recognize that the biggest terrorist on the planet is our traumatized, alienated sense of self that needs to satiate its urge for gratification and self-preservation. Reptile brains hijacked by the amygdala are our greatest threat, driving all the suffering on the planet; the neocortex attuned with others through neural circuitry is our greatest ally, responsible for optimal social redesign.

Shantideva Three of Four: Contemplate the Benefits of Altruism

Once we've seen through self-preoccupation we can contemplate the benefits of altruism. Doing so flips the rotational axis of our gravitational orbit and the flow of energy invested in self and directs it toward others. This is the one that gets me right in the center of my heart. As Asanga taught, in recognizing the kindness of others and vowing to repay them, we reflect on how every success we've had has come through the love and kindness of others. We accumulate successes like trophies, and we proudly think, *I did that*. Nope. Think about the countless, unimaginably generous, seen and unseen, known and unknown beings who helped you. Pause and think about the people, elements, and actions essential to turning on a light at night. Our world is created and delivered through kindness—a conduit for the harmonic resonance of care. It blows my mind. You can't find a beginning or end to the web of life.

It feels good to give back, pay it forward, or keep kindness flowing. It feels amazing to be altruistic, to share, love, and connect. Why? Because that is reality. You are expressing reality. I call it presence-love. With the heart-clamp released and the neural circuit open, we share love with others because we are all connected and designed to be conduits of life-sustaining love—we *are* others. We are the evolutionary expression of presence-love. Remember that the primary misperception, the thing that self-preoccupation hinges upon, is the delusion of separateness, because we are all connected, and every discrete object in the world of multiplicity is a mere reflection in a fun-house mirror. By connecting through altruism, we are expressing the way things truly are beyond delusions and appearances. We are the shared frequency, not the individual antennae. Love is the natural flow or outgrowth of the wisdom of oneness between living organisms; hate is the unnatural outgrowth of the delusion of separation.

Habit creates obstacles to this flow. For instance, I can justify buying myself an expensive phone, but when it comes to Haiti, I struggle to send a hundred dollars or even bear witness to the calamity. That is the habituated force of preoccupation that strangles the energy flow and keeps it in a self-directed circuit, which is counter to reality. No wonder we are in so much pain.

The spark of altruism is within us. We know it is, so we should contemplate it deeply and try to fan the flames until they engulf our hearts and those of all beings and melt the shell of samsara. When we do, we will make the biggest leap forward in our long evolution: from single-cell organism to mammal to self-centered human to what American economist Jeremy Rifkin calls Homo empathicus[5] to, eventually, Buddha. That is why we contemplate altruism.

Shantideva Four of Four: Exchange Self for Other

Finally, we exchange self with other. This means turning your heart inside out, shifting your energetic flow from self-concern to concern for others. Put yourself in someone else's shoes. Tap into another being's nervous system via the neural circuitry until you reach what Joe Loizzo calls the "warmth and moisture" of their humanity. We're designed this way. Think of how mothers loosen their singular "self" to include their infants. Now, gradually expand that to include other living beings, doing what the Mahamudra tradition calls "taking all reality as your consort, your muse." Life becomes a part of you, like new family members, like extra limbs in the iconography of the Tibetan deities. Altruistic exchange is the antidote for the poison of self-interest.

The moment we begin to experience empathy with no goals or endgame, we end our self-preoccupation, nonvirtuous karma, and suffering. The wall of self-delusion collapses, and we see and experience the world from another's perspective. When our partner comes home from a long day and has that look on their face, we know exactly what they are going through and can naturally respond. We can take their coat and sit them down. We make them dinner or put on their favorite music. We are exchanging our nervous system with theirs, and it feels so good for us both because we have broken through the illusion of self and truly connected with the experience of another. Even in their pain. We have removed the dam walls of self-obsession and allowed the natural expression of love—ultimate reality—to flow.

Energetic Recycling: Tonglen After contemplating Shantideva's four points of exchanging self and other, to seal its effects we perform a powerful black-belt-level meditation called "giving and taking," or Tonglen, which I've interpreted through a neuropsychological lens.

I say black belt because it's not for the fainthearted and should be approached with caution in a gradual training process. In the practice, we assume the role of a protoparent Bodhisattva, self-regulating and facilitating the "other's" secure attachment, imagining and facing the distress of living beings, and recycling their energy flow—changing it from toxic to pure—as altruism becomes our default orientation.

The practice works like a virtual-reality exercise, as if we were Lam Rim firefighters learning to increase our distress tolerance and nondual insight by performing simulated rescues of people trapped in the burning buildings of human affliction. Start by taking on reactivity and extending your presence-love to an imagined wounded child within yourself. Progress to exchanging distress with care for a loved one, a stranger, a difficult person, and finally, all sentient life. It's important that you imagine each face in distress, as this activates your mirror neurons and primes your brain's social circuits for engagement.

For the uninitiated, engaging this raw suffering may fire the amygdala and create a sense of alarm, symptomatic of too porous a boundary or an overidentification with the other's distress. You haven't learned how to put your own oxygen mask on first. Emerging research on advanced compassion practice, conducted by neuroscientist Richard Davidson[6, 7] and contemplative Matthieu Ricard,[8] gives us tools to protect the mind and brain from what is called "compassion fatigue," or overexposure to the suffering of others. Simply put, empathy must be combined with love and compassion. *Empathy* means sharing the feelings of the other's predicament and can lead you to take on their pain. But when empathy is combined with love, altruism, and the intention to do something about their pain—even if it's in the future—these prosocial emotions become the best protection from overexposure and burnout.

First, we need to recognize the difference between self and other in order to create enough space to avoid overidentification, and, second, we need to generate the wish to help them based on recognizing our sameness. This requires a cognitive dissonance that protects the mind from the extremes of detachment and overidentification. It is the compassionate wish to help others that prevents us from falling into learned helplessness and vicarious trauma, but it is the relative separation that allows us to register that we are safe even while the other feels like they are drowning.

This meditation incrementally primes new brain circuits so we can relate to interpersonal distress in robust and resilient ways, and it changes the fundamental default setting from self-concern to altruism:

1   Take a few calming breaths to disarm fight-or-flight reactivity and release the heart-clamp as you regulate. Then with secure attachment, recalibrate to the needs of others.

2   Tap and extend reassurance and care through the neural circuitry.

3   To deepen the imagery and rewire neurological pathways, connect the virtual exchange process to your breath: inhale suffering, exhale love.

4   In the pause between breaths, imagine channeling the distress to your heart where it dissolves self-centered delusion, tapping the wellspring and neurochemistry of love before sending love out. That's how the practice converts adversity into advantage and we become emotion-filtration machines, processing toxicity into compassion.

5   With each cycle of breath, imagine living beings reassured, tapping their own wellspring, developing safe attachment, and all awakening to a deeper nondual wisdom and universal compassion.

I'm often asked if this helps the imagined recipients. It's a trick question: on the one hand, no, because it's all a simulation; on the other hand, yes, because when our minds and brains change based on virtual experience, the people we interact with will inevitably benefit from our attunement and presence-love.

TSONGKHAPA'S ELEVEN-POINT SYNTHESIS

In case you were hoping for another list, here's one developed by Atisha, espoused by Tsongkhapa, and revisited by Pabongka Rinpoche in his *Liberation in the Palm of Your Hand*, which synthesizes Asanga's seven points with Shantideva's four into eleven points for developing Bodhicitta. From the fourteenth century on, this became the standard compassion method for those in the lineage of the Dalai Lamas. Like the others, this method is a stand-alone Lam Rim or part of the succession of steps toward the milestone of radical altruism. When preceded with the steps to the milestone of evolutionary self-care, and followed by the steps to quantum view, it includes the entire arc of the hero's journey to awakening.

Tsongkhapa's genius is in his gift for integration. He bridged public (sutra) and private (tantra) forms of Buddhist teachings, ultimate and conventional levels of reality, and critical theory and meditation praxis, as well as analytic (wisdom) and affective (compassion) approaches to experience. His method of generating Bodhicitta is an example of galvanizing the best of both Asanga's and Shantideva's approaches—the former more affective, the latter more cognitive. If we look at the eleven-point synthesis from a neuroscience perspective, we see how it connects the brain hemispheres—the left associated with logic and focal attention, the right with emotion and the body:

1   Meditate on social equanimity, visualizing friends, enemies, and strangers, while balancing codependent clinging to loved ones with unconditional love, disinterest of and prejudice toward strangers with genuine interest, and hostility and repulsion for enemies with genuine compassion. This inspires balanced social sensitivity.

2   Recognize all sentient beings as mothers or kin, because we all come from a common genetic source, want happiness, wish to avoid suffering, and are mutually bound within the web of interconnectivity. This inspires commonality, solidarity, and an important sense of connection, affiliation, or greater identification.

3   Remember the kindness of sentient beings whose direct or indirect efforts make everything you are, experience, and do possible. This inspires gratitude.

4   Repay kindness. Resolve to keep that kindness in the neural circuitry by paying it forward. This opens the channels and inspires reciprocity.

5   Equalize self and other by reminding yourself that all beings are fundamentally the same, equally wish to avoid suffering, and are deserving of happiness. They are like you, except there are more of them. This inspires empathy.

6   Contemplate the disadvantages of circuit-breaking self-preoccupation based on the delusion of separateness, which is the fundamental cause of all suffering.

7   Contemplate the advantages of heart-clamp-releasing altruism, which is the fundamental source of all happiness.

8   With a mind influenced by great compassion, exchange self and other using the breath. Take on the suffering of sentient beings—their clinging and repulsion rooted in fear of harm or abandonment. Do this with every inhalation.

9   With a mind of selfless love, continue the exchange by extending secure attachment and fruits of virtue through the neural circuitry to all sentient beings. Imagine them receiving your love, care, and peace as gifts that reassure and awaken them. Do this with every exhalation.

10 Based on giving and taking, generate the intention that you will be the one to save all beings, inspiring a sense of universal responsibility and purpose defined as the extraordinary intention.

11 Now seek awakening to fulfill the extraordinary intention. Let this altruistic aspiration perfume and compel your extraordinary actions of generosity, virtue, patience, effort, concentration, and wisdom as they manifest.

Whether you take the route of seven steps, four, or eleven on this phase of the Lam Rim, you will arrive at the milestone of Bodhicitta. I have chosen to combine two steps in Tsongkapa's eleven-point method, reducing them to nine steps on our road map.

Retracing Your Steps   15-23 STEPS

15 Equanimity balances social reactivity.

16 Recognize all beings as kin—inspires solidarity.

17 Remember their kindness—inspires gratitude.

18 Resolve to repay their kindness—inspires reciprocity.

19 Equalize self and other—inspires empathy.

20 Contemplate disadvantages of self-preoccupation and take on suffering—inspires compassion.

21 Contemplate the benefits of altruism and give care— inspires love.

22 Take responsibility and aspire to save all beings— inspires purpose.

23 Bodhicitta (aspiration to free others)—the milestone of radical altruism.

6 ACTION

EMBODYING THE HERO'S CODE OF IMPECCABLE CONDUCT

> The hero is the one who comes to participate in life
> courageously and decently, in the way of nature, not in the
> way of personal rancor, disappointment or revenge. The hero's
> sphere of action is not the transcendent but here, now, in the
> field of time, of good and evil—of the pairs of opposites.
> **JOSEPH CAMPBELL**, *The Power of Myth*

With minds directed toward radical altruism, we can take the next steps and train in the altruistic activities. It's not enough to conceive noble intention on the meditation cushion; we must plant the seeds of virtuous karma through thoughts, words, and actions to move from aspiring Bodhicitta to what's called engaged Bodhicitta.

The dualities of the relative world—good and evil, love and hate—don't dissolve in conventional reality, rather they define its contours and experiences within. So the hero can have no greater impact in the world than to be a champion of—and force for—good. For maximal impact in reparenting and ripening sentient beings, the Bodhisattva adheres to a set of virtuous activities that propel the evolution of consciousness toward Buddhahood—a combination of six training disciplines and a regiment of vows. I call them the "hero's code of conduct," and they were best articulated and preserved in Master Shantideva's classic eighth-century Bodhisattvacharyavatara, translated as Guide to the Altruist's Way of Life.

Hero's Code of Conduct

To manifest our extraordinary intention, we train and master six disciplines called paramitas, or Bodhisattva activities. They sync up with our road map:

24 Perfect generosity.

25 Perfect virtue.

26 Perfect patience.

27 Perfect effort.

28 Perfect concentration.

The first five paramitas amass the positive merit that produces the neural network of a Buddha's body, made of compassion, while the sixth perfection gathers the profound insights that yield a Buddha's mind of quantum openness, our final milestone:

29 Perfect wisdom—the milestone of quantum view.

One only masters these virtuous activities when fully mature wisdom-realizing emptiness is yoked with universal, spontaneous compassion. Until then, mastering the paramitas is a gradual process of purifying the mind of delusion and afflictions that leads toward that end. For example, if you feel someone is undeserving of your generosity, the virtue is not perfected. Perfection occurs when sensitivity is extended to all living beings, carried out under the influence of Bodhicitta and within the worldview of interdependence. It's under these conditions that paramitas are fully realized, and this is why I like to joke that paramitas are distinguished from other virtues as being DUIs (done under the influence) of the extraordinary intention.

Remember that generosity, virtue, patience, effort, concentration, and wisdom are natural human skills necessary to navigate the social sphere of interdependence, fine-tuning our interactions with other living beings to harness the merit that fuels realization. Saints are looking to perfect themselves in a dualistic paradigm of subject-object isolation, but Bodhisattvas understand that reality is nondual-embedded interconnectivity and so add to their training a unique set of disciplines, commitments, and vows that are prosocial in nature. The paramitas offer a guidebook for the hero or warrior to till the soil of the social field in order to ripen living beings for the abundant harvest of awakening.

Perfect Generosity   24 ROAD MAP

Generosity is the karmic cause of wealth and abundance. The perfection of generosity, or giving, is more a state of mind and less an objective action. Our motivation must be an expression of selfless compassion and not one that is tied to expectations or reward—particularly worldly ones such as gain, praise, or pleasure—which only reinforce dualism and inaccurate views about causation. Giving a dog a mouthful of food out of empathy and with the wish to alleviate hunger leads to the perfection of giving, whereas giving extraordinary sums of money to charity in the hope of being honored does not. While it is true that some merit is achieved in both instances, it is only when generosity or any paramita is undertaken with a spirit of radical altruism grounded in quantum view that it becomes the future cause for the mind and body of a Buddha.

Tibetan Buddhists divide generosity into three categories:

1 Giving resources

2 Giving protection

3 Giving dharma

The first category includes material gifts that care for the essential needs of others—from food to sacrificing one's life. Only the highest-level Bodhisattvas sacrifice their lives for others because only they have the clarity of mind to weigh the benefits of dying against the freedom and fortune of maximizing their precious human embodiment to achieve Buddhahood. For our purpose, it is more practical to remember that we should never have any regret after exercising generosity, because it cross-contaminates the potential merit. We should pay close attention to how much we give, to whom, and under what conditions. It may be better to give less, or not at all, if our generosity creates doubt, resentment, or regret, or reinforces codependency. Saying no and not giving, with the right intention and clarity, can sometimes be more skillful, depending on the recipient's need, predilection, and mental state.

The second category of generosity pertains to offering protection from fear, and it can be expressed as anything from removing an insect from a precarious situation to helping the dying face their impending transition. A turbulent, anxious mind is a condition and potential cause of reckless behavior, so by offering protection from fear, the Bodhisattva not only helps beings ease their immediate circumstance but evolutionarily protects their mental continuum from creating its own future suffering.

The third category of generosity is the dharma—the greatest gift. It's not that food and peace are insignificant, but it is through the Buddha's teachings that living beings can master their own minds and destiny. Thus, giving the dharma ends dependency on religion and potentially develops other Bodhisattvas who can exponentially spur the global mission of awakening. Although both knowledge and nourishment are required in the hierarchy of basic needs, a teaching on karma and virtue can spare someone a lifetime of future suffering, whereas feeding them allows their body to be nourished for only a day. On the other hand, if you don't feed them, how would it be possible to have the health and presence of mind to benefit from the teachings?

All six paramitas mutually influence each other. A single act of generosity should be accompanied by morality and respect for the dignity of others, particularly those disempowered or in unfortunate circumstances. If someone needs you to give repeatedly, generosity should be influenced by patience and not cross-contaminated by miserliness or resentment. Similarly, with joyous effort, one's generosity should have no limit and shouldn't tire the giver; it should inspire and energize them. We should focus on rejoicing in the innate goodness after giving, which ensures taking in, enhancing, and maximizing the merits of one's own generosity and that of others. Since wisdom dispels the notion of any reified object, subject, and interaction, perfect generosity influenced by quantum view dispels any false notion of a giver, gift, and recipient and reveals how it is a spontaneous, flowing expression of interconnectivity.

Perfect Virtue   25 ROAD MAP

From success to health to satisfaction, virtue is the karmic cause for the most important outcomes we seek in life. We achieve perfect virtue when we meet three conditions:

1 We keep our ethical vows and commitments.

2 We benefit others.

3 We act under the influence of Bodhicitta.

As we progress along the Lam Rim, opportunities arise to make more vows and commitments. Lay Buddhist practitioners vow to avoid killing, lying, stealing, sexual impropriety, and intoxicants that cloud the mind. For monastics, these vows swell in number. Bob Thurman explains the importance of moral vows from a karmic point of view, describing them as a metaphorical "second skin" that protects us from nonvirtuous intentions, speech, and action that cause future suffering. In the same way that rules and laws are designed to protect—not restrain—citizens, vows of moral conduct are liberating.

Vows are an extension of engaged Bodhicitta, designed to structure and mold behavior. If we didn't have them, our soul or consciousness might veer too far left or right off its evolutionary course, or even reverse entirely. As modern materialists who have often chosen profit over ethics, we have lost sight of the moral imperatives and standards with which to structure our behavior, so it's no surprise we've nearly destroyed our planet in three generations or that refugee children are denied sanctuary and left to drown. With vows, certain decisions are eliminated from our life's options and certain impulses are restrained—namely those that would bring about karmic repercussions and evolutionary regression. If you were dieting to lose weight, you'd fill your fridge with foods that would ensure you achieve your goal. By doing so, you could only make good choices any time you wanted to eat. Likewise, vows ensure we move toward our altruistic goal. No vows, no karmic force or merit, no progress on the Lam Rim.

It is the vows, and not meditation alone, that allow for the conscious acceleration of human development. Tsongkhapa himself said the ethical vows of the Bodhisattva were the main path to enlightenment. Vows of virtue, and the karmic merit they create, are the secret sauce that propels us through the levels of awakening. My aspiration is that the mindfulness revolution will be followed by an ethical revolution of similar impact. Think about how central and reversing that could be for our ecological crisis, global economic divide, and geopolitical instability. When the discipline of virtue is practiced under the influence of Bodhicitta, it becomes the cause for awakening oneself as well as for improving community and society through greater safety, respect, and care.

ROAD MAP 26   **Perfect Patience**

Patience is the cause for the ripening of healthy body and sound mind. There are three types of patience:

1 Not retaliating if someone harms us

2 Willingness to take on social adversity and other people's unfavorable reactivity

3 Willingness to endure the challenges posed by committed dharma study and practice

Resisting retaliation is the first form of patience, but I don't appreciate the way some traditional Buddhist teachers recommend avoiding anger—insisting it destroys merit—as doing so can lead to what psychologist John Welwood calls "spiritual bypassing,"[1] which involves using spiritual themes and practices to avoid the pain of unresolved trauma, sidestepping the messy aspects of our psyche. In my estimation, no discussion of renunciation, compassion, or meditation is complete without an awareness of spiritual bypassing. As examples, a religious authority might use karma theory to intimidate and subjugate the devout and justify maintaining power; or devotional practice toward one's guru could unknowingly reinforce childhood dynamics of subservience, fear, and shame; or compassion and altruism, without proper renunciation, could be a pious mask for neurotic self-denial and codependency.

Spiritual bypassing is ubiquitous among the yogis and meditators I receive in my psychotherapy practice and encounter at the various centers I frequent. Some people feel they are the one person on the planet who is undeserving of care. Or they have misunderstood the teaching of selflessness to mean there is no relative self and thus skipped renunciation and self-care and gone straight for the milestone of compassion without sufficient preparedness or healing. Others might skip compassion and end up at the milestone of wisdom without the sufficient level of Bodhicitta that tethers their hearts to the well-being of others and the relative world of suffering, which then manifests as an aloof overintellectualization. Even more dangerous is when individuals skip all three developmental milestones and prerequisites—evolutionary self-care, radical altruism, and quantum view—and assume a tantric or esoteric practice, allowing their narcissism to graft to the ideal archetype of a deity only to reinforce an exalted grandiosity that furthers nothing but delusion and suffering. We cannot reach the end of the Lam Rim without first going through each of the stages systematically and integrating these insights at a deeply transformational level. The realization of Bodhicitta cannot be embodied if we leave ourselves behind, if we spiritually bypass important steps on the path.

The arising of anger is a karmic ripening that cannot be avoided, but how anger is experienced and expressed is within our control, determining future ripening effects. Managing anger can be done in healthy and skillful ways, such as nonviolent protest and social activism, which is what this paramita is pointing at. When a patient becomes violent because they are delusional or is in pain, due to their condition, the doctor treating them restrains the impulse to retaliate, less as a moral obligation and more out of an understanding that these actions are not personal but the results of the patient's afflicted state of mind. This understanding helps temper the doctor's response—it is wise compassion that engenders tolerance. It's the same with an animal that bites when terrified or a tired toddler throwing a tantrum; we refrain from retaliation because of empathic understanding.

In the second type of patience—willingness to take on social adversity and other people's unfavorable reactivity—we see a sophisticated type of cognitive reframing. The underlying premise is again a karmic one, so without an understanding of causality, patience can be misinterpreted and unappreciated. Martyrs and ascetics from dualistic religions voluntarily face or seek hardship because they expect to reap rewards in heaven or an afterlife, but karmic science teaches us that because negative seeds must ripen, one actively engages in a process of reaping what has been sown to purify the mind and make it fertile ground for an abundant perceptual harvest. Black-belt-level Bodhisattvas courageously pursue unfavorable circumstances while the rest of us run and hide, naively thinking we can outrun our misfortune. This is made clear in the mind-training text called Wheel of Sharp Weapons, or, as Bob Thurman translates it, the Blade Wheel of Mind Reform, which uses the analogy of a razor-edged boomerang to illustrate how our own past negative karma returns to injure us when we wield it under delusion. In contrast, when wielded under the influence of wisdom, pursuing adverse circumstances like a karmic hunter, our past negative karma becomes a powerful weapon to purify confusion, and it finally cuts the roots of our own samsara. Totally badass.

The final type of patience is the willingness to endure challenges and hardships related to one's committed dharma study and practice. (You might be experiencing that right now as you make your way through these tedious lists!) Study presents obstacles that may anger or confuse you, that ask more of you than you feel able to give, that trigger and unhinge you. If you don't experience that edge, you're not studying the dharma correctly. It's supposed to hurt—stretching your mind and obliterating your comfort zone—so you can be reborn a child of the Buddhas.

Few things can push our limits and bring us to the brink of psychic fragmentation more than a betrayal by a spiritual teacher. Depending on how you relate to that crisis, there might also be a greater opportunity for self-discovery and growth. Scandalous and predatory spiritual teachers abound these days, and I have counseled many of their victims, which is why I'll take a detour here to highlight the potential results of spiritual bypassing and not dealing with our shadow.

A TEACHER FALLS FROM GRACE

Around the time I met Bob Thurman in 1999, I also met another American-Buddhist pioneer, Geshe Michael Roach, who alleged he was the first Westerner to complete the arduous twenty-year training of the traditional Tibetan monastic university system that had been transplanted to the refugee camps of South India. I say "alleged" because there are conflicting reports, depending upon whom you speak with. After receiving his geshe degree (the equivalent of five American PhDs) in the 1990s, Roach founded the Asian Classic Institute in New York, where he taught the central topics and practices of the Tibetan tradition that he had synthesized as his own curriculum, consisting of eighteen densely packed courses.

The first of these was based on Tsongkhapa's quintessential Lam Rim text. I was attracted to Roach's scholarly depth, the devotion and sincerity of his community, and how both he and his students were so fiercely dedicated to the pursuit of enlightenment. Roach's determination and encouragement to reach spiritual realization was in stark contrast to the message of many other Western Buddhist teachers, who tended to underplay and minimize the goal as a real possibility. (This diminishing may be because of the religious association and potential conflict that enlightenment poses in our current scientific paradigm.) I have always been a seeker at heart, ready to set my worldly house ablaze to find an ultimate solution to my and our human problems, and in Roach I thought I had found someone who shared my yearning and conviction. While I did not become his devotee and gulp the Kool-Aid he proffered, I did sip it until I realized something was off.

Sadly, the hero's journey and the Lam Rim are not composed of smooth and neatly interlocking stones along a well-manicured path. More realistically, they are ends that can become means as they twist and turn over peaks, through dark forests, and into valleys bathed in light. Despite Roach's magnetism and his audacious claim that he had reached the profound milestone of seeing emptiness directly, I wonder if important parts of his psyche may have been overlooked, left in the shadow, and underdeveloped. What can explain Roach's aberrant behaviors— crazy wisdom or psychological imbalance? His critics suggest that Roach's three-year-plus solitary retreat may have had an adverse impact on his mental health, or that the death of his parents and his brother's suicide in quick succession resulted in unresolved trauma.[2, 3]

No matter how we choose to interpret it, the growing divide between Roach's charismatic personality, compelling dharma convictions, and misguided behaviors led to much confusion, dissonance, and his fall from grace in the eyes of the greater Tibetan community, including the Dalai Lama, who denounced his activities.[4] At one time, there was a public appeal, even from Bob Thurman, that Roach disrobe and surrender his monastic vows if he wished to continue an intimate relationship with a female student. Allegations of sex, lies, manipulation, brainwashing, ritualistic violence, abuse of power, and the eventual death of a student followed and exposed Roach's human vulnerability, branded his community a cult, and mired his legacy in scandal.[5]

Like Roach, his students, and many others on the path, I have been transfixed by spiritual liberation while caught in an unconscious wish to sidestep the demons of my past. This led to my own spiritual bypassing, which is, in my estimation, the single most pervasive hindrance undermining progress on the path to awakening. Spiritual bypassing is particularly challenging for Westerners, who endure so much unresolved trauma stemming from the breakdown in attuned relationships that characterize our industrialized culture, and to which meditation alone does not necessarily serve as an immediate antidote.

Unlike many students whose teacher's fall from grace causes confusion and reaction, I was fortunate not to abandon the mentor-bonding process with my own teachers, or the guru-student institution. Instead, and importantly, I lost my naive idealism, embraced a more realistic view of devotion and reliance, and gained respect for human fallibility. As we make our way through the high ideals of the six perfections, it behooves us all to remember that they are simply that: high ideals to strive for and not benchmarks of our worth. When we fail, we do so with humility and self-compassion, only to rise again wiser and more mature for it. From Roach, I learned the hard way about the limits of an overly idealized mentor-devotion and was able to temper, with healthy realism, my reliance on and use of role-modeling visualization with my own mentors. I was able to maintain an intimate connection with Joe Loizzo without displacing or subjugating the maturation of my *inner* mentor. In other words, the real guru is always within, and while we may need an external guide to serve as a mirror to reflect our highest potential, we should never abandon our innate common sense, intuition, emotions, and wisdom. My therapist who was critical during this healing and maturation process often paraphrased the great martial artist Bruce Lee, who taught that as we progress along the path we should adopt what is useful, reject what is useless, and add what is uniquely ours.

While I grew disenchanted with Roach and how he had hurt so many people, my Buddhist and psychotherapeutic training helped me find a middle way where I could avoid the extremes of blind faith and complete disavowal, taking in those elements of his teachings that did inspire me. Chief among them was the root text, the Three Principles of the Path, which I traced back to its source in the Tibetan tradition, and I found qualified guides to reveal its mysteries. What you are receiving in these pages is based on oral and written commentaries of this text that I received from Gelek Rinpoche, Bob Thurman, Joe Loizzo, Lama Zopa, and Geshe Tenzin Zopa. Sometimes the most essential life lessons come at a price, and it's up to each of us to make them worthwhile or, as they say in the Tibetan Lojong (mind-training teachings), to transform adversity to advantage.

ROAD MAP 27   **Perfect Effort**

Enthusiastic perseverance is said to be the root of the fourth, fifth, and six paramitas, and without it one can never evolve to the state of Buddhahood. The perfection of effort is the antidote to three types of laziness that prevent our progress on the path:

1 Laziness of shame and inadequacy

2 Laziness of procrastination

3 Laziness of being committed to fruitless activities
    that don't advance one's altruistic motivation

Having motivation but being held back by a conviction that we will fail or that it's not possible to learn, grow, and change would be an example of the first hindrance. For this type of laziness, having to do with inadequacy, it's advised one work closely with a mentor—said to be the Foundation of All Good Qualities.[6] By vicariously enjoying the mentor's accomplishments and using the mentor as a psychological mirror, we can build up a realistic sense of worth in their eyes. Use them as a surrogate parent who makes you feel like a decent child. But then develop beyond needing them further for this purpose. You can also contemplate the preciousness of human life teaching to reacquaint your mind with how amazingly lucky you are. When we're depressed or ashamed, much of the time the cursor of our attention is somehow stuck on the negative, and we must shift slightly to take advantage of our wonderful qualities and experiences.

Having no motivation at all, and therefore not pursuing anything worthwhile or meaningful, is an example of the second hindrance. The antidote to procrastination is to contemplate impermanence and death. That's sure to light a fire under your ass! Pick up a newspaper and see how people like you—with hopes, dreams, health, and fortune—died unexpectedly. There's no guarantee we have any time to waste.

The third hindrance refers to being highly motivated but pursuing mundane activities that don't lead to spiritual outcomes, such as when people work tirelessly and single-mindedly to achieve wealth, fame, and power only to find these things don't result in genuine satisfaction. The same activities done under the influence of Bodhicitta could have benefited others and oneself as well. Where there is momentum directed toward mundane concerns, contemplate the defects of samsara to cut through your illusions of grandeur. That reality check is designed to expose and redirect exaggerated or wishful thinking and reprioritize your efforts toward something more sustainable and meaningful.

With all three types of laziness, the discipline of perseverance, or effort, cuts through the limiting force preventing maturation and the expression of the other virtuous activities. While there are several antidotes to misdirected effort or laziness, we can always return to some of the preliminary contemplations, such as The Four Thoughts That Turn the Mind.

Perfect Concentration

Concentration taken to its limits yields a state of mind called samadhi, characterized as complete absorption in the object of meditation to the point that the subject/object dichotomy ceases to exist, the mind is untethered from distraction, and one can remain transfixed, single-pointedly, for as long as one wishes. It's possible. I haven't accomplished this by a long shot, but I've been around adepts who have, and you can sense that they are operating in a completely distinct state of consciousness. Lama Zopa is an example of a living master who has achieved samadhi and yet lives in the world through compassionate engagement.

There is also well-established evidence in the scientific literature of outstanding feats of autonomic control by yogis that suggests humans have the ability to harness the power of concentration. Yogis voluntarily stopping their hearts, or remaining buried underground for significant periods of time, demonstrates that humans can have voluntary control of the autonomic nervous system in ways the scientific community did not think was possible. More recently, Wim Hof, the so-called "Iceman," has blown people away with his concentrative prowess and breath control, which he uses to override autonomic function so he can remain submerged for hours in an ice bath or hike snow-topped mountain peaks barefoot and virtually naked.[7]

However, such feats do not the paramita of concentration make. Concentration is a supremely powerful skill of focal attention. The problem is that mental power can be applied to either mundane pursuits or spiritual ones, can be ill-advised and maliciously motivated, or can be conducted under the influence of Bodhicitta. Military snipers and champion chess players may possess focus beyond ordinary abilities, but their skills don't lead to the type of concentration that becomes perfect when combined with other virtues, such as wisdom. Perfect concentration within the Lam Rim context is the galvanizing force that channels mental power to subsume the other five paramitas, allowing each to be perfected. Also, single-pointed focus of attention, when applied to one's spiritual vows and commitments, generates the karmic ripening that gives rise to realization and perfect wisdom—the sixth paramita and the heart of the next chapter.

Walking the Walk

Our gradual method isn't *The Secret*. It's not enough to think positive thoughts; we also need to adopt a new way to live in the world with others to awaken them from their torment and misguided reactivity. Action is as critical on the Gradual Path as self-care, compassion, and insight. Vowing to adopt the paramitas helps mold us into altruistic heroes capable of transforming adversity into advantage for both our spiritual maturation and social redesign. If we have the skills to meet the demand, nothing terrifying or overwhelming in the world need be avoided, not even the burning buildings of human affliction. But without wisdom, not even our warm, well-intentioned hearts or our black-belt meditation skills will spare us from compassion fatigue and the sheer weight of countless living beings in distress. So, let's take the next step toward wisdom, the ultimate medicine and our final milestone of the Lam Rim.

Retracing Your Steps	24-28 STEPS

24 Perfect generosity.

25 Perfect virtue.

26 Perfect patience.

27 Perfect effort.

28 Perfect concentration.

7 VISION

REALIZING THE MILESTONE OF QUANTUM VIEW

The bodhisattva, however, does not abandon life. Turning his regard from
the inner sphere of thought-transcending truth (which can be described
only as "emptiness," since it surpasses speech) outward again to the
phenomenal world, he perceives without the same ocean of being that he
found within. "Form is emptiness, emptiness indeed form. Emptiness is
not different from form, form is not different from emptiness. What is
form, that is emptiness; what is emptiness, that is form. And the same
applies to perception, name, conception, and knowledge."

JOSEPH CAMPBELL, *The Hero with a Thousand Faces*

Perfect Wisdom—the Milestone of Quantum View 29 ROAD MAP

We have worked with our motivation to develop renunciation and
opened our warm hearts with compassion, and as we reach the final
stage of our Lam Rim journey, we clarify perceptual distortions and
align with a "correct view" of reality. This is another term for emptiness, which is often misunderstood. Emptiness may be the most
advanced principle in Mahayana Buddhism, a topic that can be studied with increasing depth, each time refining the perception of the
nature of reality. Even if you have a thorough conceptual understanding of emptiness, without this wisdom becoming embodied, intuitive,
and spontaneous, it won't be relevant or have critical impact on your
life. Unlike Western philosophy, Buddhism is concerned with self-
transformation and doesn't much care about fancy abstractions. The

purpose of wisdom is to uproot ingrained mental distortions or projections and their underlying instinctual reflexive habit of reification that is the fundamental cause of suffering.

Emptiness (*shunyata*) is like a medicine that corrects the distorted view or misperception we have about how phenomena exist. It points to the absence of something we assume is there but is not there. While emptiness reveals that things don't exist in the way they appear, it neither obliterates phenomena nor proposes an alternative to replace what has been seen through. Emptiness is not an assertion unto itself; it's not another reality. This is important, because the mind likes to reify and hold on to things, and it is liable to make emptiness into a false idol. But if you replace one reality with another that seems more real than it is, you will remain fixated and stuck and continue to suffer. One needs to approach emptiness cautiously, like handling a snake, because if you grab the wrong end and misunderstand its power . . . well, look out. The great third-century Mahayana sage Nagarjuna taught this:

> The emptiness of the conquerors was taught to do away
> with all philosophical views. Therefore it is said that whoever
> makes a philosophical view out of "emptiness" is indeed lost.[1]

One false and dangerous view is equating emptiness with nothing. Read aloud and repeat this phrase: Emptiness does not mean nothingness. It's a good reminder, because the brain tends to vacillate between the extreme of existence, where things exist inherently, to the other extreme of nonexistence, where we assert that things do not exist at all.

Imagine I'm holding a water bottle. Immediately and decisively we know this is a bottle. The truth of emptiness posits that this bottle does not exist as I instinctively perceive it. Emptiness does not suggest the bottle is an illusion, rather that the bottle is real in the sense that it serves a function to hold and deliver water when one is thirsty. However, emptiness is what one discovers when trying to establish the bottle's essential nature or inherent existence (*svabhava*). It means that for this bottle, every single person *is* perceiving it but has a mistaken assumption about how it exists that they take for granted.

When we get into the wisdom teachings of Buddhism, we are not talking about metaphysical speculations about gods or the divine, but more of a practical inquiry that asks, What is reality? What are phenomena? And how do things exist? The fancy way to say this is that we're inquiring into the ontological status of an object of phenomenon. Remember, it's not questioning whether phenomena exist; we know that they exist, but *how* do they exist? Does the water bottle exist? Yes, absolutely. How do I know it exists? Because I'm holding it in my hand, and if I threw it at you, it would hit you and you would react. The water bottle does exist, but how it exists is another question.

An understanding of emptiness corrects the extreme views that things exist inherently and, the flip side, that things must not exist at all. Nagarjuna saw the extremes of false views as essentialism and nihilism. Finding an alternative between these extremes is what the Buddhist teachings refer to as the middle way. Emptiness is the sweet spot that avoids either extreme—like a womb for quantum possibility and radical altruism. This middle-way view of emptiness corrects distorted perceptions, freeing the mind to engage creatively.

I call this mind free of distortions "quantum view." I'm using this term playfully. I am a complete amateur regarding quantum physics, and I am not presenting the Buddhist wisdom of emptiness as a corollary to quantum physics; however, I use the word *quantum* because the wisdom of emptiness penetrates the nature of reality beyond appearances, beyond the superficial, atomic, or Newtonian structures. It's as if the ultimate electron microscope were aimed at an atomic core, substrate, or final essence, revealing a quantum universe of subatomic particles, quarks, and, further still, dark matter and energy, a dance of wavelike dynamic processes, multiple potentialities, and pregnant space.

So, as I like to joke, put on your quantum Ray-Bans and get ready to dive into emptiness.

THREE LEVELS OF EMPTINESS

There are three levels of analysis that help us arrive at progressively deeper understandings of emptiness:

- the emptiness of permanence—the impossibility that phenomena endure unchanging over time, despite appearances

- the emptiness of unitary substantiality—the impossibility that phenomena have a distinct, indivisible unity

- the emptiness of independence—the impossibility that phenomena have an unrelated essential nature or inherent existence

Emptiness of Permanence

The first level of emptiness concerns our gut sense that things maintain permanence—endure unchanging over time. We assume there is some *thing* here that exists and persists over time in an unchanging way. That is what our five senses perceive. Ordinarily, the way in which we relate to phenomena begins with our gut automatically assuming and responding to things as if they are permanent. By adding a critical insight of emptiness, we can challenge that assumption and engage with the world in a more realistic way, and so let go of grasping and averting, fighting and fleeing.

Here's an experiment. If I hold up a flower and ask, "Will this same flower be here tomorrow?" your gut certainty would likely be yes. However, if I ask, "Will it exist as the same flower in a hundred years?" your answer would be no. So, then we apply logic to work backward to the place and time where the flower's existence is questionable. Will it exist as the flower in ten days? In two weeks? We reach a critical point at the cusp of the flower's existence and nonexistence. It appears to exist for fourteen days, but on the fifteenth day it starts to decay, and by day thirty (let's say), it no longer exists as something we would automatically call a flower. So, the question is, what happened on the fourteenth day, at thirty minutes before the final hour of the day, right when it changed from flower to not-flower? This stalls the mind's automatic program and awakens it to a new reality, a flash of insight. *The flower has been changing the whole time.* We realize it was a mistake to think that there was constancy, a fixed thing existing and enduring over time. We realize it is *empty* of permanence.

As we continue the inquiry, the question grows subtler. Based on discerning that things are changing, the next question is, How quickly are they changing? Is the flower changing every minute? Every second? Is there a discoverable millisecond when it stops changing? Nope. You can't quantify the place where and the time when it stops changing. The progression is infinitely divisible.

Here's the kicker: If the progression is infinitely divisible and the flower is changing constantly across time, how can you say that it is indeed a "thing" that is changing? A flower that is changing? When is it ever a thing long enough to be a flower? When we find that the second can be subdivided infinitely, you can see that there is no *thing* there that is changing. A flower does not become a nonflower at a specific point in time. There is just flow. It's not apparent to our five senses that the flower is a changing thing in the moment. It's not apparent to us that it's changing so rapidly that we could never even call it a thing. Where is the flower if it is constantly changing in infinitely divisible time? Where is the *thing* that we say is changing?

When we see there is no permanent flower, the mind can go to the extreme of believing the flower must not exist at all. That it disappears—it's *all* an illusion. Remember, emptiness is not saying that it's *not* there. The flower is perfectly there. Just smell it, or prick your finger on its thorn. It is there and real; it does exist, on a conventional level. So, what doesn't exist? What is the flower empty of? It is empty of permanence.

Emptiness of permanence shows us that there are no things, there are only processes. I repeat: there are no things, only processes. Does that water bottle look like a process to you? No. We are deceived by our senses, which is what is meant when it is said that we misperceive the nature of reality. The Tibetans sometimes call conventional reality "deceptive reality."

If you saw the flower as a process, would you relate to it differently? Do you relate to things differently when you know they will inevitably arise, abide, and fall apart? If it's a thing, you want to own it, buy it, sell it, get jealous about it, and be upset when it shows you its true nature and deteriorates. In terms of karma, the way we relate to all of phenomena alters when our mind perceives phenomena as a process and expression of flow. This is the medicine of the first level of emptiness—the emptiness of permanence. What is not there ultimately, what it is empty of, is a permanent, unchanging thing. And, what is there conventionally, what does exist, is a process or flow. Why does it matter? Because we realize we can't hold on to processes, just as we can't hold a stream of water. We can savor and skillfully work with dynamic things, but we can't control or own them. Meditate on this idea; it's healing.

Emptiness of Unitary Substantiality

The second level of analysis regards the way we read objects as unitary, as singular unto themselves. Our instinct is that the flower and bottle are single, coherent objects. Here we ask, Is it one thing unto itself, or many things? The idea is that everything we encounter with our senses is constructed by and can be broken into parts. You can subdivide everything.

I hold up the flower and I ask, "Is it one flower, or many?" You say it's one flower. It is a solid, unified object. A single flower. But what are the parts of the flower? Let's put on our quantum Ray-Bans and analyze and deconstruct the parts. It has a stem, leaves, thorns, and a bud. The bud can be divided into individual petals. Therefore, we have several parts that we can further analyze: the left, right, top, and bottom of the petal. We ask, Where does the petal start and the stem end? Are the thorns the flower? Are the leaves? The petals? Clearly not. Now we have all the flower parts scattered in front of us and have agreed each is not the flower, so then where the hell did the flower go?

There is a mistaken tendency to conclude that the flower doesn't exist. That conclusion would be your mind looking for something solid—the flower either does or doesn't exist. We think, *If it's not a flower, it must not exist.* It takes a complex and mature mind to be able to hold the dissonance and to find a synthesis. There is not a single flower there because it has parts, and each of the parts can be deconstructed and never constitute the actual original object of perception. What the flower is empty of, what is not there, is being unitary—a thing in and of itself—but what is there conventionally is a collection of parts, which are themselves further divisible.

Your mind wants to make this flower into one object. It wants to call it a flower. It was one thing, a flower, and then your mind broke it down into parts. Yet, you can use reason and logic to begin to deconstruct that everything that appears whole and unitary is composed of parts, until we get to quantum particles and quarks, until they too disappear under analysis into mostly open space. *Openness* . . . there's that word again. Quantum openness is the ground of all phenomena beyond which there is nothing transcendent. It's like the circumference of infinity folding back into the center. *Inconceivable.*

We can deconstruct objects into parts to help the mind let go of and untangle from false assumptions, and to relate to the world more skillfully. Even the self can be subdivided this way. I say, "I'm Miles." The first level of emptiness is that I think *I am the same Miles regardless of time passing.* My hair gets a little grayer, I gain a few pounds, and I grow a little older, but my senses read that I am the same person: *I am the same Miles.* However, the reality is that I am always changing. You can't find a static Miles because I am changing so rapidly that there is not really a person-Miles here who is changing. There is just process. The second level of emptiness challenges the premise of a unitary self-contained Miles. If you look for the single Miles, you cannot find him. Am I the same Miles to my wife as I am to my son? Am I the same to my son when I'm angry as when I'm happy? How many of me are there?

How many parts can you divide me into? Is my body Miles? My legs? My ideas? My feelings? Buddhist psychologists have discerned the elements of a person, dividing them into five main baskets, or aggregates, called *skandhas*: physical matter or form, sensations, conceptions, emotions, and consciousness. Each of these parts can be subdivided infinitely. We ascribe the label "person" to those parts, but if we looked at each part, we couldn't find the person. Just as we couldn't find the flower in the petal, stem, or thorn, we cannot find the unitary person in the form, sensations, perceptions, emotions, or consciousness. This is what Buddhists mean by insight into selflessness.

Phenomena are empty of existing as permanent and unitary, and yet conventionally, we can still smell the flower, drink from the bottle, and shake hands. The self can be divided into parts, which means the self is empty of being a unitary thing. Because we misperceive phenomena as unitary, we objectify and create karma in relation to them. This is how we can seek to own, discard, or abuse things, or conversely, love, share, and rejoice in them. On one hand, we create negative karma based on delusion-driven afflictions that perpetuate suffering, and on the other, we create positive karma by relating to things virtuously. But to go beyond good and bad karmas, we need to adopt the correct view, which transcends the crystallization of subject, object, and interaction. We can say that delusion taints positive and negative actions equally, because at its root there is still the grasping to an essential self, other, and relationship. But when that is purified, and the root cleared, positive emotions and actions express themselves naturally without agenda or recipient, just as a pure mountain stream runs clear of impurities from source to mouth.

Emptiness of Independence

The third level of analysis is the emptiness of independence. There is a funny expression used in wisdom teachings: things do not exist from their own side. If I place a bottle on a table and you leave the room, is it still a bottle? If you left the room, went downstairs, and were thinking about a nice slice of pizza, or having a smoke, would there still be a bottle on the table? The answer is yes and no, but your gut wants to say definitively yes, doesn't it? What is happening here is that there is an important variable in addition to the parts that make the whole. This bottle is not the cap, neck, and base; it needs something else to become a bottle. It needs a mind to perceive it and label it "bottle" for it to become a bottle. It needs language. We think it has ontological independence, *existing from its own side*, but everything we encounter in the phenomenal world is interdependent with the mind that is perceiving and labeling it. It's like that famous riddle, "If a tree falls in the woods, and there is no one around to hear it, does it still make a sound?" Initially we think *yes*, because there is an energetic discharge from the displacement of matter, hence decibels, when anything falls, irrespective of if someone is there to hear it; however, there is only the sound and the tree falling if someone is around to hear it and label it as such, because sound and trees are concepts, labels supplied to processes by mind. The answer to the riddle is conventionally yes, ultimately no. Because we aren't perceiving with our ears the sound of the tree falling, nor are we labeling it with concepts from the mind, there is no sound, no tree, in abstraction. Therefore, when I leave the bottle on the table and go downstairs, because the bottle is outside of my perception and labeling of it, there is no bottle.

Remember to guard against nihilism—this doesn't mean that the bottle doesn't exist at all. Its existence is interdependent with your mind. Mind must be part of the equation for either this process or its infinite parts to become a bottle to you. If mind isn't there, and there is no perception or label, then this isn't a bottle. With no mind, it is a process. That is what we mean by *interdependence*—an interplay between processes and a mind that perceives and labels them. Mind and process meet, we name it, and it becomes a thing; but then we forget language was involved in its creation, and the thing seems to exist self-sufficiently from its own side.

We take for granted that everything exists as it appears, failing to recognize the constructive role of language. Nothing exists as it appears independent of the mind that is perceiving it. Each thing is empty of independence, empty of existing from its own side. The minute we don't think about it or perceive it, the label drops away. When the label drops, the meaning ascribed drops with it. That is why a thing that we call a pencil can also be a back scratcher, a weapon, a drumstick, and a dog's chew toy. Because it is empty of being any one of these things from its own side, it is capable of being all these things that are perceived and related to differently. The label is not inherently in the pencil, the bottle, or in the you because there is fluidity and multiplicity and possibility regarding how we see each thing.

Things exist only as a process, as a series of infinite parts, to which we assign labels that we imbue with meaning. That's one reason we call one side of the coin *conventional* reality. It's also called *relative* reality because things only exist in relation to something else. *Short* has no inherent meaning without something *long*. Short is empty and therefore only makes sense relationally.

Remember, emptiness is a negation. It is pointing to the thing we think is there but is not. The snake in the dark room is actually a rope misperceived. I'm not proposing that nothing is there, but that something we thought was there is not. When we let go of the things we think are there, we end up with relativity, mutual dependence, flow, multiplicity, and possibility. We ease the constriction of reification and free up creative interaction.

A process exists. A series of parts, infinitely divisible, exists. A label from the mind imposed upon those parts does exist. That's all. A permanent, unitary, independent object does not exist. This is correct view, quantum view. Whenever you hear Buddhists use the words *wisdom, emptiness, void, suchness*, or *shunyata*, *correct view* is what they are referring to. The way we operate, the way we perceive things to be so inherently real or fixed outside of us, is flawed. It is a misperception. Our karmic reactions to this fundamental misperception result in tremendous amounts of suffering.

From Quantum Openness to Relativity

Having glimpsed emptiness, let's return to the Three Principles of the Path:

> Even though you practice renunciation   9
> And cultivate altruistic resolve,
> Without the wisdom to realize reality,
> You can't cut the root of traumatic life—
> So, work at the art of seeing relativity.

Here we receive a caution from Tsongkhapa, reminding us that while we have made it this far in our Lam Rim odyssey, having developed evolutionary self-care through renunciation and radical altruism by conceiving Bodhicitta, these skills remain insufficient for cutting the root of suffering and ending our samsaric, or traumatic, existence. Since the root of compulsive existence is variously known as fundamental delusion, misperception, or distorted view, our noble motivations to free ourselves and others don't act as antidotes—only clearly seeing the nature of reality, or penetrative insight, can do that. We need to generate the right intentionality to redirect the evolutionary stream of consciousness and amass the collection of merit that will eliminate afflictive obscurations; but simultaneously we must amass the collection of wisdom to eliminate the cognitive obscurations that prevent us from seeing reality accurately. The collection of wisdom, like endurance on a treadmill, is developed through repeated analytic investigations or contemplations that lead to insights. As insights build and we gain karmic momentum, they displace intuitive false views with nonconceptual—or accurate—vision, like clearing condensation from a steamy mirror. To be free, we need both collections—merit and wisdom, radical altruism and quantum view. The last line of this verse is key: "So, work at the art of seeing relativity." Relativity develops both collections.

If you want to cultivate a beautiful garden of your mind, you don't just plant good seeds. Through meritorious actions guided by renunciation and Bodhicitta, you'd also want to clear the brush and weeds to make new growth possible. You don't pull out the weeds haphazardly, because they are insidious little buggers that will grow back. You remove the weeds at the root if you want to eliminate them permanently, making the garden ready to receive, grow, and flourish with a wonderful harvest. Tsongkhapa suggests a specific way to do this in the last line: "So, work at the art of seeing relativity." This is also known as dependent origination.

Dependent origination is an early, foundational Buddhist teaching on the etiology of suffering. The idea is that no experience or phenomenon arises based on its own causes; rather it arises only in relation to other interrelated factors and variables. Things arise in mutual dependence upon causes and conditions, not in isolation. Your cup of morning coffee didn't arise whole and complete out of the ether but is dependent on causes and conditions, such as the sun and soil, the coffee beans, the farmer, the roaster and delivery man, the coffee shop, and the money and resources to buy it. The same is true with a moment of joy or sorrow; each arises contingent upon a web of conditionality. Dependent origination is the inverse truth of emptiness. To help us understand this, Mahayana philosophy posits a "two truths model" that shows there are two levels—ultimate and conventional—of one reality. Ultimately, things are empty of inherent existence, yet conventionally, they arise in mutual dependence upon causes and conditions based on karma. If you see one side of the coin, you can see the other, so much so that each side bleeds into the other, becoming one. Emptiness is not something we see, it's an absence that reveals the inherent flexibility of conventional phenomena. The key is to use dependent origination to comprehend emptiness, and then to vacillate repeatedly, until you see them both as one, spontaneously, without contradiction.

> Who sees the inexorable causation of everything   10
> Whatsoever—mundane and transcendent—
> And shreds any hint of reification,
> So, enters the path that satisfies Buddhas.

Tsongkhapa makes explicit how ultimate reality, the lack of inherent existence, doesn't negate conventional reality and its inexorable karmic laws of cause and effect. The flower is empty but still arises and gives off its lovely perfume. This is critical to preserving ethics and engagement in the world as a constructive, creative altruist, rather than abandoning them out of misguided apathy or hubris. If we fall prey to thinking emptiness is nothingness, why would we bother with anything? We'd drown in the nihilism for which Nagarjuna warned there would be no cure. Emptiness, ultimate reality, doesn't obliterate the laws of karma and causality or the processes and interactions that make up conventional reality—it allows them, just as the blank screens on our computers permit various images to arise, abide, and be revised.

Here the hint of reification that Tsongkhapa is bent on shredding refers to the mind's habit of objectifying, the deep-seated instinct to calcify, to concretize everything "whatsoever—mundane and transcendent." The shredding of delusion that ends the habit of reification can be applied equally to the mundane world of phenomena and the transcendent world of oneness. Once that habit is unlearned through critical analysis, revealing there is no absolute, unchangeable self or thing, what we find is not nothingness but the openness of selves and things that allows for interdependence and constructive relationality. If you can hold in your mind that the lack of inherent existence (emptiness) and cause and effect (interdependence) don't contradict, you have (merely) entered the path that satisfies the Buddhas.

> Appearance is invariably relative   11
> And emptiness is devoid of conviction—
> So long as these two insights dawn separately,
> You've not yet realized the Buddha's intent.

Having shown no conflict between these two realities of appearance (interdependence) and emptiness (lack of inherent existence), next we train to see them as a single reality. That is the defining factor of nondualism. First, we must engage in deconstructive and constructive analysis separately, each yielding discrete insights of negation and causation. Even while it is objectively the same coin, our nervous system continues to experience this as dissonance. One of the qualities of the Buddha mind is a supreme tolerance for the cognitive dissonance that exists between appearance and emptiness, which we finally synthesized as one reality without losing the defining characteristics of each. Emptiness doesn't collapse distinctions into a pea soup puree of undifferentiated oneness, but it is the ground of fundamental openness out of which relative appearances and distinctions, causes and conditions, are permitted to arise, abide, subside, and transform. The Heart Sutra, a quintessential scripture on emptiness that Campbell refers to in the epigraph at the start of this chapter, famously states that "Form is emptiness, emptiness indeed form. Emptiness is not different from form, form is not different from emptiness. What is form, that is emptiness; what is emptiness, that is form." While form and emptiness are equated, preserving their apparent difference remains vital.

A common spiritual bypass is to privilege ultimate reality and disparage conventional reality, saying it's all one, or that the world (of phenomena) is an illusion. This leads to dispassion and detachment. The sense that conventional reality is inferior, or an illusion to be dismissed, has dangerous implications, especially if someone is holding a knife or driving a car! True nondualism preserves distinction and engenders engagement.

> But when they appear simultaneously,   12
>   without alternation,
> From the slightest unbiased insight of relativity
> Corrective knowledge breaks the reifying habit,
> And your search for genuine insight is complete.

The middle way of realizing nondual reality is a scientific method as well as an expressive art form. The science involves intensive study and critical analysis resulting in progressive levels of knowledge; the art form involves meditative internalization resulting in integration and insight. Intensive study, critical analysis, and meditative internalization are the Three Wisdoms, which I call the Three Modes of Learning, born of study, reflection, and meditation (the last of which is divided into meditative insight and quiescence).

To follow the middle way, first we intellectually study how things are constructed (that is, dependent origination and karma) and deconstructed through analytic reason (emptiness). Next, we contemplate and reflect on what we have discovered intellectually, so that our understanding deepens from conceptual to personal. Finally, that understanding needs to deepen into intuitive insight by way of meditative training, where it displaces unconscious distortions, inaccurate mental patterns, and the reification habit that creates suffering. In this sequence—concept to understanding to lived experience—correct knowledge displaces mistaken convictions, and quantum view is revealed at the deepest level of our being. Meditative analysis must penetrate to the point that the new insight becomes inherent, as automatic as was the mistaken view of inherent existence.

MEDITATIVE INSIGHT AND QUIESCENCE

To navigate this process from facts to knowledge to wisdom, we use two discrete types of meditation practice, known as insight (Vipassana) and quiescence (Shamata), combined as a single, multi-disciplinary, cross-training art form, which draws on the dual benefits of analytic inquiry and sustained focal attention. We saw this combination in Kamalashila's Five Elements of Meditation, namely the second step of contemplation (reflecting on a theme) and the third step of meditation (deepening knowledge into wisdom using the power of concentration). In the second step, you can hold a theme in mind and reflect on its lines of reasoning, or you can hold an object in mind, as if it's under a microscope, and perform an analysis. Perhaps the most famous analysis is called the Four Keys—the quintessential meditation on emptiness, originally proposed by master Nagarjuna in Mulamadhyamakakarika—or Root Verses of the Middle Way, and subsequently referred to by scholars and yogis over the centuries, including Tsongkhapa. Through analytic meditation, we examine an object for inherent existence using discursive inquiry, searching within and beyond its parts, and then transition to quiescence meditation, focusing on and internalizing the discovery of not finding the object's essential nature during our experiment. This dual process draws the learning down from the head and into the guts. That's how quantum view becomes part of you.

Meditation is the practice of becoming anew (*bhavana*) and involves successive discoveries into, or insights of, the nature of reality—by way of analytic meditation—that we then embed in the core of our being through concentrative meditation. We become what we focus on; we are the scientific experiment and its discovery, the observer and observed. If we focus on how deficient we are, the felt sense of shame, and the internal self-image of inadequacy, we become depressed; if we inquire into the nature of that assumed truly existent self, what we discover is that it is a blur of sensations, emotions, memories, and concepts that somehow have been calcified by the reification habit and mistaken to be "I" or "me." In our analysis, we accept the reality of painful feelings as a dependent origination based on causes and conditions (karma), but we also see through the superimposition of self-existence and train ourselves to let go of the absolutizing mechanism that distorts all human experience. We seal in that sense of fluidity or openness, fully owning that as a true nature.

In addition to this meditative technique of combining quiescence and the insight into the true nature of things, we must remember to practice virtuous activities to increase the merit that will facilitate realization, like greasing a pan so the cake will lift out easily. Here we see how all three disciplines, or trainings, co-emerge to mutually support one another, facilitating realization. We develop mental balance and internalization through concentration practice; we develop wisdom through study, reflection, and insight training focused on the lack of inherent existence and the interdependence of phenomena; and we develop merit through the practice of ethics and virtue that hastens the internalization process by clearing obstacles that obscure correct view.

SYNTHESIZING FORM AND EMPTINESS

Tsongkhapa suggests that when the conditions are ripe and the merit is there, our dual insights of emptiness and appearance co-emerge as a single and deep intuitive realization of reality as it is, which represents the final step of the path. Reread this line: "Without the wisdom to realize reality, / You can't cut the root of traumatic life." What's key here is to recognize that the goal is not to realize "ultimate reality" but "reality." This is because the word "reality" alone assumes both ultimate and conventional levels, which Buddhists see as the same, so by realizing only ultimate reality, one disregards how conventions work and exist.

At this point, seeing emptiness should reveal interdependence, and seeing interdependence should reveal emptiness, because they are no longer separate nor conceptual but a genuine direct perception of reality as it is. Like most art forms, in contrast to science, it's difficult to determine and quantify exactly how and when that breakthrough will happen. Slow and gradual analysis of both sides—emptiness and interdependence—deepened through concentration, leads to spontaneous realization. That realization is then deepened gradually until it supplants the final remaining reflexes of reification and distorted perception. That is how the training goes. The hallmark of the Lam Rim is that we follow a sustained, gradual process, which results in a spontaneous breakthrough, and then that breakthrough to ultimate reality is metabolized, gradually displacing every fiber of delusion in our being.

I see these breakthroughs in therapy all the time. My clients and I point out and catalog karmic patterns through a thorough case history, which is an analytic meditation at the conceptual level and is equivalent to the wisdom born of hearing or studying. Then we deepen our understanding by becoming aware and working with those patterns together as they get activated during our conversation. Technically, this is called working with the transference projection and is equivalent to the wisdom born of reflection and contemplation. This is deeper than conceptual learning alone because it's personal. Then, after sustained work at those two levels, suddenly and unpredictably a client can recognize a cognitive distortion and work with afflictive emotion in vivo, course-correcting before seeding routinized reactions. They can apply "first aid" in the moment within the gap between affliction and reaction, immediately following the ripening effect. Or sometimes they can even apply "preventative care" between misperception and affliction, immediately before an afflictive emotional response, thus averting future negative becoming. This allows for what is called a "corrective emotional experience"—a new outcome beyond the clutches of samsara's predictable production. This is the equivalent of the wisdom born of meditative or experiential learning because it has a liberating quality. Then the response must be repeated, because learning at all three levels requires reinforcement in order for old software to be displaced and new software to be "installed." Quantum view has been achieved when the old program has been displaced and the new one installed deep in the guts, not in the head. Rather than falling prey to appearances and projections, one sees through them and seizes quantum opportunities to redesign future outcomes. What good does neck-up intellectual philosophy serve if it's removed from the nitty-gritty and body-based neural wiring of our lives, from which future karma is generated?

If we return to the three types of emptiness, the emptiness of permanence reveals the chronic flow of mutually co-arising causes and conditions. We then meditate deeply on that understanding and convert it into an intuitive understanding of equally convincing, though liberating, conviction. We try to see the world not as static self-evident phenomena but as a vast tapestry of inextricably connected, mutually dependent arising that often escapes our immediate control. The flower or the cup of coffee is no more self-evident and predictable than is the moment of suffering or happiness; we cannot just wish one into being, nor can we wish one away. Instead they arise, abide, and pass based on an intricate field of factors. This view helps us accept the conditions of things we cannot control while we work diligently on the seeds that we can.

Then we move to the next level of analysis that reveals the emptiness of unitary substantiality, as well as the infinite divisibility and interdependence of parts and appearances of wholes. Not only do all things arise based on causes and conditions, but none of those causes and conditions are impenetrable things in and of themselves; they are portals to vast universes. The cup of coffee and the flower both subdivide into constituent parts, and each part breaks down under the weight of critical analysis. You can never arrive at a unitary core or indivisible essence.

The same is true of a shameful person or a moment of anger. While you can delicately hold either in the embrace of compassion, the critical eye of analysis wanders through a hall of mirrors, or a labyrinth with many passages, until you are forced to surrender to the sense of finding no ground on which to stake an identity. In this not-finding—the uncertainty principle of the quantum world—we arrive at a dynamic space where compassion and openness can frolic like passionate lovers. As we meditate deeply on this, the reality of emptiness-interdependence gets installed as the new software deep in our being.

In the final level of analysis, the search for independent phenomena, which appear to have inherent self-existence (existing from their own side), we realize that the existence of all things is dependent on our mind, which perceives and labels them. This reveals the godlike creative power of language and our verbal designations. Once we see this, we become responsible for the labels we supply the external world, can recall the unconscious traumatic projection from the assembly line, and can use virtue to rewrite a new heroic narrative. Throughout each of these meditative exercises, we see the emptiness in one moment and the interdependence in another, and we try to systematically synthesize them and then install them in our being through repetition.

> From then on, all appearance dispels absolutism,   13
> And each emptiness eliminates nihilism—
> Seeing how emptiness dawns as causation,
> You're no longer blinded by biased views.

Here is a unique perspective held by the highest philosophical school of Buddhism, the *prasangika*, or middle-way school. It's a sexy, black-belt-level mental jujitsu. Emptiness and interdependence can each be used as tools or antidotes to correct and eliminate the misperception at the root of what produces suffering: the incorrect views of essentialism and nihilism, with which we falsely ascribe either an absolute self-existence or an absolute nothingness. In both cases we give essence to something being there that's not, or else we give essence to the nothing that we find as a thing in itself. This is a natural habit of the mind, to reify and cling, just like the little kick you do when the doctor taps your knee with that funny rubber hammer. The mind will either cling to self-existence or to nothingness as firm ground to protect and orient itself—trying to establish some basis of certainty in a quantum world of uncertainty.

The respective antidotes follow; emptiness is a corrective for essentialism, whereas interdependence is a corrective for nihilism. Each antidote draws the wrong view closer to the middle from the opposite extreme. This brings us to a more accurate view of how things exist so we can more skillfully interact with the world.

How does emptiness correct the view of nihilism, and how does interdependence correct the view of essentialism? At first blush, emptiness looks closer to nihilism, appearance closer to essentialism, so aren't we in danger of slipping into and reifying the extreme position rather than letting it go? Examine that carefully. Appearance—what we see of things—is inevitably relative, or relational, because we are perceiving phenomena, thus "appearance dispels absolutism" because we see that things have and need no nonrelative being, essence, or inherent existence and therefore cannot be absolute. *Absolute* means "nonrelational," so by observing sights, hearing sounds, and tasting food, the dance of appearance is displayed out in the open for you to behold its lack of inherent, absolute existence. Ironically, then, how can you get rid of or destroy something that's not even there? Some people say the spiritual path is about getting rid of ego, as if it's a fixed troublemaker lurking in the dark that needs to be eliminated from the equation. But you can't kill what doesn't exist; all you can do is discover it is a phantom. Since there is no self-existence in a mutually relational process, there is no substantial thing that can or needs to be eliminated. Using the diamond drill of critical analysis, the clear nature of mind penetrates the appearance of self-existence, recognizing it as total interdependence, and thus prevents our binary minds from slipping into the extreme position of essentialism or absolutism.

On the other side of the equation, emptiness—the lack of inherent existence—cannot be a free-floating negation or a thing to affirm. This raises the notion and necessity of recognizing the so-called emptiness of emptiness. Emptiness is not a thing unto itself but a convention of language used like a cursor to help the mind orient to where not to find something it assumed would be there. Emptiness is only ever meaningful when referring to some relative phenomenon. That something—a flower, a bottle, an experience, or a person—is always a relational thing. Emptiness, therefore, reveals an object's dynamic nature, its causal interplay, and thereby prevents the mind from slipping into the nihilistic position that nothing exists at all. Interestingly, the translation here is "each emptiness eliminates nihilism," and I'd like to subtly emphasize the word *each*. Its use implies plurality, as if there are as many emptinesses as there are phenomena. Do you follow? If emptiness adheres and refers to things, there is an emptiness, a lack of inherent existence, to each of those things. There is an emptiness to the pen and an emptiness to the bottle. Yes, it's true they are empty of the same thing—inherent existence—but you must do the analysis for each one, coming to the not-finding for each one and resting in the mere interdependence, until the mind lets go of its insatiable reification habit. Once the reification habit has been ironed out, eliminated, then all things appear as they are. Without distortion in your mind, you no longer need to analyze each object; all things appear empty of inherent existence, and yet still arise.

I've heard one teacher say that once you jump over the puddle of emptiness, you cross every wide ocean there is; but until then, you should train the mind by jumping across each puddle—that is, analyze each object. The absence of inherent existence for the bottle doesn't reveal a dark space but the sheer relativity, the dynamic flow, and the mental projection of the bottle, all of which were there to begin with before your false assumptions obscured them like a fun-house mirror. Thus, through emptiness, the black hold of nihilism is eliminated.

The latter part of the verse pulls it all together: "Seeing how emptiness dawns as causation, / You're no longer blinded by biased views." Not only are you no longer blinded and compelled by distorted convictions, but a whole new universe of possibility has emerged in their place. We don't have a fixed concrete problem that can't be resolved, nor do we have an abyss of nothing and so nothing to worry about. What we have is a dynamic co-arising that we can intervene with. This is how we use the womb of open potentiality without bypassing or neglecting embodiment, causes, and conditions.

> So once you realize the vital points   14
> Of these three principles of the path,
> Resort to solitude and persistent effort—
> You'll quickly reach the timeless goal, child!

Here we have Tsongkhapa's final encouragement, which in its original context was directed toward monastics and yogis who, after a long course of education, would learn all three principal paths via the wisdom born of study and reflection and then seek solitude in a hermitage, or a cave for deep retreat, to facilitate the final leg of learning and meditative experience: habituating and installing quantum view and radical altruism in the fiber of their being. The hero's journey would not end once they'd accomplished their ultimate wish of achieving awakening; rather it would continue in their return to the world to help awaken others.

UNION OF EMPTINESS AND KARMA

In returning to the world, consider how emptiness (ultimate reality) and karma (conventional reality) relate. The wisdom of realizing emptiness is the lens that allows us to see the deeper nature of reality, that it's open to infinite possibilities, open to be favorably reexperienced based on the way we see and relate it to things. Like a projection screen, reality is open for the images of a projector. The ultimate openness of phenomena is what allowed us to perceive a process as a pencil *and* a weapon *and* a drumstick. This becomes important when we get into things that aren't so mundane, such as relationships and trauma.

My mother and I were walking down the street minding our business one Saturday afternoon. From across the street, I heard a guy yelling vulgarities at me. Loudly. He was instigating. At first I tried to ignore him. Then he crossed the street, stood in front of me, and began to scream, and it bothered me. He proceeded to put his middle finger right up in my face. I was upset, but I restrained myself. I didn't say anything rude or nasty or retaliatory. I didn't make eye contact because I didn't know if a knife would be next. Then he began to say some nasty things about my mother. Really nasty. I didn't bite, and he called me a coward using the most shaming words you can imagine. Then he continued barking as we walked away.

My reaction to this person was influenced by my past shame, disempowerment, and anger. I'd been around the dharma long enough to know to restrain myself, to not retaliate with violence, to not lash out, but that didn't mean that in my head I wasn't saying, *Who the hell does this guy think he is, getting up in my face? How could this happen to me?* My shame and rage kept building, my blood pressure escalating. I turned to my mother to find she was unfazed by the encounter. She smiled and said, "That guy must be crazy. Why are you so upset?"

This moment illustrates the relationship between emptiness and karma. As we can give a pencil multiple labels, even calling it a weapon, so too is the guy crossing the street open to labeling; he is also empty. He is *open* to receive my label, my interpretation, which has been conditioned by my past imprints and calcified by my mind's reification habit. I can get caught up in how he put his finger in my face and how it could have been a knife. That could have been real. I'm not saying it was *all* in my mind. I'm not negating the event, the circumstances, or the guy yelling at me. It all did happen, and that's not my karma; it was his choice to come at me and, therefore, his karma. My experience and interpretation of the event come from my mind, are my karmic ripening, and determine the quality of the interaction. The experience is not terrifying, insulting, or ridiculing from its own side any more than a bottle is a bottle from its own side. My mother had an entirely different experience based on her ripening. Same event, two different experiences.

The ultimate truth is that events are open and, therefore, can be projected upon and interpreted by the diverse karmic formations of living beings. This means that no single event or phenomenon has a singular, independent existence from its own side. As much as I don't want to agree, this guy isn't intrinsically an asshole. Nor is he intrinsically a madman, as my mom thought. Who knows; he might have gone home to his wife and kids who love him dearly. Or, if he was loved and cared for and had a meaningful job, financial security, and lived in a society without racism, he might have treated me differently. In the world of quantum possibilities, all interpretations are equally versions of relative truth. For each of us, the guy is blank, ultimately open for interpretation. Because of the force of karma, we each perceive him a certain way. What we have always understood as entirely coming at us is mostly coming *from* us, dependently originating from our past actions, coloring perception, triggering afflictive emotion, and propelling reactive actions, which color future moments of perception in an endless cycle.

I'm not endorsing moral relativism. Just because events are open to interpretation doesn't mean this guy's slander and hostile actions are okay. In the relative world, there are definite differences between pain and pleasure, violence and peace, good and bad. In the ultimate reality, these dualities lack inherent existence and are relative conventions. Fall into one extreme at the expense of the other, and something vital is missed. Get the importance of both sides of the equation, and you have a discerning wisdom.

Furthermore, the guy was being hostile, and my mother and I needed to walk away. Conventionally, there are appropriate and wise choices, and there are inappropriate, unskillful ones. Emptiness does not negate conventions, it provides fluidity for skillful engagement within them. But the more important question is, How do we experience a threat? Some are terrified and frozen in their tracks, others move toward seeming danger and are cool under pressure. Bodhisattvas with high-level emptiness training see the world of samsara on fire and aspire to rescue all living beings within it. Cool as ice. Their insight into emptiness doesn't make them passive or aloof; it makes them creative tacticians.

My friend Shastri Ethan Nichtern shared with me that one of his students didn't pay his credit card bill and justified it by saying "it was all empty." Don't be that guy. Emptiness doesn't negate conventions, like having to get out of harm's way or pay your bills; rather it allows for the multiplicity and spectrum of variety in which to experience those events. Karma is what determines that multiplicity, and more than that, virtue is how we shape-shift reality to our and others' advantage. If you never want to fear being bullied or falling into paralysis in a burning building, think about how you could train your mind and plant the right seeds to meet those experiences differently.

That guy yelling at me is there relationally, but he's not there intrinsically. The way that each of these phenomena are not there, their emptiness of inherent existence, *allows* the way that they are there to be altered by our interaction. You need both pieces—ultimate and relative—for this alteration to be meaningful and practical. Miss one, and you miss the party; or worse, you can get bit by the snake.

In other words, emptiness permits karma. This is critical. Openness permits causality and multiplicity. It is because everything is empty of inherent existence that causes and conditions come together, that processes and experiences arise, relate, and are transformed. All interactions are alterable and optimizable within the constraints of any given moment. I might not be able to change my mind or someone else's in a single moment, but given enough time, even boulders can be eroded or shifted. Emptiness allows karma to express itself. Without emptiness, everything is static, absolute, and unrelational. Because of emptiness, everything is open, flexible, and dynamic. This openness allows karmic ripening for better and for worse. Reality is the value-neutral field for living beings to express causality, create networks, and coconstruct interdepedently. Like nondualism, ultimate reality, or emptiness, doesn't negate conventional reality—it facilitates it.

The Murderer Who Changed My Life

During my clinical internship in graduate school, I worked with clients at a community mental health clinic in downtown San Francisco. Our population included those with extreme trauma and addictions. My first client there—let's call him Cyrus—was an African American man, raised in poverty in the mid-1940s. His father was a drug addict, his mother a prostitute, and gangs, drugs, and violence were all he ever knew. Right out of high school he was drafted for the Vietnam War, and while he was a teenager, our government trained an already marginalized youth to be a full-blown killer. After several years risking his life for his country, he returned home to war protests, systemic racism, and rampant unemployment.

To survive, Cyrus did what he knew: joined gangs, lived on the streets, took and sold drugs, and continued to harm people. When he was finally arrested and incarcerated in the notorious maximum-security prison at San Quentin, he did more drugs and engaged in more violence. After twenty-five years in maximum security, he was released and found his way to our clinic, where he met a young, idealistic white boy, nearly forty years his junior, who came from a privileged background. By then Cyrus, a six-foot-five man, was in his late sixties and about 250 pounds. He was an imposing figure. I was scared shitless reading his chart before our first meeting, but even more so when I met him. He was quiet in our first session, with piercing eyes and a stone-cold gaze. He told me that he walked two and a half hours each way to our forty-five-minute session because he was terrified of getting on the city bus—it was too confined, and the unpredictable movements of people made him anxious. Given his associations from war and prison, daily life brought forth post-traumatic reactions. He had been set free, but he was still imprisoned by his past, often hijacked by what remained of his nervous system.

Cyrus wanted help, even though we both believed he was beyond it. Our sessions moved slowly, mostly on an energetic level at first, each of us testing the boundaries of tolerating the silence and navigating the physical space in my small office as we sat in front of one another, sizing each other up. You couldn't have found an odder couple, like two creatures from different planets. But, nonetheless, we both had our reasons for being there, and forty-five minutes can feel like an eternity unless you slowly begin to engage. I invited him to share his story; he eventually opened up, and I listened intently. I hung on every word. I expected nothing from him, and that was mutual. I didn't offer advice in return—in fact, I didn't say much. We just hung out. Surprisingly, it didn't take more than a few months for us both to begin to let down our guard, and I lost my fear of him attacking me, reaching over and snapping my neck with those huge, weathered hands. I listened to his story each week, finding myself connecting to his humanity, looking beyond his cold killer eyes and his crimes to the emotional landscape of his inner world and the war zone of his childhood.

He grew on me. I would think of Cyrus between sessions—not only of his tragic, violent life and lack of options, but of his innate genius and perseverance that allowed him to stay alive and to dominate as an alpha male in treacherous territory. I wondered how I might have fared if the shoe had been on the other foot. I knew I would not have made it. At times I found Cyrus likable and sincere. Unprompted, I would bring cigarettes and lollipops to our sessions. (I know that was contrary to my training, but I didn't care; it was my way of saying, genuinely, that I respected him.) You may judge me as a young, naive therapist who fell under the spell of a psychopath, but I worked closely with a well-trained supervisor who knew this population well, followed my interactions, and encouraged me to drop the "professional" role and try to connect on a human level without pretense. So, I dropped the therapist act and went old-school—human.

One day Cyrus came racing into the clinic and demanded to see me earlier than our usual appointment time. I hadn't seen him so animated before. There was terror in his eyes. He was out of breath, and his body language was contorted in on itself like a child shielding himself from a beating. I sat him down in my office and asked what had happened. Apparently, on his way to the clinic, he had walked down the narrow lane to the back entrance, as he had done in all the previous weeks. This time, however, it had been a little darker outside, and there had been someone else halfway through the passage, leaning up against the wall. This man had been wearing a dark trench coat, sunglasses, and boots and had an unlit cigarette in his mouth. Upon encountering this man, Cyrus's nervous system froze with conflicting messages. Part of him wanted to push through the alleyway to connect with me, part of him wanted to flee to avoid a potentially lethal confrontation, and then a large part wanted to preemptively strike and not let anyone get in his way. As Cyrus approached the clinic, the man with the shades took his right hand and reached into the internal pocket of his trench coat . . . and for a moment time slowed down. Every part of Cyrus wanted to pounce before a gun or knife could be drawn, but by some divine act of grace, he paused instead. The man with the trench coat pulled out a lighter and lit his smoke. Cyrus's nervous system was already in overdrive and fight mode. Every fiber of his being was teleported, in what I call the time machine, back to his troubled youth, to combat-zone Vietnam, to the shower room at San Quentin. But somehow on this day, he had managed enough self-discipline to pause in the gap, restrain his impulses, and keep on walking.

I'm recounting this story in the context of emptiness, rather than renunciation, because what ended up surprising Cyrus and me the most wasn't that his nervous system constantly misperceived situations as if life-threatening based on his past, but that he sincerely—and desperately—wished to get better. Against all odds, he had the will to be a better human being. He looked at me with a tear in his eye and said, "I don't want to live this way anymore. I don't want to hurt anyone anymore." I believed him—and it split my heart wide open. Lurking deep under that piercing stare and imposing physique of a seeming natural-born killer was a child's warm, beating heart. What can I say? Cyrus was simultaneously the embodiment of our malevolent human nature, a savage caged animal wired to kill, and evidence of our Buddha nature, the flicker of the wish to #awakenwisdomlove. Both exist in us. All of us. What we choose to cultivate and feed is the difference between a gradual process of devolving or of becoming more human.

I know there are families out there who may have lost someone they loved because of the violence and drugs that Cyrus and those like him put out into the world, and who deserve to feel their anger is justified. I'm not asking them for forgiveness; that's not my place. If Cyrus had killed my boy as part of his criminal life, I may have been compelled to lock him up for life and throw away the keys, or to ask for the death penalty. My point, however, is that the stories we tell ourselves about others are always more complicated than we think. All that philosophical analysis of the bottle and the flower was to get to this critical point, so we can ask ourselves what it is that we think we see in others, and who is really there on the other side? Was Cyrus a kid who never had a chance? A victim of racism, poverty, and our military-industrial complex? A soldier who performed his duty and risked his life for our liberty? A gangbanger and drug dealer who committed many crimes? A veteran neglected by his country? A client who opened my naive eyes and prejudiced heart? Was Cyrus a killer or a teacher? A friend and father or a menace? I don't know. Perhaps he was none of these essentially and, therefore, all of them relatively. It's hard and messy when you get to the real-life application of these ancient insights and tools.

This raises a vital point about emptiness. Reality is malleable. If we are all open processes playing out different roles, seen from multiple perspectives, and equally capable of killing and saving lives, then how we interact determines everything. Wise compassion is the most constructive force for our interaction with others here and now.

Like us all, Cyrus was empty and therefore impressionable to hate and hostility, but he had a thread of goodness in him, of which I got a glimpse. What then was my role and duty to try to nurture? Should I have stamped out that last glimmer, or should I have tried to cultivate it? From an evolutionary or multilife perspective, we never leave each other. We never leave the matrix of interdependence; our well-being is inextricably intertwined with that of others, and our actions create legacies that continue long after we're gone. The racism, the violence, the economic disparity, the injustice are currents in the continuity of consciousness. The hero's training is asking us to strive to put something more positive back into the neural circuitry so that collectively we might all have a chance to elevate consciousness. Cyrus taught me many lessons, but most of all he taught me that we should never be fooled by our projections, mistaking appearances for reality. No matter how dark the prison cell, you never know when a crack in someone's window will accept your light.

Inspired by quantum possibility, let's learn how to manifest destiny.

Retracing Your Steps   29 STEP

29 Perfect wisdom—the milestone of quantum view.

8 · MANIFESTATION

MASTERING THE CREATIVE ART OF LIFE REDESIGN

And [the Bodhisattva] is filled with compassion for the self-terrorized
beings who live in fright of their own nightmare. He rises, returns to
them, and dwells with them as an egoless center, through whom the
principle of emptiness is made manifest in its own simplicity . . .
"Gift waves" go out from such a one for the liberation of us all.
"This our worldly life is an activity of *nirvana* itself, not the
slightest distinction exists between [nirvana and samasara]."

JOSEPH CAMPBELL, *The Hero with a Thousand Faces*

Once we have the confidence to self-liberate and have established
radical altruism and quantum view to free others, we should set our
sights on transforming the world, because, as Godwin taught me, the
goal of meditation is not the relief of escape but the compassion of
relationality. Our immediate relationships, our social institutions, and
the collective biosphere need our attention and intervention as much
as our individual minds. That's where *manifestation* comes in—the
bridge from inner spiritual work to what British scholar Andrew
Harvey beautifully describes as "sacred activism."

As we prepare for manifestation, it's important to consider how to
make wisdom applicable to our everyday lives and to use it as a spring-
board for reconstructive action in the world. In the Tibetan Buddhist
context, wisdom is not a general knowledge; it's a precise one. It refers to
seeing through the distortions of permanence, unity, and independence,
or inherent existence. Once our cognitive obscurations are cleansed,
as Tsongkhapa writes, we are "no longer blinded by biased views" that

create distinction between the conventional and ultimate nature of things. Only then can we intervene in the world through skillful means of the six perfections and "quickly reach the timeless goal."

Wisdom of Conventional Reality

To prepare for manifestation, we begin by considering conventional reality—the realm of dualities, appearances, or forms. No matter the label, it's governed by the laws of karmic causality. We study and appreciate how things exist through such foundational teachings as dependent origination and the characteristics of karma. Think of this exploration the way a scientist observes how processes function, seeing the flow of phenomena arising through mutual dependence based on causes and conditions. At no point during this analysis do conventions disappear. Understanding that milk lacks inherent existence at no time means it goes poof into nothingness; the absence of intrinsic reality permits milk to be churned into butter. The same is true for pain: it is not tangible or findable, but it is real in the sense that it feels irrefutably unpleasant in the moment.

This level of wisdom also integrates the first and second noble truths—the first acknowledging the suffering that characterizes the human condition, and the second delineating the links of dependent origination that trace our suffering to misperception, afflictive reaction, compulsive action, and conditioned life. To dismiss this level of reality would be to dismiss the field of human experience we all share—the textured vicissitudes and the dichotomies of joy and sorrow, me and you, past and future. We need to accept that all these dichotomies exist, and confront (rather than spiritually bypass) them. This level of wisdom refers to the first metaphoric stage of seeing the mountain, in all its pain and glory, from the point of view of the ordinary or untrained mind perceiving conventions.

Wisdom of Ultimate Reality

The second type of wisdom concerns the ultimate nature of things—their emptiness, openness, and lack of intrinsic reality. This is the penetrative analysis that deconstructs ordinary appearances and our unconscious projections upon them that we take for granted in conventional wisdom. It goes further to expose how impossible it is that anything exists in the way it appears. And further still to the ineffability of experience.

When we donned our quantum Ray-Bans, we saw that no subject, object, or interaction can be inherently found. Meditative analysis takes us from the world of forms, appearances, differentiation, and dualities into the realm described as oneness, unity, indivisibility, and spaciousness—from the infinite field of possibility that physicists call the sea of potential or the quantum vacuum into the ineffable, the indescribable, and the nameless. Bob Thurman describes the analysis as the "diamond drill of critical reflection" that penetrates further into the atom (once thought to be indivisible) and breaks through to the quantum field of reality. Bob Thurman calls this meditative realization the "space-like equipoise intuition" because an embodied awareness of the fluid, permeable, vacant, and pregnant quality of the world of static appearances replaces the habituated delusion of the atomic nature of appearance. Sacred psychedelic entheogens and near-death experiences can similarly result in the space-like equipoise intuition.

Bob Thurman describes the yogis' experience of this intuition as a "merger," an utter loss of subject-object dualism, "like water being poured into water."[1] Upon seeing, from our most subtle, intuitive level, the true nature of things beyond distortion, we can cut the root cause of misperception that perpetuates samsara—a life of self-imposed suffering conditioned and compelled by stress instincts and trauma.

Once the ultimate nature of things is revealed, there can be no further misperception, and without misperception no affliction, without affliction no compulsive action, without compulsive action no more compulsive becoming, mindless life, or tragic death. This level of wisdom is equated with the Buddha's third noble truth—nirvana, the extinction of samsara. Attaining this level doesn't mean that life is extinguished—only the compulsive, delusion-driven one is. The fact that samsara is created means it can be undone. Because the mind's fundamental nature is open, and because the world of forms is also open, we can revise both self and phenomena. That means an awakened life is possible for everyone, and the world we cocreate is as malleable as clay.

Some spiritual teachers and students stop here, in the oneness, suspended in the orgasmic radiance of the space-like equipoise intuition in which they discover that the lack of inherent existence is real, and conventional reality is an illusion. However, for true liberation we need to move through the open field of oneness and conjoin our space-like intuition with another critical and profound discovery, what Bob Thurman poetically calls the "illusion-like aftermath intuition." This will prevent us from becoming stuck in the intoxication of the realm of oneness—one of the most dangerous spiritual bypasses. If we continue further into the void, we won't disappear or drop off the edge but return to the world of dualities, this time with a more mature level of discernment that sees the reality of conventional appearances and their emptiness co-emerging in true nondualism.

In our return to the world, we realize we never left, as there was nowhere else to go, as Master Qingyuan Weixin of the Tang dynasty describes in this passage:

> Before I had studied Ch'an [Zen] for thirty years, I saw
> mountains as mountains, and rivers as rivers. When I
> arrived at a more intimate knowledge, I came to the point
> where I saw that mountains are not mountains, and rivers
> are not rivers. But now that I have got its very substance,
> I am at rest. For it's just that I see mountains once again
> as mountains, and rivers once again as rivers.[2]

Finally, there is only the mountain. Finally, there is only us, the world of differentiated phenomena, and our relationship to it. It was always there, open and awaiting our creative involvement, but obscured by our delusory projection. What changed was our release from the habit of reification, our mistaken sense of self-existence projected on phenomena. As we released ourselves, we slipped into an altered state of consciousness, set apart from forms and differentiation, wherein even the self and subject-object dichotomy ceased. From there we were in danger of superimposing self-existence onto the not-finding of phenomena, thereby calcifying the lack of inherent existence as the new independent reality, and somehow allowing the insidious reification habit to reemerge and reclaim the realm of oneness as its chief domain of substantiality. By continuing the analysis one step further, we discovered the illusion-like aftermath intuition, when the world of multiplicity returns to our clarified perception. But this time differentiated objects and mere appearances do not fool us; we see relative things just as they are and can interact with them as skillfully as an artist does with paint and canvas. Our preparation in self-care and compassion proves to be indispensable, for without it, the break-through insight into emptiness could result in an aloof detachment from the world. We can now appreciate the elegance of the gradual sequence of our training, as it ensures that foundations in self-mastery and altruism supply the moral and social impetus for creative reen-gagement once correct view has been realized.

From oneness we return to the world of dualities—conventions and multiplicities, feelings and relationships, karmic causality, body, brain, and wiring—but our illusion-like aftermath intuition under-stands that its ultimate nature is inexpressibly open, and we feel naturally inspired to intervene and change things for the better. The Buddhists call this appearance-emptiness—true nondualism, dawning unmistakably to those with quantum view. Bob Thurman eloquently describes the final push from the space-like equipoise intuition to the illusion-like aftermath intuition—a movement that can also be understood as the push from within a meditative session on selfless-ness, using the Four Keys analysis, to our residual experience between meditative sessions, when we reencounter everyday life:

> Thus, emptiness dawns immediately as the magnificent panorama of relativity, through its absolute negation of the intrinsic reality of [both beingness and] nothingness. The great death is the threshold of the dawn of enlightenment, in which the clear light of wisdom reveals the immense field of play of great compassion.[3]

I offer Thurman's description of nonduality here for two reasons: first, because cheap nonduality is big business in our spiritual marketplace and the word *oneness* has become a marketing hook, and second, because a correct understanding of nondualism serves as a solution to our sickness of paradigm. There is a difference between oneness and emptiness. While subtle, it is important, given how people mistakenly use these terms interchangeably. Oneness is *not* emptiness, but emptiness can reveal oneness as another relative state. Emptiness dissolves appearances and reveals the reality of oneness, like waves becoming the ocean, but emptiness also dissolves oneness and reveals there can be no ocean independent of the waves. Emptiness is an absence, a negation, not a thing, whereas oneness is one thing.

Emptiness can equally refer to the realm of differentiated phenomena and the realm of its unfindability. When applied simultaneously to both the waves and the ocean, it is designed to dissolve all separations, all absolutes. It can even be applied to and dissolve a reified idea of itself—*the emptiness of emptiness*. Bob Thurman suggests that it would be "senseless to claim that the lack of intrinsic reality has intrinsic reality."[4] The final disappearing act of the great magician, the great medicine itself, is that a correct view of emptiness prevents even emptiness from being the final source of clinging. The point is that we have nothing to hold on to—not the world of forms and differentiation, not the formless realm of oneness, and not even the dissolving method of emptiness. "Gone, gone, gone beyond, gone utterly beyond, hail awakening," as the Heart Sutra pronounces.

Oneness is the unified field, the single ocean from which the world of multiplicity—the waves—emerge. Emptiness is the lack of inherent existence and is applied to conventional reality, exposing the ways in which people and objects seem to appear, but it also dissolves the subtle sense of substantiality superimposed on oneness. Emptiness exposes how the appearance of oneness set apart from multiplicity is also a reified projection or distortion, which, like all projections and distortions, leads to suffering. The only definitive teaching in Buddhism is that everything is empty of self-existence (svabhava), even emptiness; all other teachings, such as multiplicity and oneness, wave and ocean, karma and continuity of mind, are considered interpretable. That is, they are relative and contextual, so, interestingly, even oneness belongs to the conventional teachings on the relative level of reality, no matter its profundity.

Buddhism sees both realities as equally empty, which brings us back to manifestation. This realization is what provides the relationality between the two truths—form and emptiness, conventional and ultimate, duality and oneness, karma and wisdom—which we use to justify the reconstruction of the world. A true realization of nonduality supplies the rationale and motivation for inner and outer system change.

Wisdom of Skillful Means

Remember Godwin's teaching? *It's not about breaking out, it's how we break back in.* True nondualism is inspired toward life redesign and engaged with the troubles of the world with the knowledge that they are empty, and yet still arise. Within the quantum vacuum lies probabilities and potential solutions for everything, if we can align with and cultivate them. Our hero's journey combines two arcs: the inward arc involving leaving home, slaying the demon, and gaining insight into selflessness, and the outward arc involving finding the treasure of compassion and returning home with the elixir. The Dalai Lama, Lama Zopa, Bob Thurman, and Joe Loizzo aren't sitting back, relaxing, and enjoying oneness. They're engaged without fear. Proponents of mature nondualism have seen the mountain and seen it disappear and, as a result, have come back to seeing the mountain again with creative solutions—skillful means—driven by the warm heart of compassion and protected by the wisdom of emptiness. Nondual wisdom and compassion open the heart to a suffering world, but they offer the best medicine of protection and healing.

Mature nonduality leading to action brings us to the final type of wisdom: *upaya*, or skillful means. Upaya includes the creative ability to intervene in the illusion-like world of differentiation in the most effective manner relative to the needs and predispositions of beings in order to awaken them from their delusory nightmare. We first beheld the mountain from the delusion of fixed appearances and were overcome by fear. Then, with the space-like equipoise intuition, we saw there was no mountain and basked in the radiance of selfless liberation. The original mountain reappeared, but this time we beheld it anew, not as static but as dynamic and guided by the illusion-like aftermath intuition. Now we have the tolerance of cognitive dissonance necessary to work with the co-emergence of appearance-emptiness. The realizations of the space-like equipoise and illusion-like aftermath intuitions are themselves psychological milestones in our process of becoming fully human. Combined, they allow us to appreciate how things are simultaneously empty and yet arise, abide, and cease—and therefore can and must be redesigned and reexperienced. Motivated by compassion, the Bodhisattva conceives to transform the world by accessing the womb of emptiness and impregnating it with the seeds of virtue. What is born is the sacred mandala of the manifest world reinforced by the inspiration of the Jewel Tree flight simulator of love.

Bodhisattvas know by what means everyone will be drawn into the process of their own conscious unfolding. *Skillful means* is the art of recognition and creative engagement that allows the hero to inspire, model, teach, and offer others whatever is necessary to ripen them along their Gradual Path. As Shantideva taught:

> My own body and all that I possess,
> My past, present and future virtues—
> I dedicate them all, withholding nothing,
> To bring about the benefit of beings.[5]
> Withholding nothing . . .

Virtual Engagement: Manifesting in Meditative Rehearsal

There are several ways to prepare and practice for skillful engagement with others. One is housed within the Five Elements of Meditation—the scaffolding of practice we explored in chapter 3—and is recommended by Master Kamalashila:

1 Preparation

2 Contemplation

3 Meditation

4 Dedication

5 Application

After the fourth step of dedication, and while still on the cushion, pre-visualize connecting meditative learning and inspiration to practical life and experience. For example, if you seal in the experience of urgency because of the contemplation on inevitability of death, then after you dedicate the merit imagine how your priorities and routines might be impacted accordingly. Then, in the fifth step, because of the meditative study and practice, you will be more compelled by the force of this conviction and habituation to make a concerted effort to live differently. This is a way of manifesting learning and psychological gains in the world as postmeditation integration.

The skillful means method is also housed within visualization practice. Steps five and six are key stages within the Seven-Step Mentor-Bonding Process from chapter 3:

1 Admire qualities.

2 Make offerings.

3 Disclose negativities.

4 Rejoice virtues.

5 Request guidance.

6 Request presence.

7 Dedicate merits.

Having asked for the blessings and guidance of the mentors in step five, imagine receiving waves of nectar and rainbow lights from them that carry the bejeweled affirmation and wisdom intuitions you seek. Coming to your crown, slipping past your throat, dissolving in your heart, you feel empowered by the lineage, blessed by the mentors, and anointed as an emissary of the path. You become a mirror, refracting the harmonic resonance of enlightenment from the mentor and lineage through you to the world. Those harmonics ripple out like moonlight on a still lake, to the ends of the earth, through all the hearts and minds of living beings, kindling their own diamond-like intuition, awakening them, and then rippling back to us and the Jewel Tree refuge field like a wave of solidarity so we all feel the warm embrace of the divine frequency of love. At that point, having been thoroughly blessed and in an altered, awakened, and receptive state, one can pause and insert any type of meditation practice one wishes, from a period of deep concentration to savor and internalize the sense of ecstatic activation (called the great bliss state) to an analyzing meditation on the emptiness of self or an object. Or one can contemplate one of the thirty themes of the Lam Rim, or read a text, or even practice a yoga sequence—each with the understanding that this is the best state in which to learn, retain, and deepen any of the insights gleaned.

At step five we are role-playing, being an emissary of the mentor and lineage, extending love and rehearsing how to heal and awaken the world. There is a slight, but important, difference in step six. The mentor and the lineage dissolve entirely, and all their wisdom and compassion coalesce as a raindrop that again comes to your crown, passes through your throat, and dissolves inseparably at your heart—the raindrop merging with the ocean. This time you are not reflecting your mentor's great qualities as an emissary; you and the mentor are one, so you now role-play being the mentor, arriving fully at the end state, trying on Buddhahood for size, tasting what it would be like to embody and manifest your ideal. The simulation can continue from there as a ripple effect once you imagine the suffering of all living beings and, out of compassion, send them your wisdom and care, which they receive, and as a result they awaken from their samsara nightmare, restoring the world to sanity.

There is real power in this simulation, because you can't manifest anything "in reality" without first visualizing an outcome with clarity. If you can't first imagine yourself as awakened, positively affecting others, and restoring the world to balance, then you are left trying to develop confidence in a slow and unpredictable manner, reliant upon trial and error in real-world experience, which we know can be intermittent and mixed at best. What we are intentionally doing is maximizing this special awakened and inspired state in the nervous system to test-drive prosocial engagement based on the Bodhisattva vow, including the anticipated successful completion, thereby banking the internal reward, karmic impressions, psychological memories, and neurological associations. Try to see the world restored to peace and harmony among living beings, the ecosystem restored to balance, the planet becoming verdant and alive, and all beings safe and protected. It's a good seed to plant, a good simulation program to run. Most of the time we're visualizing how that's all gone to hell, but here we commit to manifesting a more optimistic vision with the science to back it up.

There is nothing stopping you from playing jazz and ad-libbing to tailor this phase to your developmental needs. Sometimes, diverging from the classic Tibetan script toward how guided imagery is used by athletes and executives puts us in the position of accessing our highest ideal, "acting as if" we have already reached our goal. We simulate specific maneuvers that we know will prime mind, speech, and action for real engagement in the world. For example, if I have a difficult client who triggers me adversely, I might simulate a best intervention with them during my visualization, rehearse working through expected blocks and reactivity, and previsualize a successful outcome. In doing so, I tap my highest ideal in the future and strengthen my muscle memory and felt sense so that I can recruit them during real-life interactions, when my ordinary "limited" self might feel incapable or scared.

Through repetition we can see how this process begins to dislodge the fixated, neurotic self-image and habituated fearful programming.

If, in my ordinary state, I become anxious the hour before seeing my difficult client, I'm predisposed to the worst-case outcome. With my amygdala hijacked and my prefrontal cortex compromised, I'll be short on patience, more defended, and cut off from my empathic circuitry and healing intuition. The terror-based anticipation brought on by visualization can have an actual effect, even if subtle, on the real interaction, so why wouldn't the opposite be true? That's why we role-play manifestation during our visualization practice. This is the secret art form responsible for the Dalai Lama's famous presence and connection. He has primed his entire way of being through role-modeling virtual reality, which carries over into everyday reality.

ROAD MAP 30   Manifestation (Using MAPS)

Requesting guidance and requesting presence are how we rehearse manifesting during meditation and visualization practices, respectively, to create confidence, prime for compassionate engagement, and wire the brain for heroic, real-life encounters. Next, I'd like to offer a method for actual engagement that will draw on the muscle memory and inspiration acquired during practice sessions. I've developed the acronym MAPS to help you synthesize the core themes from the Lam Rim—refuge, karma, emptiness, and ethics—in a practical method for manifesting and applying heroic altruism and agency:

Maturity   Take responsibility for your ripening.

Acceptance   Feel the burn with presence-love.

Possibility   Recognize quantum openness.

Seeding   Be a gardener of virtue.

These four points are a synthesis of all the material in this book, but the list is not meant to serve as a cheat sheet or a shortcut, or to be featured as "everything you need to know" clickbait.

MATURITY

Remember that the way we view things in any given moment is conditioned by our past. Most of us look outside ourselves for guidance or to blame people, places, and circumstances for our internal experiences. In contrast, the mature Bodhisattva takes equal responsibility for their mind's distortions and creative power, thus becoming their own source of reliable refuge for healing and transformation. They put blame where blame is due: on the faulty psychological wiring and evolutionary program that is distorting reality and making us feel alienated, threatened, and reactive. They also take refuge where it's most reliable—in innate Buddha nature and innate capacity to transform. I must reclaim and understand that the way I might experience authority as manipulative and uncaring, or myself as a humiliated and powerless child, is my psychological default program. At the same time, I take refuge in my capacity to unlearn and relearn the program—to shape-shift consciousness.

Even if conceptually we can understand that our perception is mostly a projection upon a blank screen, that its ultimate nature is open, in each moment we must perceive and experience it as a ripening of the past. If we can catch the true source of experience in the gap of awareness, we can use the illusion-like aftermath intuition to see life more like a phantom, resisting future destructive actions that reinforce the projection. That's nonduality—wisdom recognizing appearances as open projections and yet still karmically arising as unpleasant experience. We understand with wisdom the ultimate open nature of things, and yet we embrace with compassion the conventional ripening of past action. The first point of MAPS is the maturity it takes to recognize that microreactions at the level of your own mind are creating all of your experiences, which proliferate into entire worlds. So, take responsibility for your life-making.

ACCEPTANCE

Accept the sting in any given moment—it must be experienced. You cannot avoid your karmic ripening. There is no clemency, no escape. The sadness or shame is unavoidable. The joy and success fade. The unpleasant sensations arising during meditation are unavoidable, and the pleasant sensations are ungraspable. We didn't ask for the ripening to be there; the conditions were perfect, and yet our experience is unbearable or tumultuous and painful because it is a seed that has already been planted.

Lama Zopa advises seeing the unpleasant ripening of negative deeds as an adventitious opportunity for purification and for training the mind. Yogis actively pursue adverse circumstances. Like karmic hunters to purify their mind stream, they create a space for negative ripening to extinguish past actions while cultivating better seeds for the future. In other words, because the seed has already been planted, we must experience the flower and fruit. So, don't avoid the seeds. Let them come up, feel them with courage and compassion, and let them be extinguished rather than reinforced in karma's cycle.

It's how we relate to the current experience that decides the future. That's where we plant a new seed to grow favorable outcomes. Does shame beget blame, or do you meet anger with more violence? Do you stuff it, avoid it, or bypass it? These actions only seal an unpleasant fate. Instead, meet the ripening with presence-love. Presence-love is the medicine or safe container for past ripening. Imagine a child who is terrified and whose overwhelmed parents either neglected them or blamed them in a moment of reactivity. Their terror is compounded with abandonment or hostility. When we relate to our inner experience this way, shame further fuels the fire of fear. The hero knows to meet negative ripening as the parent they wish they had: attuned, present, nonjudgmental, loving. We can't fix it or take the pain away in the moment, but we can train to meet it with unwavering attention, unconditional love, and disciplined nonreactivity to stop the cycle of violence. That hero's stance of radical acceptance purifies negative karma.

POSSIBILITY

The third point is to remember that even when something difficult befalls us, its ultimate nature is vacant, open, and pregnant with possibility. This is not easy, but what a worthwhile application of mindfulness. When something negative happens, remember that its nature is empty, therefore it is transformable. Even while it burns, you have one leg standing in the flames of past ripenings, feeling deeply with presence-love, while the other leg is active and mobile, emerging from the empty womb of quantum possibilities to plant causal seeds for the future. Most of us haven't trained sufficiently to even recognize the first point of maturely taking responsibility, or the second point of accepting pain with presence-love. As a result, we react to experience and objects as if they were as substantial as they appear, compelling our karmic wheel to further deepen its rut. MAPS is a conceptual training model at first, but if we study, meditate, and apply it to our immediate circumstances, we will catch ourselves in a painful moment and not only endure it without reactivity but also recognize it as a portal to the quantum vacuum of possibilities. Every encounter and experience has within it multiple outcomes. We can sometimes recognize this in retrospect, but if we work hard to close the gap, one day we may recognize it in the moment—the nondual insight co-emergent with feeling the burn—so that ripening the past and seeding the future are concomitant. Life is a choose-your-own adventure, not a fait-accompli tragedy.

When I spoke with my accountant about saving for my kids' college educations, I was in shock and then horror to hear how exorbitant tuition had become in the United States. I examined my anger as it arose. I saw how the anger wanted to blame someone—this time the government and the banking cartels. I had a moment of recognition and choice. First, I took responsibility for the external trajectory of my mind blaming others, which forced me to consider what I was reacting to. I saw anger, and as I looked a little deeper, I saw the residual legacy of my past fear and shame. Under my outward-directed anger was a sense of scarcity, a fear that my children will be exposed and vulnerable in a cold, hard world. As I looked deeper still, I could see the insecurity, the sense of sheer incompetence, that I wouldn't be able to support them. The default setting for my entire life, the perpetual refrain of my inner, karmic monologue, was that I am unworthy, incapable, and in danger. It's a subtle and all-pervasive story, but in that moment I caught a glimpse of it for what it was: one story line among countless possibilities of equally empty interpretations. Usually that level of shame leads to anger and overcompensation that keeps my hamster wheel spinning, but only—secretly—reinforces the shame. Because the fear is the karmic residue, or ripening, of past actions, in the gap I could meet the terrified child within with subtle awareness, presence-love, and a sense of reassuring compassion—showing up as the parent I wish I had had, in the same way I wanted to show up for Cyrus and his traumatized inner child.

Based on reassurance and reactivity subsiding, the mind's capacity to see things reemerges as the prefrontal cortex comes back online. In that moment, I could see what was always there and will always be there, like a buried treasure obscured by affliction and delusion: possibility. From a clear state of mind, I could see many solutions for my kids: ways to create financial opportunities, realization that I am not alone in making financial contributions for the family, the possibility that society will offer more scholarships or create solutions in the next fifteen years to make university programs more affordable, or perhaps that my sons will grow up free of my scarcity mentality.

From a place of inner safety and presence-love, what can arise is what Tibetan Master Chögyam Trungpa calls basic goodness, or confidence—solutions born of seeing the possibilities. All the solutions to the world's problems exist right here and now, not as reified, complete alternative realities but as potentials in the quantum vacuum. Solutions exist if you can prime and open your mind to them. That's what a breakthrough insight is—a moment when the mind reveals something that was there all along but had been hidden in plain sight. First there is a mountain of confusion, then there is no mountain, and then the inner eye of wisdom reveals the mountain of possibilities that had been there all along. Truth reveals itself in the dawn light of quantum view. Possibility is about sharpening the mind to detect quantum openness in any given moment.

SEEDING

While the ripening of past karma is not under our control, what we *do* with that ripening is, and this becomes the cause for future ripening. We've taken responsibility that mind is our creator-god, we have met the past with presence-love, we have recognized the realm of quantum possibilities in each moment, and now it's time for conscious, virtuous action. You have control over what you do with your pain, what you do with your breakup, what you do with the guy's middle finger in your face, what you do once the shame underneath the anger is unearthed, what you do with the arising of your joy and abundance. The present moment comes from your past and must be experienced, hopefully with presence-love. There is nothing you can do about it except bear witness with restraint. How you relate to that experience is entirely up to you, but what you do in that moment plants a seed.

When we do giving and taking (Tonglen), for example, we are doing a practice that exchanges our nervous system with another. We send out all our good qualities and take on another's suffering. And when we do that, we don't think that, magically, some person in Africa is feeling better. It is a simulation for *our* mind, to transform it from self-centeredness to altruism, samsara to nirvana, suffering to freedom. However, it's not only for your mind, because when your mind is free, the heart-clamp has been released, and the energy and information in neural circuitry is flowing, you have an immediate impact on others. The mind that is free from deluded constriction can help others to become free, and together we can save this planet—we can save all sentient beings. It's not just a virtual simulation; it carries over to manifestation.

The last point is about virtuous seeding in the quantum field of possibility. Lead with your ethical foot forward, and be a good gardener.

The Art of Manifestation

I'm reluctant to use the high lamas as examples for fear they are too advanced for us to feel that dramatic life changes are possible for us mere mortals. But from the Tibetan perspective, that's exactly what heroes are for—to inspire awe and galvanize our motivation. Even if we don't reach their lofty extremes, we'll move one step further in our own development of becoming more fully human. Lama Zopa Rinpoche effortlessly makes every single activity he does a mind-training practice, converting everything from mundane activities to the most intense adversities into a purification process, as well as an offering to all living beings. He's transformed his entire life into a continual, ritual offering, resulting in a rain of blessings. While he was traveling in Tibet with his students, Lama Zopa stopped the entire pilgrimage group to pray for the welfare of tadpoles in a drying puddle. His chief attendant, Venerable Roger, also told a story of how Lama Zopa, when given his onboard meal on a short flight, began his prayers and dedications, offering the benefit of the food to all sentient beings. This lasted for more than half an hour. When the plane was preparing to land, the flight attendant insisted that she take back the tray of food even though Lama Zopa had not eaten. He gladly gave her back the tray, saying, "It has served its purpose." That is a mind thoroughly suffused in Bodhicitta.

In 2011, Lama Zopa Rinpoche had a massive stroke. Despite his otherworldliness, he is still a human being with a body, which has its own causal process. He lost use of his left side, and with it, his precious speech. He was in a hospital for months, undergoing intensive rehab. What do you think Lama Zopa was doing during his time in the hospital? In an email I received, he wrote, "All this suffering I am experiencing, may it ripen upon me so that His Holiness the Dalai Lama is spared. So that His Holiness may have a long life and benefit others." That's what Lama Zopa was harboring in his mind. That's his karma. Although the stroke had its own biological causality, it was not his karma; rather, his subjective experience of immense gratitude for the stroke was the ripening effect of his past action, and his present relationship with the stroke—his extraordinary compassion—was the causal seed for his future ripening.

There is the event (the stroke), there is the ripening from the past (his experience of gratitude), and there is the cause for the future experience (which is compassion and generosity). There's Lama Zopa following MAPS, demonstrating how a new operating system based on radical altruism and quantum view runs for self and others. That's why he teaches his students, such as myself, prayers, including "May the suffering I experience relieve whatever harm might befall His Holiness the Dalai Lama. Let *me* be the one to take it on." This kind of reaction is a perfect embodiment of Shantideva's Four-Point Exchange of Self and Other, resulting in the reorientation of flow and an exchange of self-interest with altruism. Radical altruism is not a highfalutin ideal, and Lama Zopa's relationship to his illness exemplifies this.

Technically, you can't take on another person's karma, otherwise Buddha, Jesus, and the other saints and sages would have purified the world for us, and we wouldn't have to do a thing. So why did Lama Zopa say what he did about the Dalai Lama? Because it's an intention, a seed, even if it's technically not possible to wash away the karmic seeds of others; only they can clean their mind stream of past imprints and residue. Lama Zopa's intention is a flight simulator for his burgeoning Buddha mind and body. He reaps the karmic benefit of thinking this way.

Is the intention selfish if it's just for his personal development? It turns out that while it karmically benefits him, practically and by extension it also helps others. People who have trained their minds like this do have enormous impact on other people's lives and, by extension, the world. They are manifesting awakening qualities that shift the dynamic of the interactions with those they meet in increasing numbers and expanding circles, networks, and systems. If a bad apple can spoil the barrel, what can an exceptional apple do? The historical Buddha's awakening and teaching campaign are still having a tsunami-like impact, rippling through the world twenty-five centuries later. Now do you get why I call it radical altruism?

In another email, Lama Zopa wrote something like *for every being who has suffered in this hospital, every being in the hospital suffering right now, and every being who comes into this hospital in the future, may I take on their pain and suffering. May I be the one who takes the pain away. May all beings be free.* He thought this repeatedly, like a prayer for humanity, every hour of each day—an unbroken mantra seeping out of the stiff lips of his sagging, paralyzed face. Think about a mind that has trained to exchange self and other like this, embodying that there is no fixed Lama Zopa, no fixed stroke, no victim there, no sorrow, no sadness. However, the world hasn't disappeared—he recognizes that the suffering of others still exists for them. He chooses to embrace them and foster goodwill with his infectious smile and warm heart. With that mind-set, great delight naturally arises.

Lama Zopa was incredibly kind, grateful, and respectful to all the doctors, nurses, and hospital staff—he honored and appreciated each person for their kindness, mumbling prayers, words of jeweled validation, through his paralyzed mouth. He walked room to room with a cane, attendants on either side of him, meeting the other patients, blessing them, praying for them, and spreading good cheer with his half-sagging smile. The entire hospital, normally a place of hardship, sadness, and fear, was transformed into a circus by the Tibetan monks all praying, chanting, and giggling, with their bald heads, crimson-and-yellow robes, worn beads, lightheartedness, and infectious smiles. At the center of it all was the great Bodhisattva, Lama Zopa, semiparalyzed yet undaunted, a ringmaster of love.

What tangible impact do you think that resonance circuitry had on the recovery of the other patients in the hospital? What tangible impact did it have on the morale of the doctors and staff who endured long hours and faced unending challenges? It motivated them all to do better. It motivated them to recover faster, from their DNA and cells to their psychology and immune system. It made people happy and helped them heal despite their circumstances, and Lama Zopa wasn't even able to speak a single coherent sentence through his paralyzed mouth, yet he conveyed far more from his pure being than you or I might ever do in a single lifetime. His was a magnet that drew everyone into the medicinal resonance of interconnectivity, goodwill, and universal compassion—medicine far more potent than anything being administered in the hospital, and one that is available in each of us, if only we had a model to know that was true.

Maybe in this lifetime we won't all reach the final milestone of the great masters or be capable of exhibiting the totally transformational impact they have. I'm under no delusion that this will happen for me, but it doesn't stop me from pursuing the path with vigor all the same. You see, it's not an all-or-nothing proposition; it's not sudden, full enlightenment or bust. That's the wonderful thing about the gradual approach we're on; we each get to taste some truth, grow a bit more mature, and feel a bit more human with every step. We each have something to learn, to realize, and to manifest for the collective good of the planet. I know you feel it too. Otherwise you wouldn't have made it this far in our odyssey. Some amount of spiritual progress is good enough, a treasure for humanity that no amount of material accumulation, power, or fame could ever compare with. While Lama Zopa and my other heroes might have resounding harmonics of liberation emanating from the Jewel Tree at the center of their hearts, in all modesty we can each say something kind, respectful, and inspiring that can have a kindling effect, igniting others' hearts and minds in the matrix we share.

The Jewel Tree isn't just a visualization or a child's fantasy. The ripple effects are real, because we are mammals, sensitive creatures, and open systems subtly made of energy and connected by resonance. We are evolutionarily designed like tuning forks to have communal impact. If the entire nation can be vicariously traumatized and paralyzed by 9/11 or Hurricane Katrina, it's also possible that a tsunami of love can wash over an entire city, country, or planet. That's what happened when the Buddha awoke under the Bodhi tree, and now Bodhgaya, India, serves as ground zero for a worldwide movement of awakening. Perhaps now is what high periods were like in Tibet when the dharma flourished. Certainly not all were awakened, not by a long shot, but a critical mass was committed to conscious evolution in a gradual process of training the mind. That legacy of awakening trickles down to us today, giving us a direction and renewed hope for our modern societies that have lost their way.

The Dalai Lama insists that if we were to teach children compassion in schools, along with all the other modern arts and sciences, within one generation we could stop wars and bloodshed. With the mind suffused by evolutionary self-care, radical altruism, and quantum view, an army of sacred activists could launch a movement to transform a planet hell-bent on greed-based exploitation and fear-driven nationalism destined for nuclear implosion and environmental matricide. If we prized minimalism, ethics, shared equity, and sustainability as much as we do hedonism, consumerism, competition, and capitalism, then one day every industrial factory pumping out toxic waste could be retrofitted to be a recycling plant to clean up our mess. Every bank profiting from interest at the expense of the working poor and the debt-based economy that enslaves developing nations could be replaced by local cooperative initiatives, the sacred economics proposed by Charles Eisenstein,[6] or the circle economy proposed by Pearce and Turner.[7] If we moved toward vegetarianism, the restorative impacts on the environment and animal welfare alike would be astronomical. Every oil well could easily be replaced by a renewable energy source, and clean energy could be stored and distributed freely in the way we will eventually share everything—horizontally across an integrated internet of things—as envisioned by visionary economist Jeremy Rifkin.[8] There is no need to despair. Creative solutions for our new world in every sector of human activity are already emerging, and Pinchbeck beautifully chronicles them in a recent work.[9] Imagine every rooftop from New York City to Beijing converted into a vertical vegetable garden, harvesting its own power, food, and water, and every basement repurposed as a yoga studio, soup kitchen, or community center for contemplative learning. It's within reach. Because of emptiness and karma, anything is possible, and love heals. From quantum view and sacred activism come awakened manifestation.

The Dawn of Integration

The current climate crisis that threatens the planet is but a symptom of inherently disenfranchising economic and political structures, which are themselves the outer manifestation and amplification of the all-too-human inner root afflictions of greed, hatred, and the delusion of separateness that the Buddha discovered during his awakening. The planet in peril offers us the greatest karmic opportunity in human history to put our individual, national, racial, cultural, and religious differences aside—all merely constructs anyway—and look courageously within and without to collectively address the challenges that threaten us. The days are numbered for industrialism, which has rendered itself nearly obsolete while bringing us closer to extinction. Likewise, the sun is setting on materialism, as a new paradigm based on science reuniting with spirit is emerging. We have entered the dawn of integration.

Spiritual awakening, whether spontaneous or gradual, via the Buddhist, shamanic, or other tradition, is only provisional and incomplete without practical steps toward social transformation. The inner revolution is a necessary precursor to an outer one. The platitude "Change your mind to change the world" is dangerously simplistic. After twenty years of commitment to spiritual development, it's clear I have so much more to learn from those who have evaluated the flaws of our economic, political, and energy systems, and who are at the forefront of proposing new equitable, regenerative, and sustainable alternatives. The age of integration is best epitomized by the historic, cross-cultural, and interdisciplinary dialogues between the Dalai Lama and neuroscientists, the shamans of the Amazon and medical anthropologists, Christian mystics and quantum physicists, and yogis and ecoactivists. Joining together in mutual discussion and shared ceremony, our goal is to bridge the divide between science and spirit, inner and outer, personal and social, left and right brain, masculine and feminine energies.

What will emerge as a result is a more complete map of mind and universe, a more strategic call to action for systems change guided by altruism, and a paradigm shift based on insight into interdependence. It seems to me that this transition won't be centralized and top-down; no single figurehead will lead us. It appears that a new worldwide movement with a common higher purpose to both spiritually awaken and save the planet will actually be composed of multiple but linked and highly specialized grassroots submovements. That means each one of us will have a role to play in our own respective domains while forging strategic connections with others—networking, like neurons in the brain, organs in the body, or sites on the internet—preserving diversity while becoming one. The future is ours to manifest, but time is not on our side.

There have been predictions of the emerging paradigm shift prophesized in ancient history by the elders of the Indian, Tibetan, Hopi, and Mayan cultures, each of which foretold not the end of the world but the end of a dark age and the dawning of a new golden era. Even while the ice caps melt and another dictator unlawfully rises to power, we can see the marginalized masses across the planet beginning to awaken, reclaiming their intrinsic dignity and innate power and rising to assert the collective will of the people. Worldwide, we see growing social unrest, mobilization, and resistance at the local level, with millions of ordinary people opting out of indentured servitude, confronting unjust authority, and reconfiguring inherently disenfranchising systems. From the Occupy movement and Standing Rock in the United States to other grassroots revolutions around the world—the Arab Spring, Mexico's *Zapatista* movement, South Africa's Rhodes Must Fall movement, the anti-austerity movement in Europe, and the *Indignados* movement in Central America—it's clear the uprising is in effect, challenging the current paradigm. But will social activism be conjoined with sacred view? Or will these movements be misguided by equally polarizing and fanatical views rooted in separateness and us-versus-them binary thinking? Can those working on systems change be enticed to explore and embody the inner revolution proposed by the Lam Rim or the equivalent methodology prescribed by other authentic wisdom traditions? Can those sitting on their meditation cushions be mobilized to go beyond the Three Principles of the Path to manifest social redesign?

It's taken but a nanosecond in evolutionary time for man to destroy what took the galaxy, human evolution, and culture countless millennia to develop. The irony is that the spiritless agenda of corporate capitalism, and the materialism and nihilistic worldview that compose its grotesque underbelly, affects the Western world and those who wield its power as much as it does all the colonized and subjugated developing nations. And this internal disease, with its disenfranchising social systems, will engulf us all, for even those who profit most at the expense of others, while hiding in their ivory towers, can't withstand the wrath of climate change and the resistance of the masses. Their billions in profits and their fearmongering won't protect them when the planetary boundaries are breached and the carbon dioxide, global temperature, and sea levels exceed their thresholds, displacing millions of people and sending the entire planet into geopolitical chaos.

Interdependence truly means that we either flourish or perish together. As I learned from Cyrus, you can never objectify somebody—every person is open, so our misguided governments and corporations are likewise not fixed entities but empty labels composed of ordinary people who have been hijacked by delusionary propaganda and are slaves to their evolutionary survival wiring, animalistic impulses, and childhood traumas. They breathe the same air and drink from the same water sources that we do. Their brains are neuroplastic and their minds express Buddha nature. Their children's fates are inextricably linked with those of our children and the children sold into sex slavery in Bangkok and working in the sweatshops in Mumbai's Dharavi slum. Misguided oligarchs, high on their supply of power, are merely strung-out addicts, hungry ghosts who are never far from hitting rock bottom and are primed for a rude awakening—a swift, wrathfully compassionate kick in the ass that can bring them back to their humanity. From a multilife perspective, we cannot banish or kill them but must see them as kin and vow to rehabilitate them. We share but one ship, and the choice is ours: sink our vessel or transform it into the Jewel Tree mandala inspired by sacred view.

Spirit and ecological balance are intimately connected endeavors we must return to. Both are vital for our survival, and each is mutually reinforcing in an age of integration. For the Hopi tribal elder, the Polynesian way-finder, the Peruvian shaman, and the Tibetan mystic, the realms of spirit and nature, the divine and material worlds, have always remained one and the same. It is only Western culture that forged the divide three centuries ago, abandoning spirit to dominate matter. The gamble only paid short-term dividends and has left us exposed. Now our collective fate rests on a revival, on bringing together twins separated at birth during the age of reason: spirituality without dogma, and science with heart. The former focuses on the internal cultivation of sacred view and prosocial qualities such as compassion that recognize our common kinship, the latter on the redesign of external systems, technology, and science sensitive to our humble place within the delicately balanced biosphere. In our near future, shamans and Bodhisattvas, steeped in perennial wisdom, will wield the tools of science and technology along with their feathers, ritual drums, sacred plants, and bells, channeling our collective energies not toward material gains but toward what Rifkin calls "biosphere consciousness."[10] When we realize that our place is not to master dominion over the planet's diverse life-forms, resources, and habitats but to serve as custodians, we will all inevitably come to a deep appreciation for how utterly interdependent we are within the complex web of life. This shift in perspective will allow us to move beyond personal, national, and even racial boundaries to identify with the totality of the planet in a final transpersonal awakening, so that we can relate to all life-forms with the same concern, love, and respect with which we regard our own bodies or children.

A New Paradigm of Wisdom and Compassion

If a new paradigm emerges to supplant the old, it will be because we engage in more sacred activism in the years to come, rising as empathic warriors committed to manifesting radical altruism and quantum view in the trenches of social and global redesign. For this to happen, each of us will have to awaken from our self-centered, hedonic slumber. We'll need to be diligent on and off the cushion, resolving internal and psychological obstacles as contemplative yogis, and working through external and environmental challenges as uncompromising activists. Then, as the lovers of freedom, hope, and shared equity have done at Standing Rock, we will stand bare-handed, openhearted, and united against corporations, governments, and militaries that live only for profit and represent the last effort of our current paradigm on life support. That's how Gandhi, King, and Mandela helped manifest their respective country's freedom movements against all odds. That's what Campbell's epic hero's journey and Atisha's Lam Rim are meant to offer us, beckoning our nascent heroes and heroines to return to the world with life-giving elixir. But we can't wait for a select few to rise and lead us; we'll each be called upon to play a role in the paradigm shift and rebuilding effort. Every vote we cast and every choice we make will count toward this aim. Every dollar we spend will be channeled purposefully. Every moment of collective consciousness we tap will be our weapons of mass destruction. We will dismantle the Berlin Wall of separation we erected, brick by brick. It takes only a flicker of the light of wisdom to dispel the vast darkness of ignorance.

Our manifesting mission is a *White Op*, a term based on the military *black op*, or black operation, a clandestine plot usually involving highly trained government spies or mercenaries who infiltrate an adversary's position, behind enemy lines and unbeknownst to them. *White Op*, coined by my best friend Bunny, stands for what I see needing to happen on the planet: a group of well-intentioned, highly trained Bodhisattva warriors (appearing like ordinary folk), armed with the six paramitas and restrained by ethical vows, begin to infiltrate their relationships, social institutions, and industries across all sectors of society and culture. Ordinary Bodhisattvas infusing the world with sacred view and transforming one mind at a time from the inside out until a new paradigm based on wisdom and compassion has totally replaced materialism and nihilism. The White Op is in large part how I envision the work and intention of my colleagues and me at the Nalanda Institute for Contemplative Science; we aspire to fulfill it by offering a Buddhist-inspired contemplative psychotherapy training program, infused with the latest neuroscience, to therapists, health-care workers, educators, and savvy business leaders.

The Buddha didn't proselytize, and his mission was not to convert the masses. He set up an educational system that taught the inner science and meditative technologies that make his personal transformation both accessible and reproducible, drawing people from across Eurasia like a magnet. Over the centuries, some of his most devout students were kings, such as Ashoka, and high members of society, while others were warriors and members of the working class. Together, over time, they transformed the Indo-Gangetic Plains of North India into an epicenter for contemplative learning featuring the world's first public universities: Nalanda, Odantapuri, and Vikramashila. Centuries later, with this awakening legacy and curriculum migrating east and north, a similar paradigm shift occurred in Tibet, leading to the near-complete demilitarization of the region and the widespread institutionalization of a vast network of monastic universities that preserved the treasury of Buddhist knowledge like a time capsule, until the Chinese invasion in 1950.

Today the Kingdom of Bhutan, a mandala nestled between industrial giants India and China, serves as one of the latest bastions of the Buddha's great legacy of contemplative living and learning. Bhutan is a tiny but noteworthy model for the rest of the world. It's a modern society where a spiritual worldview and values permeate culture, coexisting alongside modern disciplines of science, technology, and commerce, and where individual well-being, social harmony, gross national happiness, and ecosustainability are prioritized. No society is perfect, and utopia is but an ideal to strive for, but Bhutan is a real-world example of an attempt to manifest an enlightened society based on an ancient educational movement. If considered without its theocratic rule, Bhutan could serve as a prototype, or at least inspiration, for future societies looking to integrate science and spirit in the new world.

A New Beginning

My hope is that I have shared the depth of the vast tradition of Buddha's awakening that has been preserved and hidden for centuries in Tibet's land of snow. I hope that by translating it through the modern idiom of neuroscience and psychotherapy it can be relevant and accessible to you. I selected and presented our road map of thirty themes for you to follow, calling out Tsongkhapa's three main principles of evolutionary self-care, radical altruism, and quantum view to serve as developmental milestones that help plot your progress of becoming fully human. In the audio recordings associated with this book,[11] I offer a compilation of guided meditations to lead you through the practices to help embody your experience. And in this training manual, I shared my four-point MAPS—Maturity, Acceptance, Possibility, Seeding—which synthesizes refuge, karma, emptiness, and virtue in order to help you integrate and manifest the most liberating insights and skills in your everyday life. May this serve as a manifesto for gradual awakening and a curriculum for future sacred activism.

With all this, I pray that we each repeatedly reacquaint ourselves with our fundamental natures—#awakenwisdomlove—so that we can all aspire to benefit others and collectively rescue this planet before it's too late. To do this will require systematic study, reflection, practice, and application, with us seeking refuge at the Jewel Tree within us to transform our hearts and minds, and then venturing out to transform societies and manifest a sacred mandala, a pristine planet. Our spiritual and ecological goals can be simultaneously realized with the leap toward biosphere consciousness, with each of us collectively experiencing the entire world as an expanded sense of self and relating to life's diversity with presence-love. One day we will feel the great winds and sky in all directions as our own breath; the streams, rivers, and oceans as our own veins, arteries, and blood; the natural habitats and continents as our own organs and body; and all sentient creatures and beings as our very own limbs. We will recognize the world is within us, and we are the world. With this recognition, having turned our hearts inside out, we will naturally work for the benefit of others and the planet as much as we once did our limited ego, before this transpersonal shift had occurred.

So even as we near the tail of this book, please don't think you're finished. This is not the end but a new beginning. Treat this book the way you do your grandmother's favorite cookbook, keeping its worn pages within arm's reach of the kitchen countertop—in our case, your altar—and returning to it repeatedly to revisit the "recipe" needed to advance in the phase of development most pressing and relevant to you. Return to it repeatedly, like counting prayers on a string of weathered beads or *mala* (like the one on this book's cover), slowly and steadily purifying your mind, one Lam Rim step at a time.

Don't worry about reaching enlightenment. Know that it's always here and possible, as great masters confirm this, but instead, focus on the next incremental step ahead of you, and awaken gradually. If you make it to the final breakthrough and its integration, that's most auspicious; if you don't, you still will have taken full advantage of your precious human life, becoming a more mature, aware, insightful, and loving human being, and, as a result, having brought a little more light into the world. In short, even making one small incremental Lam Rim step for yourself is a giant leap for human evolution. Guided by your Bodhisattva vow, armed with refuge, emptiness, karma, and ethics, we'll cast our sights on the outer world we collectively cocreate and usher in a new paradigm based not on nihilism and the quiet desperation of modernity but on quantum interconnectivity and universal compassion. Always remember, there is only the mountain.

As we stand at the crossroads of evolution and extinction, there has never been a more monumental or critical opportunity as there is now. No greater a purpose, no pursuit more meaningful, no mission more pressing than that of our collective awakening achieved when each of us embarks on the Gradual Path of becoming fully human. With my deepest, most sincere plea, let's continue in earnest. Together, let's dedicate:

> By virtue of this practice and all my efforts,
> May I quickly become a mentor-archetype,
> And lead all beings without exception
> To the exalted state of full enlightenment!

STEP 30   **Retracing Your Steps**

30 Manifestation (using MAPS):
   i **M**aturity
   ii **A**cceptance
   iii **P**ossibility
   iv **S**eeding

ACKNOWLEDGMENTS

This book, like all human endeavors, co-arises from a tapestry of inter-woven threads, the living expression of love and devotion of countless beings. In short, this is not my book; I cannot claim its inspiration, message, or production as my own. It belongs to all the teachers who came before me, all the seekers who come after me, and all my fellow travelers who walk with me on the hero's path. I silently bow in all directions, for to thank each one for their kindness becomes an impossibility.

I'm especially grateful to a select few, foremost my wife and spiritual partner, Emily Jane Wolf, the heroine who makes everything I do possible. Emily, you will always be my first thought, love, and inspiration. To our sons Bodhi and Pema, my youngest teachers, thank you both for choosing to come my way. My life's mission was clarified with your births, and I will do whatever I can to leave you and your peers a better planet than the one I inherited. May this book inspire you to one day seek out Tibetan masters, serve them well, preserve their lineage, and further their legacy as heroic custodians of a brave new world.

I endlessly bow my head to the lotus feet of all my heroes, the life-bestowing teachings they impart, and the wish-fulfilling Jewel Tree lineage they represent. To the late Acharya Godwin Samararatne, embodiment of mindfulness and loving-kindness, for helping me to trust human intimacy again and for teaching me how profound wisdom can be brought down to earth, I reverently bow. To His Holiness the Fourteenth Dalai Lama, thousand-armed Chenrezig, embodiment of radical altruism, beacon of world peace—for all you accomplish with your endless and universal compassion, I bow with pure devotion. Please remain, always. To Professor Robert Thurman, the Thurmanator, the wild, buffalo-headed Yamantaka himself, the Death Slayer, one-eyed embodiment of wrathful wisdom, for the Lam Rim bliss bombs you dropped in *The Jewel Tree of Tibet*, including your translation of the Mentor Devotion that stole my heart and captured my imagination, I bow and vow to continue your challenge of materialism. To Lama Zopa Rinpoche, embodiment of quantum view, you epitomize Tsongkhapa's Foundation of All Good Qualities, and your space-like equipoise intuition on the nature of reality leaves little doubt that enlightenment exists. Thank you for offering me refuge, the Bodhisattva vows, and an extensive transmission of the Lam Rim at Kopan Monastery. I bow in awe; please bless me. To Geshe Tenzin Zopa, gifted protégée of the great Kopan Bodhisattvas, embodiment of evolutionary self-care, your immaculate guru devotion brings tears of joy. Thank you for reaffirming my refuge and Bodhisattva vows at Bodhgaya, for the oral transmission of the Three Principles of the Path on Vulture Peak, and for your endless rain of blessings. I bow and vow to serve you lifelong; please stay close. To the late, great Gelek Rinpoche, last of the old guard born in Tibet, embodiment of Vajrayogini's infectious bliss, exemplar of the hero's impeccable conduct, your legacy is without blemish. Thank you for revealing the secrets of the diamond way and for bestowing profound Lam Rim oral transmissions and commentaries, including Shantideva's A Guide to the Bodhisattva Way of Life, Pabongka's *Liberation in the Palm of Your Hand*, and your seminal *Odyssey to Freedom* that inspired this book. In reverence I endlessly bow, prostrate myself, and make offerings. And foremost among them all is my peerless mentor, Dr. Joseph Loizzo, embodiment of Nagarjuna's precision and eloquence, renaissance man, juggernaut of sciences East and West. Though I'm not cut from as fine a cloth, nor will I ever wear a black beret as well as you do, with you as my role model, I've actualized a life beyond my wildest dreams. For the artful translation of Tsongkhapa's text and the prayers shared in this book, and for offering us all a contemporary version of the Lam Rim in *Sustainable Happiness* that will last centuries, I bow in endless gratitude.

Beyond my teachers, thanks to a small band of dharma bums: Bunny Batliwala, Michael Sheehy, Dan Hirschberg, and, recently, Ethan Nichtern and Marco Mascarin. I could not wish for better companions to walk with on the path. While completing prostrations at Bodhgaya, I had a vision that Bunny and I had been spiritual brothers in prior lifetimes, forging our bond and commitment to pursue awakening in the sweat and tears of purification. May we all continue to meet each other in future lives until our Bodhisattva vows have been fulfilled.

I am grateful to all my students, particularly those who completed my iteration of Nalanda's Four-Year Program in Sustainable Happiness in 2016. Our Lam Rim sojourn was one of the most enriching experiences of my life. Over those epic forty-nine classes and eight retreats we shared, it was in the crucible of your love that I came of age. To those who then joined me on our once-in-a-lifetime hero's pilgrimage to North India, our connection was sealed for eternity during that group embrace at Sarnath, while receiving the Bodhisattva vows under the Bodhi tree, and on Vulture Peak after the oral transmission of the Heart Sutra by Geshe Tenzin Zopa. These memories typify the Three Principles of the Path: renunciation, Bodhicitta, and correct view of emptiness. I will never forget you, Johanna, Antonia, Michael, Stew, Peter, Patrice, Walter, Andi, Myckie, Stamatia, Mark, Virginia, Carrie, Ivy, Bunny, and Kanchi. This book is the tsunami of merits we created together; may they ripple out and fulfill our White Op.

Thanks to those who participated in the process of this book, itself a gradual unfoldment, from its genesis in 2010 to its fruition some eight years later. Thank you to Kaitlin Lennon, Neil Roberts, Angela Russo, and Jenna Fillia Canty for editing the transcriptions of my original Lam Rim lectures. Without their early insistence and dedication, this book would have never been born. The attention and beauty that Tiffany Chandler and Virginia Crawford applied to the transcript have left a sweet perfume on its pages. At that point, the book was still being conceived of as a self-published ebook. If it were not for the highly skilled and deeply committed editor Alice Peck, whose vision for the book exceeded my own, it would have never been rewritten and sent to Sounds True for consideration. Alice pushed me beyond my own limiting beliefs, and her wordsmithing is what has brought this dream to life. She was the potter; I was the clay. Along the way, Alice and I transformed the writing process into a purification practice— a modern-day version of prostrations. Each editing session began by evoking Tsongkhapa and concluded with a dedication of merit. Alice's name should be placed right alongside mine on the front cover, but she's too humble.

Thanks to my agent, Linda Loewenthal, for her diamond-sharp intuition and skill in putting this deal together, and to Tami Simon and the whole team at Sounds True, all Bodhisattvas who live to help authors share their wisdom with the world—I rejoice in their merits. I'm especially grateful to Jennifer Y. Brown for believing in me over the years and for allowing me to share my unconventional truth without compromise. Thanks to Duane Stapp for his illustrations, Cory Richards for sharing his photographs, and Tashi Mannox for his calligraphy seal.

A final word of appreciation for the beautiful nuns of Khachoe Ghakyil Ling Nunnery in Nepal, to whom the earnings and merit of this book are dedicated. Their commitment to pursuing the Gradual Path to Enlightenment against all odds is beyond inspiring. When I struggled during the writing process, I thought of them—a reflection that keenly put life's priorities into perspective and provided a source of perseverance. We have so much to learn about mature spiritual practice in the West, and the Kopan nuns and the Tibetans in exile offer a glimpse of the grace and grit it takes to evolve and become fully human. Nothing we can offer them will ever reciprocate what they give us with their contagious joy, devotion, and courage. A quote on the donation page of the Kopan Nunnery website sums it up best: there is nothing higher than the joy of "making enlightenment possible for others."

Om Ah Hum.

ROAD MAP, TEXT, AND PRAYERS

Lam Rim Thirty-Step Road Map

1 Create a sacred space.

2 Set up an altar and make offerings.

3 Prepare your body and mind.

4 Evoke the mentor and the Jewel Tree refuge field.

5 Initiate the Seven-Step Mentor-Bonding Process:
   - i Admire qualities
   - ii Make offerings
   - iii Disclose negativities
   - iv Rejoice virtues
   - v Request guidance
   - vi Request presence
   - vii Dedicate merits

6 Offer the mandala and final prayers.

7 Find a mentor.

8 Become a suitable student.

9 Preciousness of human life inspires appreciation.

10 Death inspires urgency.

11 Refuge offers evolutionary safe-direction.

12 Causality inspires agency.

13 Defects of samsara inspire distaste in compulsive existence.

14 Renunciation (aspiration to be free)—the milestone of evolutionary self-care.

15 Equanimity balances social reactivity.

16 Recognize all beings as kin—inspires solidarity.

17 Remember their kindness—inspires gratitude.

18 Resolve to repay their kindness—inspires reciprocity.

19 Equalize self and other—inspires empathy.

20 Contemplate disadvantages of self-preoccupation and take on suffering—inspires compassion.

21 Contemplate the benefits of altruism and give care— inspires love.

22 Take responsibility and aspire to save all beings— inspires purpose.

23 Bodhicitta (aspiration to free others)—the milestone of radical altruism.

24 Perfect generosity.

25 Perfect virtue.

26 Perfect patience.

27 Perfect effort.

28 Perfect concentration.

29 Perfect wisdom—the milestone of quantum view.

30 Manifestation (using MAPS):
    i **M**aturity
    ii **A**cceptance
    iii **P**ossibility
    iv **S**eeding

Text

Three Principles of the Path

lam gyi gtso bo rnam pa gsum

by Lama Je Tsongkhapa
translated by Joseph Loizzo

Homage to all Spiritual Mentors!

[In this brief text] I'll explain as best I can   1
The quintessence of all Buddha's teachings—
The path revealed by his noble heirs,
As the crossing for fortunate freedom seekers.

Listen with open minds you lucky people   2
Who break the addiction to worldly pleasures,
And work to give leisure and opportunity meaning,
Trusting the path that satisfies Buddhas.

The drive to survive binds all embodied beings,   3
And no cure can stem the pleasure seeking
Tides of mere survival but real transcendence,
So first of all work to renounce [mindless pleasure]!

Leisure and opportunity are hard to find,   4
And a lifespan leaves no time to waste—reflect on this
And you'll counter the obsessions of a worldly life.
Compulsive action and reaction inexorably cause
Future cycles of pain—repeatedly contemplate this
And you'll counter obsession with an afterlife.

With practice, your mind won't entertain   5
Even passing fantasies of mundane wealth or fame,

But will aim for freedom day and night—
Then you've developed transcendence!

Since transcendence without altruistic resolve   6
Can't yield the collective happiness
Of [a Buddha's] full enlightenment,
The wise conceive the spirit of altruism.

Swept away by the torrents of birth, illness,   7
     aging, and death,
Tightly bound by the chains of relentless compulsion,
Imprisoned in the iron cage of self-protectiveness,
All caught up in the blinding shroud of delusion,

Endlessly living and reliving the cycle of trauma,   8
Constantly suffering in body, speech, and mind,
Such is the state of beings, all dear as mothers—
So, from your natural response build heroic resolve!

Even though you practice renunciation   9
And cultivate altruistic resolve,
Without the wisdom to realize reality,
You can't cut the root of traumatic life—
So, work at the art of seeing relativity.

Who sees the inexorable causation of everything   10
Whatsoever—mundane and transcendent—
And shreds any hint of reification,
So, enters the path that satisfies Buddhas.

Appearance is invariably relative   11
And emptiness is devoid of conviction—
So long as these two insights dawn separately,
You've not yet realized the Buddha's intent.

But when they appear simultaneously,   12
    without alternation,
From the slightest unbiased insight of relativity
Corrective knowledge breaks the reifying habit,
And your search for genuine insight is complete.

From then on, all appearance dispels absolutism,   13
And each emptiness eliminates nihilism—
Seeing how emptiness dawns as causation,
You're no longer blinded by biased views.

So once you realize the vital points   14
Of these three principles of the path,
Resort to solitude and persistent effort—
You'll quickly reach the timeless goal, child!

Prayers*

Taking Refuge in Altruistic Resolve

From now until enlightenment, I take refuge
In the Buddha, his Teaching, and Community—
By virtue of practicing [transcendences] like generosity,
May I reach enlightenment to benefit all!

(Repeat three times.)

Four Boundless Emotions

May all beings have happiness and its causes.
May all beings be free from suffering and its causes.

May all beings know pure joy untouched by suffering.
May all beings live in peace untroubled by anger or clinging.

Seven-Step Practice

I honor you, Buddha, in body, speech, and mind.
I offer you all that is dear to me, real and imagined.
I regret all faults I've acquired in this life and throughout
    evolution.
Gratefully I enjoy the virtues of all beings, mundane and
    transcendent.
Buddha, please shower me with your guidance and blessings,
And please stay in my heart until I break the cycle of trauma.
By virtue of this may I reach enlightenment to benefit all!

Paradise Offering

This gemlike earth filled with sweet smells and wildflowers,
Adorned with mountains and continents, sun, moon, and stars,
I envision as Buddha's paradise and offer you—
So all beings may inhabit so perfect a world.
Mentors, please accept this precious environment!

Dedication

By virtue of this practice and all my efforts,
May I quickly become a mentor-archetype,
And lead all beings without exception
To the exalted state of full enlightenment!

May the supreme spirit of altruistic resolve
Be conceived wherever it has not yet spread,

And may that spirit already conceived not decline
But continue to flourish and spread ever more.

Although I and all beings are objectively empty,
By virtue of all the positivity I have acquired
Together with all enlightened beings through all time,
May I reach the state of perfect enlightenment,
And lead all beings, who are all equally empty,
As quickly as possible to that supreme state!

*Translations by Joseph Loizzo

NOTES

For ease of reading, Sanskrit words have been rendered without diacritics.

1 INITIATION — EMBARKING ON THE GRADUAL PATH

1   John Welwood, *Awakening the Heart: East/West Approaches to Psychotherapy and the Healing Relationship* (Boston, MA: Shambhala, 1985), 3.

2   Robert Thurman, *Inner Revolution: Life, Liberty, and the Pursuit of Real Happiness* (New York: Riverhead Books, 1998).

2 PREPARATION — READYING SPACE, BODY, AND MIND FOR THE JOURNEY

1   Robert Thurman, *The Jewel Tree of Tibet: The Enlightenment Engine of Tibetan Buddhism* (New York: Atria Books, 2006), 3–4.

2   Traditionally there are two sets of Preliminaries; six constitute the *Ordinary* Preliminaries, and another set of four composes the *Extraordinary* Preliminaries, known as *ngondro* in Tibetan. The former set leads to the latter set in training, or it can be stand-alone as presented here, whereas the latter set readies the practitioner to benefit safely from the esoteric system of the Tantras—advanced deity practices with subtle body-energy work. All of this is to say that the Preliminaries I'll present are a safe and effective way for beginners who are new to meditation, as well as practitioners seasoned in other traditions, to learn a complete visualization system with the option of going further into the most advanced, mind-blowing practices Tibet offers.

3   The Chinese philosophical system of harmonizing the environment.

4   Stephen M. Kosslyn, Giorgio Ganis, and William L. Thompson, "Neural Foundations of Imagery," *Nature Reviews Neuroscience* 2, no. 9 (September 2001): 635–42.

5   Joseph Campbell and Bill Moyers, *The Power of Myth* (New York: Anchor Books, 1991), 115.

3 VISUALIZATION — TRAINING IN THE FLIGHT SIMULATOR OF INSPIRATION

1 "First Law of Thermodynamics," Glenn Research Center, National Aeronautics and Space Administration, updated May 5, 2015, grc.nasa. gov/www/k-12/airplane/thermo1.html.

2 Joseph Campbell, *A Joseph Campbell Companion: Reflections on the Art of Living*, sel. and ed. Diane K. Osbon (New York: HarperCollins, 1995), 8, 18.

3 Evan Thompson, *Waking, Dreaming, Being: Self and Consciousness in Neuroscience, Meditation, and Philosophy* (New York: Columbia University Press, 2017).

4 Matthieu Ricard and Trinh Xuan Thuan, *The Quantum and the Lotus: A Journey to the Frontiers Where Science and Buddhism Meet* (New York: Three Rivers Press, 2004).

5 Daniel J. Siegel and Tina Payne Bryson, *The Whole-Brain Child: 12 Revolutionary Strategies to Nurture Your Child's Developing Mind* (New York: Bantam Books, 2012), 27.

6 Thich Nhat Hanh, "The Universe is a Single Flower," TNHAUDIO, February 18, 2011, tnhaudio.org/2011/02/18/ the-universe-is-a-single-flower.

7 Daniel J. Siegel, *The Developing Mind: How Relationships and the Brain Interact to Shape Who We Are*, 2nd ed. (New York: Guilford Press, 2012).

8 Pabongka Rinpoche, *Liberation in the Palm of Your Hand: A Concise Discourse on the Path to Enlightenment*, 2nd ed., trans. Michael Richards (Somerville, MA: Wisdom Publications, 2006).

9 Aryashura, Ashvaghosha, and Geshe Ngawang Dhargyey, *Fifty Stanzas on the Spiritual Teacher*, 2nd ed. (Dharamsala, HP: Library of Tibetan Works and Archives, 2001).

4 RENUNCIATION — REACHING THE MILESTONE OF EVOLUTIONARY SELF-CARE

1 Alexander Berzin, "Refuge: A Safe and Meaningful Direction in Life," Study Buddhism, August 2010, studybuddhism.com/en/ tibetan-buddhism/about-buddhism/buddha-s-basic-message/ refuge-a-safe-and-meaningful-direction-in-life.

2 Joseph Loizzo, "Buddhist Perspectives on Psychiatric Ethics," in *The Oxford Handbook of Psychiatric Ethics*, vol. 1, eds. John Z. Sadler, Bill Fulford, and Cornelius Werendly van Staden (Oxford: Oxford University Press, 2015).

3   Traditionally described as one of the Six Realms of Existence one is reborn in, or as a pervasive psychological state: god realm (narcissistic), demigod (envious), human (dissatisfied), animal (anxious), hungry ghost (addicted), and hell (traumatized).

4   The Four Opponent Powers are (1) the power of refuge that counteracts the karmic object, (2) the power of remorse that counteracts the karmic intention, (3) the power of the remedy that counteracts the karmic action, and (4) the power of resolve that counteracts the karmic completion.

5   Adapted from Joseph Loizzo, *Sustainable Happiness: The Mind Science of Well-Being, Altruism, and Inspiration* (New York: Routledge, 2012), 115–16.

5 COMPASSION — ACTUALIZING THE MILESTONE OF RADICAL ALTRUISM

1   Siegel, *The Developing Mind*.

2   John F. Kennedy, "Commencement Address at American University, June 10, 1963," John F. Kennedy Presidential Library and Museum, accessed January 13, 2018, jfklibrary.org/Asset-Viewer/BWC7I4C9QUmLG9J6I8oy8w.aspx.

3   Alison Luterman, "What We Came For," *The Sun*, October 1996, thesunmagazine.org/issues/250/what-we-came-for.

4   Joseph Loizzo, *Sustainable Happiness*, 162–63.

5   Jeremy Rifkin, *The Empathic Civilization: The Race to Global Consciousness in a World in Crisis* (New York: J. P. Tarcher, 2009).

6   Richard J. Davidson and Anne Harrington, eds., *Visions of Compassion: Western Scientists and Tibetan Buddhists Examine Human Nature* (Oxford: Oxford University Press, 2002).

7   Richard J. Davidson, "The Neurobiology of Compassion," in *Wisdom and Compassion in Psychotherapy: Deepening Mindfulness in Clinical Practice*, eds. Christopher K. Germer and Ronald D. Siegel (New York: Guilford Press, 2012), 111–18.

8   Matthieu Ricard, *Altruism: The Power of Compassion to Change Yourself and the World* (New York: Back Bay Books, 2016).

6 ACTION — EMBODYING THE HERO'S CODE OF IMPECCABLE CONDUCT

1   John Welwood, *Toward a Psychology of Awakening: Buddhism, Psychotherapy, and the Path of Personal and Spiritual Transformation* (Boston, MA: Shambhala, 2002), 11.

2   Scott Carney, *The Enlightenment Trap: Obsession, Madness and Death on Diamond Mountain* (Denver, CO: Foxtopus Ink, 2015).

3   Nina Burleigh, "Sex and Death on the Road to Nirvana," *Rolling Stone*, June 6, 2013, rollingstone.com/culture/news/sex-and-death-on-the-road-to-nirvana-20130606.

4   "Dalai Lama's Office Disapproves of Geshe Michael Roach," Michael Roach Files, May 28, 2009, michaelroachfiles.wordpress.com/2009/05/28/dalai-lamas-office-denounces-geshe-michael-roach.

5   Fernanda Santos, "Mysterious Buddhist Retreat in the Desert Ends in a Grisly Death," *New York Times*, June 5, 2012, nytimes.com/2012/06/06/us/mysterious-yoga-retreat-ends-in-a-grisly-death.html.

6   Lama Tsongkhapa, *The Foundation of All Good Qualities* (Portland, OR: Foundation for the Preservation of the Mahayana Tradition, 2008), fpmt.org/wp-content/uploads/teachings/foundation_of_all_good_qualities_bklta4.pdf.

7   Radboud University Nijmegen Medical Centre, "Research on 'Iceman' Wim Hof Suggests It May Be Possible to Influence Autonomic Nervous System and Immune Response," ScienceDaily, April 22, 2011, sciencedaily.com/releases/2011/04/110422090203.htm.

7 VISION — REALIZING THE MILESTONE OF QUANTUM VIEW

1   C. W. Huntington and Geshe Namgyal Wangchen, *The Emptiness of Emptiness: An Introduction to Early Indian Madhyamika* (Honolulu: University of Hawaii Press, 1995), 3.

8 MANIFESTATION — MASTERING THE CREATIVE ART OF LIFE REDESIGN

1   Robert Thurman, *The Central Philosophy of Tibet: A Study and Translation of Jey Tsong Khapa's "Essence of True Eloquence"* (Princeton, NJ: Princeton University Press, 1991), 168.

2   Donald S. Lopez Jr., "First There Is a Mountain (Then There Is No Mountain)," *Tricycle*, Fall 2008, tricycle.org/magazine/first-there-mountain-then-there-no-mountain.

3   Thurman, *The Central Philosophy of Tibet*, 169.

4   Thurman, *The Central Philosophy of Tibet*, 169.

5   Śāntideva, "Fully Adopting Bodhicitta" in *Bodhicaryāvatāra: An Introduction to the Bodhisattva's Way of Life*, trans. Adam Pearcey, Lotsawa House, 2007, lotsawahouse.org/indian-masters/shantideva/bodhicharyavatara-3.

6   Charles Eisenstein, *Sacred Economics: Money, Gift, and Society in the Age of Transition* (Berkeley, CA: North Atlantic Books, 2011).

7   David W. Pearce and R. Kerry Turner, *Economics of Natural Resources and the Environment* (Baltimore: Johns Hopkins University Press, 1989).

8   Jeremy Rifkin, *The Third Industrial Revolution: How Lateral Power Is Transforming Energy, the Economy, and the World* (New York: St. Martin's Griffin, 2013).

9   Daniel Pinchbeck, *How Soon Is Now? From Personal Initiation to Global Transformation* (London: Watkins, 2017).

10 Rifkin, *The Third Industrial Revolution*, 242.

11 Miles Neale, *The Gradual Path: Tibetan Buddhist Meditations for Becoming Fully Human* (Boulder, CO: Sounds True, 2018), audio.

BIBLIOGRAPHY

Aryashura, Ashvaghosha, and Geshe Ngawang Dhargyey. *Fifty Stanzas on the Spiritual Teacher*. 2nd ed. Dharamsala, HP: Library of Tibetan Works and Archives, 2001.

Berzin, Alexander. "Refuge: A Safe and Meaningful Direction in Life." Study Buddhism. August 2010. studybuddhism.com/en/tibetan-buddhism/about-buddhism/buddha-s-basic-message/refuge-a-safe-and-meaningful-direction-in-life.

Bryant, Edwin F. *The Yoga Sūtras of Patañjali: A New Edition, Translation and Commentary with Insights from the Traditional Commentators*. New York: North Point Press, 2009.

Byrne, Rhonda. *The Secret*. New York: Simon & Schuster, 2006.

Campbell, Joseph. *The Hero with a Thousand Faces*. 3rd ed. The Collected Works of Joseph Campbell. New York: New World Library, 2008.

Campbell, Joseph. *A Joseph Campbell Companion: Reflections on the Art of Living*. Selected and edited by Diane K. Osbon. New York: HarperCollins, 1995.

Campbell, Joseph, and Bill Moyers. *The Power of Myth*. New York: Anchor Books, 1991.

Dalai Lama. *Kindness, Clarity, and Insight*. Translated and edited by Jeffrey Hopkins. Ithaca, NY: Snow Lion, 2006.

Dalai Lama. *Stages of Meditation*. Translated by Geshe Lobsang Jordhen, Losang Choephel Ganchenpa, and Jeremy Russell. Ithaca, NY: Snow Lion, 2003.

"Dalai Lama's Office Disapproves of Geshe Michael Roach." Michael Roach Files. May 28, 2009. michaelroachfiles.wordpress.com/2009/05/28/dalai-lamas-office-denounces-geshe-michael-roach.

Dass, Ram. *Be Here Now*. San Cristobal, NM: Lama Foundation, 1971.

Davidson, Richard J. "The Neurobiology of Compassion." In *Wisdom and Compassion in Psychotherapy: Deepening Mindfulness in Clinical Practice*. Edited by Christopher K. Germer and Ronald D. Siegel. New York: Guilford Press, 2012.

Davidson, Richard J., and Anne Harrington, eds. *Visions of Compassion: Western Scientists and Tibetan Buddhists Examine Human Nature*. Oxford: Oxford University Press, 2002.

Dharmaraksita, Atīśa, and Geshe Ngawang Dhargyey. *The Wheel of Sharp Weapons: A Mahayana Training of the Mind: In Tibetan, "Theg-pa-chen-pohi-blo-sbyong mtson-cha-hkhor-lo."* Dharamsala, HP: Library of Tibetan Works and Archives, 1994.

Eisenstein, Charles. *Sacred Economics: Money, Gift, and Society in the Age of Transition.* Berkeley, CA: North Atlantic Books, 2011.

Gelek Rimpoche. *Odyssey to Freedom in Sixty-Four Steps.* Ann Arbor: Jewel Heart, 1998.

Germer, Christopher K., and Ronald D. Siegel, eds. *Wisdom and Compassion in Psychotherapy: Deepening Mindfulness in Clinical Practice.* New York: Guilford Press, 2014.

Geshe Sonam Rinchen. *Atisha's Lamp for the Path to Enlightenment: An Oral Teaching by Geshe Sonam Rinchen.* Translated and edited by Ruth Sonam. Ithaca, NY: Snow Lion, 1997.

Hanh, Thich Nhat. "The Universe is a Single Flower." TNHAUDIO. February 18, 2011. tnhaudio.org/2011/02/18/the-universe-is-a-single-flower.

Hanson, Rick. *Hardwiring Happiness: The New Brain Science of Contentment, Calm, and Confidence.* New York: Harmony Books, 2016.

Huntington, C. W., and Geshe Namgyal Wangchen. *The Emptiness of Emptiness: An Introduction to Early Indian Madhyamika.* Honolulu: University of Hawaii Press, 1995.

Kabat-Zinn, Jon. *Full Catastrophe Living: Using the Wisdom of Your Body and Mind to Face Stress, Pain, and Illness.* New York: Bantam Books, 2013.

Kabat-Zinn, Jon. *Wherever You Go, There You Are: Mindfulness Meditation in Everyday Life.* New York: Hyperion, 2005.

Kennedy, John F. "Commencement Address at American University, June 10, 1963." John F. Kennedy Presidential Library and Museum. Accessed January 13, 2018. jfklibrary.org/Asset-Viewer/BWC7I4C9QUmLG9J6I8oy8w.aspx.

King, Martin Luther, Jr. "17 May 1957: 'Give Us the Ballot,' Address at the Prayer Pilgrimage for Freedom, Washington DC." Martin Luther King, Jr. and the Global Freedom Struggle. King Encyclopedia. Accessed January 13, 2018. kingencyclopedia.stanford.edu/encyclopedia/documentsentry/doc_give_us_the_ballot_address_at_the_prayer_pilgrimage_for_freedom.

King, Martin Luther, Jr. "Loving Your Enemies, Sermon Delivered at the Detroit Council of Churches' Noon Lenten Services." The Martin Luther King, Jr. Research and Education Institute at Stanford. Accessed January 13, 2018. kinginstitute.stanford.edu/king-papers/documents/loving-your-enemies-sermon-delivered-detroit-council-churches-noon-lenten.

Kosslyn, Stephen M., Giorgio Ganis, and William L. Thompson. "Neural Foundations of Imagery." *Nature Reviews Neuroscience* 2, no. 9 (September 2001): 635–42. DOI: 10.1038/35090055.

Lama Tsongkhapa. *The Foundation of All Good Qualities.* Portland, OR: Foundation for the Preservation of the Mahayana Tradition, 2008. fpmt.org/wp-content/uploads/teachings/foundation_of_all_good_qualities_bklta4.pdf.

Loizzo, Joseph. "Buddhist Perspectives on Psychiatric Ethics." *The Oxford Handbook of Psychiatric Ethics.* Volume 1. Edited by John Z. Sadler, Bill Fulford, and Cornelius Werendly van Staden. Oxford: Oxford University Press, 2015. DOI: 10.1093/oxfordhb/9780198732365.013.47.

Loizzo, Joseph. "Personal Agency across Generations: Evolutionary Psychology or Religious Belief?" *Sophia* 50, no. 3 (September 2011): 429–52. DOI: 10.1007/s11841-011-0231-y.

Loizzo, Joseph. "Personal Agency across Generations: Translating the Evolutionary Psychology of Karma." In *In Vimalakīrti's House: A Festschrift in Honor of Robert A. F. Thurman on the Occasion of his 70th Birthday.* Edited by Christian K. Wedemeyer, John D. Dunne, and Thomas F. Yarnall. New York: American Institute of Buddhist Studies, 2015.

Loizzo, Joseph. *Sustainable Happiness: The Mind Science of Well-Being, Altruism, and Inspiration.* New York: Routledge, 2012.

Lopez, Donald S., Jr. "First There Is a Mountain (Then There Is No Mountain)." *Tricycle.* Fall 2008. tricycle.org/magazine/first-there-mountain-then-there-no-mountain.

Luterman, Alison. "What We Came For." *The Sun.* October 1996. thesunmagazine.org/issues/250/what-we-came-for.

Nāgārjuna. *The Fundamental Wisdom of the Middle Way: Nāgārjuna's Mulamadhyamakakārikā.* Translated by Jay L. Garfield. New York: Oxford University Press, 1995.

National Aeronautics and Space Administration. "First Law of Thermodynamics." Glenn Research Center. Updated May 5, 2015. grc.nasa.gov/www/k-12/airplane/thermo1.html.

Neale, Miles. *The Gradual Path: Tibetan Buddhist Meditations for Becoming Fully Human.* Boulder, CO: Sounds True, 2018. Audio.

Pabongka Rinpoche. *Liberation in the Palm of Your Hand: A Concise Discourse on the Path to Enlightenment.* 2nd ed. Translated by Michael Richards. Somerville, MA: Wisdom Publications, 2006.

Pearce, David W., and R. Kerry Turner. *Economics of Natural Resources and the Environment.* Baltimore: Johns Hopkins University Press, 1989.

Pinchbeck, Daniel. *How Soon Is Now? From Personal Initiation to Global Transformation.* London: Watkins, 2017.

Radboud University Nijmegen Medical Centre. "Research on 'Iceman' Wim Hof Suggests It May Be Possible to Influence Autonomic Nervous System and Immune Response." ScienceDaily. April 22, 2011. sciencedaily.com/releases/2011/04/110422090203.htm.

Reich, Wilhelm. *Character Analysis.* New York: Farrar, Straus and Giroux, 1990.

Ricard, Matthieu. *Altruism: The Power of Compassion to Change Yourself and the World.* New York: Back Bay Books, 2016.

Ricard, Matthieu, and Trinh Xuan Thuan. *The Quantum and the Lotus: A Journey to the Frontiers Where Science and Buddhism Meet.* New York: Three Rivers Press, 2004.

Rifkin, Jeremy. *The Empathic Civilization: The Race to Global Consciousness in a World in Crisis.* New York: J. P. Tarcher, 2009.

Rifkin, Jeremy. *The Third Industrial Revolution: How Lateral Power Is Transforming Energy, the Economy, and the World.* New York: St. Martin's Griffin, 2013.

Śāntideva. "Fully Adopting Bodhicitta" in *Bodhicaryāvatāra: An Introduction to the Bodhisattva's Way of Life.* Translated by Adam Pearcey. Lotsawa House. 2007. lotsawahouse.org/indian-masters/shantideva/bodhicharyavatara-3.

Santos, Fernanda. "Mysterious Buddhist Retreat in the Desert Ends in a Grisly Death." *New York Times.* June 5, 2012. nytimes.com/2012/06/06/us/mysterious-yoga-retreat-ends-in-a-grisly-death.html.

Siegel, Daniel J. *The Developing Mind: How Relationships and the Brain Interact to Shape Who We Are.* 2nd ed. New York: Guilford Press, 2012.

Siegel, Daniel J., and Tina Payne Bryson. *The Whole-Brain Child: 12 Revolutionary Strategies to Nurture Your Child's Developing Mind.* New York: Bantam Books, 2012.

Stevenson, Ian. *Twenty Cases Suggestive of Reincarnation.* 2nd ed. Charlottesville: University Press of Virginia, 1980.

Thompson, Evan. *Waking, Dreaming, Being: Self and Consciousness in Neuroscience, Meditation, and Philosophy.* New York: Columbia University Press, 2017.

Thurman, Robert. *The Central Philosophy of Tibet: A Study and Translation of Jey Tsong Khapa's "Essence of True Eloquence."* Princeton, NJ: Princeton University Press, 1991.

Thurman, Robert. *Essential Tibetan Buddhism.* New York: Castle Books, 1997.

Thurman, Robert. *Inner Revolution: Life, Liberty, and the Pursuit of Real Happiness.* New York: Riverhead Books, 1998.

Thurman, Robert. *The Jewel Tree of Tibet: The Enlightenment Engine of Tibetan Buddhism.* New York: Atria Books, 2006.

Thurman, Robert. "Religion as a Natural Phenomenon." Daniel C. Dennett in conversation with Robert Thurman. February 13, 2006. Accessed January 13, 2018. web.archive.org/web/20060503091655/http://blog.mindandreality.org/files/den_raft_transcript.html.

Tsong-kha-pa. *The Great Treatise on the Stages of the Path to Enlightenment.* Volumes 1–3. Edited by Joshua W. C. Cutler and Guy Newland. Boston: Snow Lion, 2014.

Vaidya, P. L. "Madhyamaka Shastra of Nagarjuna." Archive.org. March 15, 2016. archive.org/details/MadhyamakaShastraOfNagarjunaDr.P.L.Vaidya.

Welwood, John. *Awakening the Heart: East/West Approaches to Psychotherapy and the Healing Relationship.* Boston, MA: Shambhala, 1985.

Welwood, John. "Human Nature, Buddha Nature: On Spiritual Bypassing, Relationship, and the Dharma." Interview by Tina Fossella. 2011. Accessed January 13, 2018. johnwelwood.com/articles/TRIC_interview_uncut.pdf.

Welwood, John. *Toward a Psychology of Awakening: Buddhism, Psychotherapy, and the Path of Personal and Spiritual Transformation.* Boston, MA: Shambhala, 2002.

INDEX

ABOUT THE AUTHOR

Miles Neale, PsyD, is a Buddhist psychotherapist in private practice, assistant director of the Nalanda Institute for Contemplative Science, and faculty member at the Tibet House (US)—all initiatives that aim to preserve and assimilate Tibet's rich curriculum of awakening into contemporary life. With more than twenty years integrating the mind science and meditative arts of Tibetan Buddhism with neuroscience and psychotherapy, Miles is a forerunner in the emerging field of contemplative psychotherapy, offers public teachings and professional trainings worldwide, and is coeditor of *Advances in Contemplative Psychotherapy* (Routledge, 2017). He is based in New York City. Visit milesneale.com for more information.

ABOUT KOPAN NUNNERY

Most of the proceeds from *Gradual Awakening* will be donated to the nuns of Kopan Nunnery in Kathmandu, Nepal. Opened in 1994 as a branch of the Kopan Monastery founded by Lama Thubten Yeshe and under the spiritual direction of Lama Zopa Rinpoche, the nunnery was given the auspicious name of Khachoe Ghakyil Ling, or "Pure Land of Bliss."

One of the largest nunneries in Nepal, it is home to nearly four hundred women, many of them orphans and refugees from Tibet and other impoverished areas of the Himalayas, and all of whom wish to follow their spiritual calling. Each nun receives housing, meals, health care, and education in modern subjects such as languages, science, and math, as well as ancient Buddhist philosophy, all free of charge. Many of the women attain the geshe-ma degree—a Doctorate in Buddhist Studies—and go on to become teachers in their own right.

Kopan Nunnery's website urges us all to "Give others the opportunity to attain enlightenment." By purchasing this book, you do just that.

For more information, please visit kopannunnery.org

ABOUT SOUNDS TRUE

Sounds True is a multimedia publisher whose mission is to inspire and support personal transformation and spiritual awakening. Founded in 1985 and located in Boulder, Colorado, we work with many of the leading spiritual teachers, thinkers, healers, and visionary artists of our time. We strive with every title to preserve the essential "living wisdom" of the author or artist. It is our goal to create products that not only provide information to a reader or listener, but that also embody the quality of a wisdom transmission.

For those seeking genuine transformation, Sounds True is your trusted partner. At SoundsTrue.com you will find a wealth of free resources to support your journey, including exclusive weekly audio interviews, free downloads, interactive learning tools, and other special savings on all our titles.

To learn more, please visit SoundsTrue.com/freegifts or call us toll-free at 800.333.9185.

SOUNDS TRUE
many voices, one journey